Forty-Two Minutes

A Novel

by

Jenny K. Percey

Copyright Page

Paperback ISNB: 978-0-578-29783-5
EBook ISBN: 978-0-578-29784-2

Printed in the United States of America

Dedication

I dedicate this book to my birth mother. I would not have a story to tell if it wasn't for you. Your alcoholism affected and shaped me in ways I am still coming to terms with and will never fully be able to explain to you. My new life started the day you gave me up, and I am eternally grateful for the sacrifices you made. This is what I did with what you did. I hope it makes you proud. All I can say is thank you.

Acknowledgments

I've waited a very long time to be able to thank my parents in a book. Thank you Bill and Jodeen for believing in me and in this story. You both rescued me from a life of addiction and fear and unspeakable pain. I would not be who I am today if it wasn't for your love and support. Thank you for fighting so hard for me and for keeping me.

I would also like to thank my sisters, Sarah and Rising, who never once treated me like I didn't belong to them. I never for one second doubted I was your sister. You all are my family, in every sense of what that word means, and I couldn't have asked for a better one.

To my dear, beautiful friend, Brenda, your encouragement, unwavering faith in my gifts. goals, dreams and passion, means more to me than I can ever tell you.

And lastly, thank you to all those who choose to read this gritty, raw and painfully personal story. I've been writing this book for over twenty years. It grew and healed as I did and is a purging and reckoning for me. My hope for all of you is that you find a bit of yourselves in the middle of me trying to find myself.

Author's Note

I get asked all the time what the title of my book means. Forty-Two Minutes symbolizes a few things in the story. I was fascinated with the concept of time and how quickly life can change, for better or worse, and literally in a matter of minutes.

The first line of Chapter One is the first hint. It takes forty-two minutes to get drunk. It also represents the short amount of time between when Victoria is sober and her next blackout. I have woven the number forty-two throughout the book in conversations, clocks on the wall, and in seemingly simple moments that are anything but ordinary.

There are 42 chapters in this book and each one is told from a different character's perspective as alcoholism affects all people involved, not only the person drinking. I wanted everyone to have a voice in a situation where too many are forced to stay silent.

Whenever you see the number, know that something important is happening, shifting, changing, awakening, and being realized. I've used it as a boundary marker and breadcrumb for those traveling on this journey with these perfectly flawed people.

I hope you will enjoy discovering the number tucked away within the tapestry of this story, and that each time you see it, you are reminded how even a split-second decision can impact a whole life. Tragedy and heartbreak can happen in a matter of minutes, but so can hope, redemption, forgiveness, healing and love.

-Jenny

Contents

Chapter One
LEXY

D id you know it takes the average person about forty-two minutes to get drunk? I've counted. From my experience, I can tell you that statistic is painfully very true. It can change a bit, depending on your sex, size, weight, and tolerance level. How fast you're drinking. If you're already hungover. If you've eaten. The proof of the vodka.

If you're actually average or normal and the alcohol isn't already permanently in your blood.

I've learned to gauge how drunk my mom is by how far down the vodka is in the bottle, how many swallows, the clumsy sloshing into the glass, the slurring of her words, and the unsteadiness of her footsteps. I can tell by how unfocused and glazed her eyes slowly become as if she's disappearing right in front of me. She will swing from euphoria to depression in exactly eleven minutes.

Even the air around me changes. It becomes heavier, thicker, and suffocating. The rooms in my house get darker, colder, lonelier.

Haunted.

The walls start closing in as the addiction sneaks through like shadows, seeping through windows, slithering along the floors, scratching underneath doors, until it takes over everything in its path.

She usually goes through three bottles before she can no longer stand. One more before she blacks out. And then there's nothing but deafening silence until she comes to and does it all over again.

I told my first lie when I was four. While my mom was lying passed out on the bathroom floor, I told our next-door neighbor that everything was fine and we didn't need any help. Even at such a young age, I had already learned to protect her at any cost. Before I ever lost my first tooth, I started keeping her secrets and have never stopped.

The lies got easier to tell. *She's sleeping, she's sick, she's not home, she's on the phone, she's busy, she'll be right back.*

I don't know if anyone ever believed me, but the neighbors eventually stopped checking on us, and my mom kept drinking.

I constantly wonder what it's like to be normal. I've never known. To look at me, you'd think I am. On the outside, my life looks almost boring. My name is Lexy Monroe, and I live in the suburbs of Los Angeles. I just turned eighteen two weeks ago. My dad's name is Richard. He is a lawyer at a firm downtown.

My mom is Victoria, and she used to laugh, and she used to sing me to sleep at night, and she used to be involved in the PTA when I was in elementary school.

My mom used to do a lot of things. But now, she's just an alcoholic.

If you drove down our street, you wouldn't see anything on the outside that made you think anything was wrong. Minivans in the driveways, swimming pools and summer BBQs, soccer balls, and bicycles on the lawns. Normal, everyday people living their normal everyday lives.

Our house is a yellow and white two-story near the end of a court. You wouldn't look twice at it. Nothing stands out, and nothing looks different. It's how we've kept our secrets for so long. No one ever suspects what is really going on. No one would ever believe the hell we live in. No one would guess because the minute we walk outside, we lock all our secrets up behind closed doors.

If you come inside—not that anyone ever does—you wouldn't see it, at least not right away. Our house is clean; floors vacuumed, furniture dusted and polished, dishes done, laundry folded, beds made. I make sure of it. I have to keep some sense of order in all the dysfunction and chaos. I've been cooking my own breakfast since I was five. I'd burnt the toast, and the eggs were runny, but it had been better than starving.

If you stay long enough, you'd start to see the little cracks. You won't find any family photos anywhere on the walls or the mantle above the fireplace. And you won't want to stay very long. The atmosphere will be too quiet, too uneasy, and strangely hushed. My mom may or may not make an appearance, depending on how wasted she is. You'll start to realize something is off, and you'll be right. You'll be uncomfortable, and you won't even understand why.

What you won't see is what happens after you leave. My mom is locked up in her room, and I won't see her again for four days, maybe a week. She hides out and drinks. She can't *not* do it. I've never known the reason. She won't ever tell me, and I've learned not to ask. If she goes too long without a drink, she shakes, sweats, vomits, and gets blinding migraines.

She always keeps a bottle of vodka stashed somewhere nearby. She won't stop until she passes out. Once she resurfaces, she'll offer me desperate, slobbering apologies, promising to stay sober this time, swearing she'll change, but I learned years ago her promises mean nothing.

She'll manage to stay sober for a day, two at the most, and then there's always something that happens, some trigger I don't see coming, and the cycle begins all over again. The alcohol and addiction are stronger than her, than me, than all of us. It's winning, and we all know it.

And the sickest part is, I think she likes it.

I've spent every second of my life waiting for her to put the bottle down. But she never does.

This is my normal. This is my life. I wonder if you'd even want to know me. I don't. It's too hard trying to act sane all the time. It's exhausting.

You always hear that home is where the heart is and where you are supposed to be safe. When you go to bed at night, you lock your doors and fall asleep with the security that all the danger has been kept outside.

But there is nothing safe or secure about my home. My doors are locked, but it's too late. The monster has already found its way inside. And it's after my mother.

Chapter Two
LEXY

I don't know very much about how my mom grew up. She rarely ever talks about her childhood, and the few times I've dared to ask have sent her into a devastating tailspin.

I don't ask anymore. Questions cause too many consequences.

She's from somewhere out in Tennessee. A ranch just outside Nashville, I think. She has a younger sister named Becca, who she hasn't seen or spoken to since she was eighteen and left home. She won't tell me why. The only thing I've ever been able to get out of her was that her sister cut her out of her life and wants nothing to do with her. Both her parents have passed away. She refuses to talk about her father, and I know only the flimsiest details about her mother. Her life is a mysterious black hole to me.

I know something happened to her, something so horrible and frightening, she falls apart if the subject of her past is ever mentioned.

She's terrified of me leaving her. She's constantly making me promise I never will. I don't know where she's afraid I will go. I tell her over and over I won't, trying desperately to keep her from the next blackout. The addiction holds me captive just as much as her.

The irony is that she's always leaving me. I have an invisible shell for a mother. The alcohol has gutted everything out of her. I've always felt too guilty to even think about leaving. What would my mom do? Who would take care of her? What if she couldn't make it? With my dad hiding at work all the time, my mom has no one.

I never realized the day would come when I would break my promise to her.

I found the letters by accident. My mom was passed out in her room, and I was hiding her car keys in the locked drawer of my dad's study. We have a secret agreement to put them in the cigar box he keeps at the bottom of the drawer. I hide them so she won't sneak out to buy more vodka.

She thinks she's fooling us by putting it in water bottles or a thermos or taping a spare bottle under the toilet tank and behind the couch. She thinks I can't smell it on her, but I can. The alcohol oozes from her pores, her breath, and her hair. I swear even her shadow is drunk. The stench covers every wall in our home.

I've always thought it ironic how much vodka looks like water. So clear and pretty when the light hits just right. Deceptively harmless. But just like with water, my mom would die of thirst without it.

When I unlock and open the desk drawer, I'm surprised to find a stack of letters bound in a rubber band on top of the box we normally hide the keys in. Confused, I stare down at them a moment. How come they're in here? Had my dad left them for me? Why would he do that?

As I pull out the envelopes, I suck in my breath and stare in complete shock at the name on the return address. Becca Ryan. My mom's sister. My aunt.

Lightheaded and dizzy, I sink weakly down to my knees on the floor, the stack of letters clutched in my lap. My hands are trembling as I remove the rubber band and flip through the envelopes. There have to be hundreds of them. The postmarks go back at least twenty years. They've all been opened and read. She's been writing to us all this time? But, that doesn't make any sense. My mom said Becca wanted nothing to do with us. Why would she contact us?

Quickly opening one, I frantically skim the pages. It was sent three years ago. She writes of the death of their mother. My grandmother, I realize. Lily Mason. She'd been in a care home since the progression of Alzheimer's and had died of pneumonia. Becca writes of how much she misses my mom, how much she loves her, and hopes they can finally speak one day.

My gaze falls on a manila envelope from a law firm in Tennessee. Pulling it out from underneath the others, I open it and see it's been notarized. As I scan the paperwork, I realize it's a deed to the ranch. Both Becca and my mom are listed as the beneficiaries. We'd inherited the ranch in Tennessee? I never knew about any of this. Why didn't my mom tell me? Why haven't we ever been there?

Another letter tells of Becca getting married to Ben Ryan, and she sent a photo of their wedding. They had been married on the ranch twelve years ago. The wedding took place outside, under a canopy of thick oak trees. Mesmerized, I stare down at the picture of my aunt, beautiful and smiling, in flowing, filmy white, and my uncle, tall and handsome, in his tuxedo. They look so happy. So normal. They look like people I would want to know. My aunt looks like my mom, like me. It's an odd sensation to recognize so much of myself in someone I've never met.

Time seems to slow to a stop as I open every letter, read every word, and realize everything my mom ever told me about her sister and her past was a complete and total lie.

The pages are soft, worn, creased, some of the words blurred, smeared, and stained, as if tears had fallen on them or from fingerprints holding and reading them over and over and over. My mom's eyes and hands and tears. Folded and refolded. Again and again and again. She had known about these for years. And each time, she'd made a choice not to tell me.

They even smell like her. Desperation, vodka, cherry almond lotion, fear, and loneliness. Of family history and the past and childhood secrets.

A jolt goes through me when I pick up a pink envelope and see my name on it. Checking the postmark, I see it's recent, dated only a few weeks ago. The seal is cut. My mom had read this one, too, I realize, a cold sweat breaking out over my body. She hadn't said a word and purposefully hid it.

I'm surprised she was even coherent enough to go outside and get the mail. She must have done it while I was in school and my dad was at work. Because she knew the letters would come. She knew she had to watch and make sure I didn't find them first.

Anger and betrayal surge through me, churning my stomach. I bite my lip to keep from screaming out in frustration. Not that it would matter. She wouldn't hear me. She never does. She's not even conscious.

Opening it, I find a birthday card Becca had sent for my eighteenth birthday. I had no idea she even knew. She tells me how much she wishes she could say happy birthday in person but hopes I know she is thinking of me on such an important day. She writes of life on the ranch, the abandoned, abused horses they help rescue and take care of, and how beautiful the land is. She'd included pictures, and I flip through snapshots of lush, green pastures, the old white farmhouse, the stables, and the barn.

She ends the letter by telling me she would love to get to know me and hopes I will come to see her someday soon. She signs it, "Aunt Becca."

Tears blur my eyes and spill hotly down my cheeks, onto my hands and arms, and the pile of letters and lies still in my lap. I sit on the floor, holding the card close against my heart, and cry quietly as the last of the daylight fades.

My mind is reeling. How come I have never seen these letters? Why has my mom never shown them to me? What happened on that ranch that made my mom want to leave and never speak to her family again? Why has she lied all this time?

I realize my dad must have put the letters here for me. He's the only one who knows about our hiding place. Does he understand what he gave me? Does he know the door he just opened? I have so many questions that I'm terrified to ask. I already know what it's going to do to my mom when she finds out I've discovered the truth about her past and her family. All hell will break loose.

Becca sounds nothing like my mom said she was. She sounds beautiful and kind and loving. Nothing is matching up with the scattered bits and pieces I've been told. She's written to my mom for years. She's sent pictures and postcards. She hasn't missed one holiday, anniversary, or birthday. She's waited for her, for all of us. She still is.

As the reality starts to sink in, it dawns on me that there is barely any mention of their father—only a small, short sentence telling of his death fifteen years before. I can't find any other information on what happened to him. It's as if the subject of him is too dangerous and traumatic and volatile, off-limits and painful.

Cursed.

Excluding him feels deliberate somehow, hushed, shrouded in shame and secrecy, as if neither of them dares speak his name. But I can't figure out why.

No wonder my mom has dreaded this. She must have known there would be a day when I would want to know the truth. Discovering the letters has made me even more determined to find out what happened to her. And maybe, even more than me leaving her, she's feared that most of all.

Chapter Three
LEXY

Two days later, my mom finally came out of her room.

I'm waiting for her when she does. I'd already known she was waking from the blackout. I'd heard her stumbling into the bathroom, coughing until she gagged and choked. Spit. Retch. Violently vomit. The toilet flush. A clumsy, heavy thud against the wall that I know is her bracing for balance as she tries to stand. And then the shower running.

Almost an hour later, she shuffles into the kitchen, looking haggard and hungover. Her eyes are swollen, runny, and bloodshot; her skin mottled and blotchy. Her dark hair is wet and uncombed. She's wearing the navy blue robe my dad bought her for Christmas a few years back. Her feet are bare.

No one but me sees her this way. I keep the blinds and curtains closed. The morning light will be too bright and harsh for her. Our house stays shut and dark to the outside world.

My heart is heavy as I stand quietly by the counter and wait for her to realize I'm there. I'm used to her not seeing me even though I'm right in front of her. How on earth did we ever get here? I wonder, fighting back tears. I'm so tired. Even my bones ache. I don't want to do this. It's going to destroy her. I'm already shaking.

She used to be so beautiful, I think, as I watch her simply try to survive being alive. Is this who she wanted to turn into? I realize I can't remember her sober. She's been drunk most of my life. I have a vague memory from years before of her singing me to sleep. As a child, I remember thinking she looked like one of the dark-haired fairy princesses in my storybooks. Her eyes are the clearest, purest green I have ever seen. They can penetrate straight into you. I used to be able to look into them and see every part of myself. Now when I look at her, I can't find either one of us. Only the addiction is left and has stolen her away from me.

I know her routine, and she follows it like clockwork. I feel like all I ever do is track time, counting her every step, breath, and movement, trying to stay ahead of the next blackout. A pendulum swinging from one extreme to the other.

Tick tock. Tick tock. Tick tock.

She goes to the cabinet, gets the bottle of aspirin, and pours three into her palm. She moves with the frailty of an eighty-year-old to the coffee pot and pours herself a cup. She drinks it black and downs the aspirin. She won't be able to eat, not yet. Her ravaged system won't be able to handle it.

In a little while, she'll ask me to make her a fried egg and dry toast. The protein and grease will absorb her nausea and help fight the migraine. But her favorite cure for the hangover is a Bloody Mary. I learned how to make them when I was seven.

She's like a quiet hurricane, slowly barreling through our lives, ruthlessly ripping up and flattening everything around us until there's nothing left. And we've just kept living in the destruction and debris, pretending we don't notice our house has fallen down around us.

"Morning, baby," she murmurs and brushes a clumsy kiss over my hair. No regret. No apology. No acknowledgment of what she's put me through. As if she hadn't disappeared on me for days. As if I haven't been scared to death that she's stopped breathing or won't come out of it this time. Gingerly carrying her coffee, she sits down at the kitchen table, zones out, and stares off somewhere she never lets me follow.

Saying nothing, I walk over to the table and set the stack of letters down in front of her.

She's not sober enough for this conversation, but I don't think there will be a time when she ever is. Because her mind is sluggish, it takes her a good two minutes to realize what she's looking at. I see the moment the reality registers, watching as her color slowly drains away, even her lips fading to a pale shade of gray. Her hands are visibly shaking as she picks up the letters, but I can't tell if it's from the hangover or the shock of me laying her past in front of her.

"Where did you get these?" she asks hoarsely. I've often wondered if the sound of her own voice hurts her; if every time she speaks, she's reminded of where she comes from. It's still deeply southern, even with all the years she's lived in California. Her drawl stands out even more when she's drunk and has no control over what is coming out of her mouth. It's the one part of her she can't change or get rid of and proof she used to be someone else.

"In Dad's study." I keep my voice quiet so I don't trigger the migraine, and a wave of hysteria rises up at the irony of thinking a headache would be the worst of our problems. Who has conversations like this? I feel insane.

"His study?" she repeats dumbly, looking confused. "That's not where I put—" she suddenly gags, pressing her arm to her mouth to swallow back a wave of nausea.

"Why did you lie to me?"

"I didn't mean—" she stammers. "You don't understand. I wanted to protect you," she manages to rasp out. She blindly reaches out for me and tightly grips my hand. Her face crumples as she begins to cry. "Please. You have to believe me. You don't know what it was like out there."

I wince as her nails cut into my skin. Her hands are clammy and cold, but she doesn't loosen her hold as if she can't dare let me go. "What happened to you?"

Her head is shaking frantically back and forth. "No, no, no, no," she blubbers, sounding small and pitiful, like a cornered child. She looks so frightened. "Please don't do this to me. I can't tell you."

"Why?" I ask desperately. I still smell the vomit on her, the stench of the vodka that she can never get out of her skin. I don't know why people say it has no smell. It seeps out from her every pore. *This can't be my life,* I think helplessly. This madness can't be all there is. This can't be how she wants it to be. I kneel down next to her, hoping for one last attempt to break through. "Mom, please tell me. I want to understand. I love you. I want to help you."

"You can't help me." Tears stream down her cheeks; her nose is grossly running over her lips, chin, and neck. She doesn't even bother to wipe it away. She's completely ruined. "No one can."

"Becca has been waiting for us all this time. She's written to us for years. Why won't you talk to her?"

"I can't." Her voice is suddenly empty of all emotion, and my stomach drops as if I just fell off the edge of a cliff I should have seen coming. I can feel her spiraling further from me as her past creeps out from where it has been hiding. She no longer has anywhere to run. "You don't know what he did to us."

"Who?" I realize I'm literally on my knees, begging her for answers. How has it come to this? "Please talk to me."

But she doesn't say anything. She's staring blearily down at the stack of letters in front of her. She almost reaches out to touch them but then quickly pulls back as if afraid they will swallow her. Maybe they will. Her hand falls into her lap, and she leans weakly back in the chair as if all her strength is gone. "You're going to go find her, aren't you?" she asks dully, her lips barely moving. "You're going to leave me. I told you one day you would."

"I'm sorry, but I have to." I blink back tears, wrestling violently against the guilt. I almost give in and swear I won't ever go. But I can't live like this anymore. I won't make it. None of us will. "I need to know the truth." I'm losing her again. I can feel her slipping away, sinking down into that bottomless abyss where no matter how hard I try, I can't ever reach her and drag her back to the surface. "I want to know what happened."

When she finally looks over at me, her eyes are shockingly clear and steady on mine. She hardly ever makes eye contact with me anymore. Her self-hatred won't let her. It's one of the most lucid moments I've experienced with her in years. I almost could think she was sober. "I wish I could burn that place to the ground."

Five...four...three...

The countdown starts ticking in my head. The warning sirens are about to go off. I know the inevitable is coming. The meltdown is here before I can catch up and stop it.

Shoulders hunched, my mom heavily moves her chair back. I flinch as it scrapes loudly across the floor. She gets unsteadily to her feet, sways, and has to grab onto the table before she falls, her palms leaving sweaty imprints on the wood. I immediately reach out to help her, to somehow keep her with me, but she slaps at my hand and pushes me off, another attempt to punish and make me pay.

Two...one...

That was fast, I think, wearily glancing at the clock on the wall. 10:42. My mom has only been awake for two hours and is already spiraling back down into the blackness.

She stumbles away from me, bracing herself against the wall as she weaves and staggers back to her room. I jolt when the door slams and locks. I want to run down the hall and bang the door down, but even if I got in, it still wouldn't do any good. She's already made her choice, and I realize my last shred of hope is gone. I don't even cry. I'm not sure I have any tears left.

I'm already packed and call an Uber. There's nothing left for me here. There's nothing else I can do. I'm surprisingly calm, considering the destruction I'm causing. I can't seem to feel anything anymore. Maybe I'm in shock. Or maybe I'm just suicidal and can't care. I've thought about it. In the darkest places of my mind, I've thought about exactly how I would do it. But I couldn't ever go through with it. Who would keep her alive if I wasn't?

I have to go before I change my mind. I'm terrified to leave, but it's the only way I know how to help her. I have to find out what happened on that ranch. I have to understand why and how she ended up like this. Maybe I'm delusional in thinking I'm going to find that one thing that is going to miraculously bring her back to me, but I have to try. I have to believe it even if it's futile. I don't know what else to hang onto.

I've heard the truth will set you free. I just hope once I find it, it doesn't end up killing us.

Pulling out the letter that was addressed to me, I leave the rest on the table for my dad to find when he comes home. It's the only explanation he will need. He must have known I would leave once I found them. Is this why he put them in the drawer for me? Is this the only way he knew how to save me? I wish I could ask him, but I can't wait any longer. If I do, I'm afraid I won't go. I had used his credit card to pay for the ticket to Nashville. He'd given it to me to use in case of an emergency. I think this qualifies as one. Gathering my things, I walk out the front door, closing it quietly behind me.

As I lock the door, I realize I've never been keeping her safe. I've been keeping everyone on the outside safe from us.

The car pulls up. I get in, and we drive away from my ordinary suburban house on my ordinary street, where it looks like nothing out of the ordinary could ever happen. I keep my eyes focused straight ahead and don't dare let myself look back.

Chapter Four
RICHARD

She's gone.

The house is dark. Quiet. Blackout quiet. It's late. I stand in the kitchen and stare down at the letters on the table. The relief I feel is intense. I hoped Lexy would find them and that she would let herself leave. I fiercely pray she made it to Nashville, and she's finally safe.

When the birthday card arrived for her, I knew the time had come for her to know about her family. I couldn't keep lying to her. I still don't know how Victoria managed to keep the letters from her for this long. She promised years ago she'd tell her the truth, but as time went on and the drinking grew worse, I knew she was never going to say anything. She was too fragile and unstable to handle it. If I hadn't moved them to a place I knew she'd look, I don't know if Lexy ever would have discovered them.

I waited until she was eighteen, until the choice would no longer be up to us, and she would finally be out of our reach. Where we would no longer have a say. She had a right to know where she came from, and I couldn't live with the guilt of keeping the truth from her any longer.

Even though I'm dreading what I will find, I make myself go down the hall to Victoria's room. The door is closed and locked. I try to turn the knob, but it doesn't give. I stand outside and listen, but of course, I hear nothing. I knock, but there's no answer. There never is. I'm being punished for betraying her and giving Lexy the letters. I already know she's passed out.

I feel as if I am living with a fatal gunshot under my clothes. I know it's bad, that I'm close to bleeding out, but I'm too afraid to look at how much damage has been done, so I ignore the gaping hole in my gut and force myself to push through the pain and stagger forward with an open, seeping wound that is slowly killing me.

It's strange what you get used to, how easily you adapt to the panic, what you learn to endure. Fight or flight kicks in. Pain becomes somehow normal. It's cruel how much tragedy a person is expected to take.

Seeing empty vodka bottles all over the house is just a typical day. Your wife lying passed out in the toilet is just another Tuesday night. You become numb to trauma, desensitized. The reality is too much, so you shut down. You tell yourself it's not as bad as you think it is. That you can handle it. That you're fine.

It's infuriating when I hear people say that something like this could never happen to them. Or that they would never let it happen. That they could somehow outsmart the addiction, and they are above the rest of us foolish mortals who were stupid enough to give in to temptation in the first place. What a joke. Their ignorant arrogance makes me want to laugh in their faces or punch them.

Don't think for one second that it couldn't happen to you, me, or any one of us, at any time. You have no idea what you would do until you're in the vicious, sinking pit of it, and you do the only thing you can to survive.

It's almost as if the rest of the world is crazy, and yours becomes the one that is real. How isn't everyone else also living in this kind of chaos?

I know I could call Lexy or get on a red-eye flight to Nashville, find my daughter, and try to convince her to come back home. I could tell her everything would be different, desperately apologize, and beg her to forgive me. But what would be the point? It wouldn't do any good. What would she be coming back to? Cleaning up Victoria's vomit, desperately waiting to see if her mother would make it through the night, dragging her from the bathroom floor into her bed? Staying up until dawn to make sure Victoria was still breathing?

Nothing has changed. Her mother is still an alcoholic. And she would still expect Lexy to be the one protecting her.

I can't do it anymore. She's our child. We are supposed to be the ones taking care of her. I can't ask her to be responsible for us any longer. I can't ask her to come back into our hell. She's too young to have to be this brave.

I haven't known what else to do to protect the people I'm responsible for. I've just survived this madness, thinking one day my wife would choose to get sober and we could somehow find our way back to each other.

All I've known how to do is cope. I've gone to work, paid the bills, kept food on our table, our electricity and water running. Those were the only things I could control. But what they've most needed from me, I've had no idea how to give them. And, have failed at every turn.

Somewhere along the way, we somehow made a sick pact that the addiction could have us. It feels as if she's the one who really gets to live, and I'm the one who is the ghost. She's the one who decides what happens to all of us, and when we get to move and breathe and exist again.

And when we don't.

I've tried for years to get Victoria to go into rehab but that only made her drinking worse. She would quickly shatter at the slightest mention of treatment; scream and wail and cry hysterically, slam doors. The fallout was horrific and disturbing. She would threaten to kill herself and I was terrified she would do it. It just became easier not to risk or push it.

The final tipping point came around the time of Lexy's birthday. The binges were getting worse, extreme, violent. The closer Lexy got to eighteen, the more reckless and frantic Victoria became.

Lexy had just graduated and applied for the community college nearby and would start in the fall. She'd somehow managed to keep her grades up even in the middle of trying to make sure her mother stayed alive.

But there was only so long we could keep her here. She was growing up and was now legally an adult, even though I feel as if she's unfortunately had to be one her entire life. Victoria was panicking that Lexy would leave her, punishing her because it was the only way she knew to control her.

Over the last few months, Victoria had become more dangerous in her drinking, pushing the edge with a toxic combination of pills, as if she had a death wish. I lived in constant fear that one more time would be her last time. She is completely losing her grip on reality and is too drunk to care.

My worst nightmare is that Victoria will go through with hurting herself and somehow take Lexy with her. Or worse, that my daughter would witness it happen. I knew I needed to rescue her before Victoria took them both out.

Life outside my front door is coming together as it should. I go through the motions of taking a shower, getting dressed, and driving to work. The routine helps keep me sane. It's a surreal existence and one that I'm so used to that the magnitude of the damage doesn't even register. I won my case. We gained a new client, a lucrative one. I look like I have it together and know what I am doing.

I live in the constant irony of what I do and the humiliating reality of what I don't know how to do. My life has been spiraling out of control for years, and the only person that held us together is now gone.

I should have intervened for my family years ago. Gotten a court order, forced Victoria into rehab. AA, support group, counseling—anything. I'm a lawyer, for crying out loud.

But it's different when it's your own family. And I know better than anyone how flawed the system is and that it isn't always on your side. What if they had taken our daughter away from us? Victoria would never have survived that, and I couldn't put Lexy through more trauma. She's suffered enough already.

I've felt trapped between my love and the fear of losing both of them. I convinced myself we were the lesser of two evils. Right and wrong isn't as concrete when it's your own flesh and blood. I was too afraid of the fallout and justified that having an alcoholic for a mother was better than her not having a mother at all. But the sick truth is, she hasn't had one either way.

It's only a matter of time now, I realize, before one of us falls apart. I'm not sure who will be first. My only solace is that my daughter is far away. She's finally safe. I offered her the parachute, and she found the courage to jump. I wasn't sure if she would. Her loyalty to Victoria keeps her trapped in a never-ending cycle of dysfunction. Some would call it classic textbook codependency. The victim trying to save the person claiming to be one.

All I know for sure is I needed to get her out. I wanted her to have a chance. It's the only time since she was a little girl I've done the right thing for her.

I feel like a zombie as I walk back into the kitchen—empty, cold, nothing. I've been dead inside for years. I carefully put the rubber band around the letters, binding them all back together into neat and tidy little time bombs. I have no idea if they have saved our lives or just blown them up completely.

Chapter Five
LEXY

My plane lands in Nashville a little after six in the morning, and I get a cab to my aunt's house. I give the driver the return address on Becca's letter. He enters it into his GPS, and we drive out of the airport.

It's still early, and there isn't much traffic on a Saturday morning. The radio is playing on low, and I recognize Reba McIntyre's voice drifting out, singing about Fancy not letting her down. I make small talk with the driver, who tells me his name is Joe. He's been married fourteen years and has two kids. Their photo is taped to his sun visor. As I look at their smiling faces, I can't help wondering if there is such a thing as a happy, normal family. Does everyone have dark secrets they don't talk about? Is everyone pretending?

He has the front windows down, and I notice the breeze is already warm and smells of the silt and sediment from the Cumberland River that winds and flows through Nashville.

The sights and sounds should be beautiful, but I can't get my anxious mind to stop racing. I didn't sleep much on the plane and feel dazed, edgy, and wired. I still can't believe I'm here, that I actually went through with leaving. I haven't been able to stop worrying about my mom for one single second.

My phone is on silent in my purse. I'm too afraid to look at it. I'm not sure if I'm more worried that she's called or that she hasn't. Fear and guilt hang heavily around me as we cross over the Gateway Bridge and drive into the heart of downtown.

Nashville is known as the Country Music Capital of the World, and I can see why. Billboards with the latest country stars are plastered on every corner, on the side of buses and park benches. It's the birthplace of the blues and rock and roll. Singing legends Johnny Cash and Elvis lived and recorded their music here.

As we drive down Broadway, I look up at steel skyscrapers glistening in the early morning light. They tower over the faded brick buildings, charming cafes, and colorful shops that line the waterfront. There aren't a lot of people out; a few joggers, a couple walking their dog.

Since it's my first time here, Joe takes me the long way around and points out landmarks such as the famous Ryman Auditorium, The Country Music Hall of Fame, the Grand Union Station Hotel, and the replica of the Parthenon in Centennial Park.

Excitement fills me as we follow the signs for Music Row, and Joe drives down the middle of a musical wonderland. I lean forward in the seat so I can see better. The entire street is lined with brightly colored buildings and neon signs for famous honky tonk bars and clubs such as Tootsie's Orchid Lounge, The Bluebird Cafe, Second Fiddle, and Tomkats. I feel like I'm in a completely different world, one I've always secretly dreamt of being a part of.

With it being so early, the neon signs are dark, and the streets quiet and deserted. I would love to see what it looks like at night with the music blaring and voices spilling out, the lights lit up and flashing, while people dance and laugh.

Singing has been my escape and salvation since before I could talk. Knowing that music is always there, even when nothing and no one else is, has been the one thing that has gotten me through the darkness and devastation. It's been the only thing I can count on, the only place where I know who I am. I don't talk about it and have never told anyone. No one has ever heard me sing; it's too personal. It's mine, and it's the only part of me she hasn't been able to take away. Being able to channel all my fears, pain, and guilt into a song helped me survive and gave me a safe place to disappear. Singing is the only way I can speak in a world where I've had no voice. It's the only truth I have.

Once we get further from downtown, the buildings become fewer and farther in between until they all but disappear in the rearview mirror. The land flattens out into miles and miles of lush, green farmland.

Barns, silos, and stables begin to pop up along the backroads. Peach orchards drift fragrantly past the landscape. A scarecrow stands in the middle of a cornfield, the stalks so high they tower clear over my head. On the other side of the road, I notice wheat bales neatly rolled and stacked as they are prepared for harvest. The golden fields are starkly beautiful against the wide blue sky above.

A glittering flash catches my eye, and I see a blackbird swoop down and perch on top of a fence post, its wings glossy black in the sunlight. Its beady eyes seem to pierce and follow me as we pass. An eerie feeling comes over me. What if it's a warning? I hope it's not a sign or an omen. I've heard they are bad luck. I watch the bird get smaller and smaller in the side mirror of the passenger side. I swear it's still watching me.

Objects are closer than they appear.

Spooked, I make myself breathe. I'm psyching myself out. Stress and exhaustion are making me delirious. Shaking off the uneasy feeling, I look straight ahead and focus again on the green spread out in front of me.

I lurch forward slightly, my seatbelt holding me in place when we suddenly brake. Looking out the dusty windshield, I see a man on a tractor pull out in front of us and begin driving leisurely down the middle of the road, unconcerned with speed or traffic or being in anyone's way. Joe doesn't seem to mind and simply waves and moves around him, and the man tips his hat, as if it's the most normal thing in the world.

Life is definitely different and much slower out here, I think, as I look out the window at horses and cattle lazily grazing in wide-open pastures. Sprinklers sprint far and wide over the fields, stirring up the scents of soaked earth and freshly cut grass. Somewhere in the distance, I hear a train going by.

Even the air feels clearer, purer somehow, unpolluted by lies and hurt and the stench of addiction.

"Here we are," Joe says as he pulls up in front of the ranch gates.

My nerves are jumping as I lean over to look out the window at the thick timber posts standing strong and proud on either side of the dirt road. Arched high above is a sign, and I notice that branded deep into the wood are the words "Montgomery Ranch, Established 1871." Something stirs in me, some pull I have never felt before and don't understand.

I thought I'd have more time to prepare myself, but Joe is waiting, the meter is running, and I have to get out of the car. He's already getting my suitcase and guitar from the trunk. I haven't brought much. I wasn't sure how long I'd be staying or if my aunt would even let me past her front porch.

As I step out onto the road, the heat swirls up and steals my breath. I hadn't expected it to be so hot and humid here. The air is thick and feels as if I'm swallowing water. Clumsily, I pull out my wallet, fumbling a bit as I hand him the money. My palms are sweating. "Thank you," I manage, still trying to find my bearings.

"Enjoy your stay in Nashville," Joe says as he gets back in the cab. I watch as he does a U-turn and drives back down the road into town and wonder if it was a mistake to let him leave me here. Good thing I kept his card, just in case. Shading my eyes, I look to my left and then back to my right. The road is long, and there's not one car coming in either direction. I suddenly feel very alone and stranded.

Turning around, I look back up at the tall gates, again feeling that strange longing for connection and belonging. *They have to be handmade,* I think, running my fingers over the rough, grainy wood that has turned crimson with time. The heat has already made it warm. I wonder who built it. I don't know anything about my family who settled on this land.

My brows come up in surprise when I notice an old cowboy boot perched up on one of the posts. Strange. I don't know why someone would hang it there. A large, rusted wagon-wheel rests up against the side of the gate. Gathering my courage, I pass underneath the arch and start the long walk up towards the house.

The dirt lane stretches out like a carpet in front of me, flanked on either side by mossy, ancient oaks. Beyond the trees, I can see endless miles of green pasture and horses grazing or simply standing under the early morning light. White picket fences follow and barrier in the land, and I wonder how many acres are here. Glancing to my left, I see glimpses of scattered outbuildings, a large red barn, and stables on the far side of the ranch.

The air seems to shimmer from the heat, making the road ahead look like a mirage that will disappear under my next step. Even so early, the morning is already warm and sticky. *Welcome to summer in Tennessee,* I think, pulling at my shirt, which is now damp and clinging to my skin. I wish I'd thought to change into shorts and sandals instead of the jeans and sneakers I'd worn on the plane.

The land is so quiet and hushed and still. All I can hear is my shoes crunching over the dirt lane, the hum and swarm of insects, the song and call of the birds in the trees overhead. Thick, gnarled trees, the kind you only see in the deep, deep south, create a canopy of mossy, dripping vines that brush against my hair and shoulders as I pass under them. Sunlight filters through the branches, patterns shifting and dancing along the dusty ground. The light seems different out here, lazy and peaceful and dreamy.

And then the trees open up, and the house is suddenly in front of me.

My breath catches, and I stop and stare at a three-story white Victorian farmhouse with a wraparound porch and lace curtains drawn back in an upstairs window. The roof is steep and high and pitched. Sunlight glints off the glass from the bay window on the first floor. The paint is warped and peeling from the years of weather and age, making it seem even more sentimental and cozy. Honeysuckle vines twirl up the posts around the porch and weave through the trellis, and I smile a little as the light, sweet scent drifts over to me. The house is simple and pretty and somehow feels as if it's been waiting for me.

This home is where my mom was born, where she grew up, and where she ran from. *It doesn't look anything like how she described it,* I think, confused. What did it used to be like? The house I'm looking at now isn't run down and ugly. There is nothing frightening or threatening lurking in the shadows. Where are all the ghosts and monsters she told me haunted this land? What was she so terrified of? Who hurt her here?

My eyes scan over the land, looking for any small sign that she might have left behind. Which room was her bedroom? Did she run and play in the pastures? Did she swing on the old tire swing still hanging from a branch of the large oak? The house is beautiful, like something straight out of a Hallmark movie. I can't figure out why she would want to leave so badly. What had happened to her that has made her never want to come back and lie about the people who stayed behind?

It's too hot to keep standing still, and I walk the rest of the way up the drive. I don't know if every step is getting me closer to the truth or more pain. I wonder if my aunt and uncle are awake and try to see movement through the front windows as I come up the porch steps. Doubt creeps in. What if coming here was a mistake? What if Becca has gotten tired of waiting and decided she no longer wants to know us? What if all our years of silence have hurt her too much, and she sends me away? Where would I go? I can't go back home.

My stomach is in knots as I set down my suitcase and guitar. Blowing out a nervous breath, I bang the brass knocker.

As I wait, I look around and notice an old golden lab sprawled out in the shade under the porch swing. I smile as the dog barely stirs and lazily wags its tail at me, too hot to do anything else. I feel the same way and use my hand to fan myself from the thick, sweltering heat.

I hear the heavy thud of footsteps, and the face that peeks out at me through the aged glass is distorted and rippled and then comes into clear view as the front door opens.

The man on the other side of it doesn't look much older than me but somehow feels older than he should. He has dark hair and brown eyes that look much too weary and sad for someone so young, as if looking out at the world is painful for him. A white, jagged scar is above his right eyebrow. Curiosity has my eyes flickering to it before I quickly look away.

He's not my uncle. I don't recognize him from the pictures Becca sent. Was he the one who helped out around here? My aunt had mentioned him in the letters. Mike? Nick? I can't remember his name. I can barely remember mine at the moment. He seems to know who I am, though. He does a double-take, and his eyebrows come up in surprise. I think he's shocked to see me because he just stands and stares for a minute. I don't know what to say and again wonder if I should never have come.

"She's waited a long time for you." His voice is deep and southern, and I wonder if I hear an edge of anger underneath it. Is he accusing me, or do I just fear everyone is? Before I can ask him what he means, I hear a woman's voice come from behind him.

"Who's at the door, Nick?" She pushes it open wider, and I'm suddenly face to face with my mom's sister.

She recognizes me immediately, and I watch as her eyes widen and hear her gasp. She instinctively raises her hands to her mouth in shock. "Lexy?" My name is a whispered question as if she's trying to believe I'm really in front of her. I notice how close Nick stays to her side, as if he's protecting her from me.

I try to soak in as much of her as I can. She has the same green eyes as my mom. Her hair is curly and dark like ours. She has hers pulled back off her face, which is clean of makeup. She's wearing a red and blue plaid button-up shirt, faded jeans, and boots. Small hoop earrings are in her ears, and a gold locket is around her neck. The half of a heart looks familiar but at the moment, I can't place it.

I take all these things in, desperate for a connection, and feel my throat tighten and close up. I thought I'd know what to say; I'd rehearsed it in my mind the whole way here, but all that comes out is, "I just found your letters." I awkwardly held up the pink envelope I'd been carrying. It was now crinkled, some of the writing smeared off from being read over and over. "I didn't know where else to go."

Tears are in her eyes as she nods and steps towards me. "Oh honey, you came to exactly the right place." She doesn't even hesitate as she pulls me into her arms. Exhausted and relieved, I let myself be held close, grateful to finally be somewhere safe. She smells like strawberry shampoo and lavender lotion, and I breathe her in, committing every detail to memory. "Please come inside, sweetheart. It's terribly hot out here."

Picking up my suitcase and guitar, I follow as she leads me through the front doorway. Nick steps back, but I notice he continues to stand guard over Becca as he gauges me. I can feel his eyes tracking my movements and wonder what he's worried

I'm going to do. Becca has me put my things in the entryway. She notices my guitar case but doesn't mention it.

The house is cool and dim and as charming as the outside. We pass the front parlor with its cozy floral chairs, antique tables, and stained glass lamps. An ornate wood fireplace is the room's focal point, a large, gilded mirror perched above. To my left is a narrow staircase leading up to the second floor, photographs lining the wall. I think I see one of my mom, but my aunt has my hand and is leading me into the kitchen.

"Ben, look who's here."

My uncle glances up from his breakfast, his coffee mug stilling halfway to his lips as recognition dawns. "Well, hello there." He must see how unsure and nervous I am because he smiles at me, his blue eyes crinkling up at the corners. His face is kind and warm, just like in the pictures Becca had sent. Relief makes me smile, too. "Now, this is definitely a surprise."

Feeling awkward, I stand by the table, unsure of what to do. I don't know what to call him. Or Becca. They are my family, and I'm their niece, but we don't know each other. They are strangers I am related to. And with all the years of silence and things left unresolved between us, I can't expect the familiarity and connection yet. I wonder if they will let me stay long enough for that to change, and I fervently hope they do.

I thought they would be angry, but both my aunt and uncle are smiling and happy, holding nothing against me. I'm stunned to be welcomed in so willingly. Only Nick doesn't seem to want me there. He stands in the doorway, silently watching me. I don't look at him. His suspicion and mistrust crowd me. I can't seem to move without bumping up against them.

Becca walks toward the stove. "Are you hungry? We were just about to have breakfast."

To be polite, I was going to tell her I wasn't, and I didn't want to impose, but my stomach growled, betraying me. I hadn't eaten anything since yesterday morning when I left California. I'd been too upset to keep anything down. "I guess I am," I admit, giving her an embarrassed smile. "Thank you."

"Please have a seat, honey." She flutters around the kitchen, full of nervous energy, getting an extra plate and some silverware. She scoops a big helping of eggs, plucking off two strips of bacon from the pan. "There's coffee or juice if you'd like."

Still feeling completely out of place, I find the first chair I see and sit down across from my uncle. "I'll have some coffee, please."

She pours me a cup and hands it to me. I notice the blue mug has a rooster and the words *Rise and Shine* painted on it. "Sugar and cream are on the table." She turns back to the stove and carries over a pan of cornbread.

I take a quick second to look around. The kitchen is the heart of the house. The warmth surrounds me as I take in the exposed beamed ceilings and handcrafted cabinets and the brick hearth blackened by over a century of fires burning within it. Copper pots dangle above the large range stove; the pantry is stocked full of food and tin canisters, sacks of flour, and spices. Delicate floral china plates are displayed up on a shelf above the doorway. Sunlight streams in and spills over the scarred plank floors. Scents of coffee, baked bread, and bacon fill the room, along with the warm breeze drifting in from the screen door that leads out towards the pastures. It makes me feel strangely content.

My peaceful mood quickly fades as Nick sits down next to me. He doesn't say a word, but his silence and hostility are like a foghorn blaring. My body tenses up. I don't even try to defend myself. He couldn't be thinking anything about me I haven't already beaten myself up for. Needing the comfort of the heat, I hold my coffee between my two hands and stay quiet as I sip it.

Becca brings over butter and jam and sets both down next to the cornbread. If I hadn't been looking at her, I wouldn't have caught the way she brushed her hand over Nick's shoulder, almost as if she's reassuring him. "Lexy, this is Nick Walker. He helps us out around here. He lives in the cottage out back. He and Ben grew up across the road from each other. Ben has known Nick since he was in diapers."

Nick scowls at her. "Thanks," he mutters. The sound of his voice again makes me want to look over at him, but I don't dare. I remember how dark his eyes are. It's unnerving.

"I don't think she needs a picture of that, Becca," Ben says and winks at me, and I manage to relax a little more. Something about him puts me at ease.

"Probably not," Becca says and laughs; the sound is pretty and light and fills the kitchen. I don't remember the last time I heard my mom laugh, much less smile. Fascinated, I can't help but stare at her. She is so much different than what I expected. She isn't cold or angry or bitter. In fact, there's nothing about her that gives me any clue as to why my mom would want to shut her out of her life. Becca is still smiling as she sets a plate full of food in front of me. "Anyway, Nick has been living with us for a couple of years now. We couldn't run this place without him."

"You help with the horses." I remember him now. "You mentioned him in your letters."

Nick gives Becca a sharp look that seems to speak to something no one was supposed to talk about. A tense quiet falls over the table. Becca flushes and seems to stammer a little before quickly changing the subject. She gives me a bright smile that seems forced. "I wish I would have known you were coming. I would have cleaned the house up a little bit."

The food suddenly loses its taste. My fork clumsily clangs onto my plate, the sound much too loud. I have a hard time swallowing it and drink some coffee. It's hot and burns my tongue, but I barely feel it. I had thought about calling her to let her know I had found the letters and wanted to come see her, but how was I going to tell her I hadn't known when my mom was going to wake up from the blackout? There had been too much I would have had to explain over the phone. It had been easier to just come before I had a chance to change my mind.

"It was kind of a last-minute decision," I say quietly. I can barely look at her, too afraid she'll see everything I've done, what I am, how I've failed. "I flew out yesterday."

Becca knows there's more. I catch the worried look she exchanges with Ben. I can tell she wants to ask, and I tense up, waiting for the questions I have no idea how to answer. But thankfully, all she says is, "Oh honey, you must be exhausted."

Her kindness is making me feel guilty. I don't deserve it. "I slept a little on the plane." I hadn't, but I want to make this as easy as possible for her.

Becca sits down next to Ben. "After breakfast, I'll take you up to the guest room, and you can get settled and lay down for a bit."

I can feel Ben watching me, reading me. My anxiety builds as I wonder if he's figured everything out. I already know his first instinct is going to be to protect Becca from more hurt and disappointment. From me. What if he asks me to leave? Nervously, I bite my lip and risk looking over at him, but all I see in his eyes is concern, and realize he feels sorry for me. I hadn't expected him to. It flusters me. I must not be hiding my fear very well.

"Nick, why don't we give these two some time to catch up?" he says, still looking at me. Without waiting for an answer, Ben gets to his feet and gives me another easy smile. "Glad you're here, Lexy. Hope you'll stay for a bit." He brushes his hand over Becca's hair as he moves past. I notice how sweetly she smiles at him and feel a pang of loneliness. My parents never looked at each other like that. I can't even remember the last time they were actually in the same room together.

Nick reluctantly pushes his chair back and stands up. He doesn't look at me as he carries his cup of coffee and silently follows Ben out the back door. I don't let out my breath until the screen closes after him. I can't figure out why he makes me so nervous. I don't even know him.

When it's just the two of us, Becca finally asks the question I'm dreading. "Does she know you're here?"

At least I don't have to lie. "Yes." I press my lips together as I cautiously gauge her expression, wondering if she'll ask how my mom is, what her life is like, if she ever talks about her, if she misses her. Why she's done what she's done. The blame of all her choices rests on me.

Becca must sense my torment because she doesn't push for more, although I can tell how badly she wants to know. Her eyes, my mother's eyes, search over my face. "You look a lot like her," she murmurs, resting her chin in her hand.

"So do you," I say, my throat tight. I want to tell her how sorry I am for not coming sooner, for not trying to find her before now, for believing the lies. I want to explain what it would have done to my mom if I had tried. I want to tell her I just hadn't known, but I can't. The words won't come. I don't know where to start. All I'm able to say is, "Thank you for the birthday card."

Tears fill her eyes, and she lets out a shaky sigh. "You're welcome, sweetheart." Sniffling, she gently pats my hand. "Now finish up your eggs. You must be starving."

I was, in so many ways, I didn't know how to talk about. Saying it all out loud would hurt too much, and I'm still feeling too overwhelmed and fragile. I'll break down completely. The kitchen is bright and sunny, and I finish every bite on my plate. It's the first breakfast I've eaten in years with more than just me at the table.

Chapter Six
BECCA

Resting my arms on the fence, I smile to myself as I watch the horses leisurely graze. The sky beyond is streaked in shimmering shades of lavender, pink, and gold. Summer sunsets on this ranch are unlike anything I've ever seen before. The heat has eased just a little, and a gentle breeze rustles the grass and trees, stirring my hair. The scents of honeysuckle and gardenia always seem heavier later in the day, and I can taste their sweetness and nectar on my tongue.

Our golden lab, Abraham, has followed me across the pasture and is rolling happily around in the grass, trying to itch his back and find somewhere cool. He'd been a stray that had wandered onto our land a few years ago and decided he wanted to adopt us. He's useless as a guard dog but is so sweet; you can't help but love him. He must sense I'm hurting because he doesn't go far.

Closing my eyes, I listen to the sounds of the evening—crickets, cicadas, the whinnying of the horses. This land is so deeply a part of me and has been since I was born. Even the dust is ingrained into my blood, whether I want it to be or not.

Some could ask how I can stand to stay, and it would be because of moments like this, where the rest of the world begins and ends right here. I have rediscovered and reclaimed the beauty here. I'd had to strip it down to its barest core and completely start over, but I finally found it.

I remember what happened here. Not one moment passes that I am not haunted by what he did to us. And, I have to remind myself to put one foot in front of the other so my past won't bury me. Every day I choose to move forward is one more day I don't end up like him.

Nights like these, with brilliant sunsets, summer grass, and wounded horses that used to trust no one, now prancing joyfully across the fields, are what make me smile, give me a sense of hope, and get me out of bed in the morning.

And now, my niece is here. I've waited so long to meet her, to know her, to have my family back. I never gave up hope that someday, one of them would come find me. Year after year, I wrote Victoria, desperately hoping for some acknowledgment, some tiny flicker of response.

But there had been nothing.

My sister's wall had been impenetrable and excruciating. Silence really can scream. I've cried over it, raged, prayed, and lost sleep. I understand why she left; he left her with no other choice. The day she was legally able to escape, she ran and never looked back, leaving me behind to pick up the pieces alone.

The abuse was worse for her than for me. I was invisible to him, which is terrible in its own way. He targeted her more. They were too alike, and he knew it. He punished her for it, for reminding him constantly of his failures and everything he hated about himself.

That's why I couldn't give up on her. No matter how far away she ran or how many letters went unanswered, she was still my sister. And my hope has always been that one day she'd remember that she needed me and every secret promise we'd made to each other.

I'm so grateful I kept believing because finally, after years of waiting and wishing and wondering, my niece has arrived on my doorstep.

But, along with her comes my past. I instantly flash back to hiding under the porch with my sister while our father staggered, shouted, and swore above our heads. I don't even know how many hours we spent under there, in the sweltering heat, in dirty clothes, with no food, and bare feet, having to listen to our mother cry and beg him to stop hurting her. I flinch as his slurred, angry voice echoes in my ears.

There will be more I will have to deal with and remember. I know Lexy will ask me what happened to us, and I'll have to relive every terrifying, violent moment of my childhood. I'll do it for her because I believe she deserves to know the truth. I just hope I'm strong enough to stand on this side of the destruction and not get sucked back under. That fear is why I hold on tight to moments like these where there is peace and quiet and no tears.

"There you are."

Ben always knows where and when to find me. My heart still quickens whenever I look at him. I would have thought the sweet rush would disappear the longer we were together, but my love for him has only grown deeper. He's my best friend, the only one I want to tell everything to. I smile as he comes up beside me. The way he looks at me still makes me blush. He stands close enough to where our arms touch.

He falls into the silence, absorbing it and me. We watch the horses together as the sun sinks lower behind the trees.

"How're you doing?" he finally asks.

"I can't believe she's here." Looking over at him, I drink in his face, his smile, his eyes, the way the sun has kissed his skin. "She's so sad, Ben," I murmur, thinking of the shell-shocked girl with dark, haunted eyes that had stood on my front porch a few hours before. Was it really just that morning? "I've never seen someone so sad. Except for my own sister. What was happening to her out there?"

He shook his head, his expression grim. "Whatever it is, it's bad enough that she came all the way here to get away from it. She looks scared to death."

"She said she just found my letters." I think of Lexy holding up the wrinkled pink envelope. "I've been writing to them for years. How come she only found them now?"

"I don't know," Ben says. "What do you think Victoria will do?"

I lift my shoulders helplessly. "I have no idea." My eyes fall from his as I realize that the sister I've held onto all this time is basically a memory. That's all I have left of her. We've both become different people in all the space and time that has been forced in between us. I wonder if we would be able to recognize each other now. "I used to know her better than anyone. But it's been years since I've even heard her voice."

"Have you called her?"

"No. Lexy said they know she's here. I don't want her to feel I'm betraying her trust by contacting them. Besides, I doubt Victoria would even answer. She never has before."

"Maybe Lexy being here will finally push Victoria to do something."

"Maybe," I murmur. I'm almost afraid to hope for it. I've waited so long but up until now, nothing has changed. I look back towards the horses, feeling the dark threat of the past looming over the land. The sun is barely a shimmer behind the trees as night approaches. I want the light to come back. I felt so much peace before. Now I feel unsafe and exposed and fight the urge to look over my shoulder, to lay low. He's gone, I remind myself, and wonder if I will spend the rest of my life telling myself that.

Instinctively, I move closer to Ben, absorbing his safety and warmth. Understanding, he wraps his arm around me, his lips brushing my temple.

"Have you been able to find out anything more from Lexy?" he asks.

I shake my head. "Not much. The poor thing was exhausted when she got here. She's been asleep the whole day."

"She looked worn out. It's like she ran for her life to get here."

I wince. "I know. I thought the same thing. But from what?"

"I'm sure you'll find out soon enough. I imagine she has a lot of questions for you."

"I'll bet she does," I agree quietly. "I just hope she's able to handle the answers." I hope we both are. I tilt my head, so I can see his eyes. "She looks so much like her, Ben. It's like looking at Victoria twenty years ago." Past Ben's shoulder, I see Nick walking one of the horses back into the stable. "Nick doesn't seem too happy that she's here."

Ben follows my gaze and turns his head. "He just doesn't want to see you hurt. You know how he is with new people. He doesn't know her yet."

I pull back. "Neither do I."

"You will," Ben soothes, tucking one of my curls behind my ear. "She's here because she wants to know you. You're her family."

"I'm scared, Ben," I admit helplessly. "How am I going to tell her what he did to us?"

"You'll figure it out." He gently rubs my back. "Just spend time with her. That's all she wants."

What if she decides she doesn't want to know who I am? What if she regrets coming to find me? What if we both shatter under the crushing weight of the truth? Sensing my uncertainty, Ben pulls me back to him, and I rest my head on his shoulder. I've always believed him. There's no reason to stop now.

The trees and barn are shadowed silhouettes against the horizon. The horses are playing and whinnying. And my niece is finally here and is sleeping up at the main house. I again focus on this one moment where I am safe and loved and no longer have to hide under porches and beds.

Morning will be here soon enough, and I'll face a young girl who, just by knocking on my front door, has opened up Pandora's box.

Chapter Seven
LEXY

My cell phone jolts me awake. Disoriented, I open my eyes and groggily look around the shadowed room, not remembering where I am. It's dark outside. As I fully begin to resurface, I remember what has happened and what I've done.

I quickly sit up and realize I'm in my mom's childhood bedroom, and I've been asleep since after breakfast this morning. I slept in my clothes. I'd only meant to lay down for a few minutes. I can't recall the last time I actually slept without having to wake up and check if my mom was still conscious and breathing.

My phone vibrates again on the nightstand. I thought I had turned it off and blearily pick it up, seeing that I have another voicemail. It's after one in the morning. I already know it's my mom. I don't even bother to listen to the message. I can't bear to hear her tears and desperate apologies. I'm too afraid I'll cave.

She's already left me ten messages since I left. That's not including the times she's called and hung up or the text messages she continues to send me, begging my forgiveness, promising me she's going to get help, swearing she'll change.

Or I get guilt trips, accusations, and angry rants telling me she no longer has a daughter and to not even think about coming home. Most of the messages are slurred and rambling and don't make a lot of sense. It's more of the same, getting worse the farther away I got from her and the longer I was gone.

Feeling vulnerable, I pull my knees tight up to my chin. The house is so quiet. It makes me nervous. My thoughts seem much louder and accusing. I already know I'm not going to fall back to sleep. The fear has found me again.

Dragging my hands through my hair, I look dully out the window. It's a full moon tonight. I can see it resting largely over the trees through the lace curtains. The air is so still, trapping the stifling heat in the room along with my thoughts. I feel like I can't breathe through the pressure in my chest. My phone vibrates again, and I see a text message light up the screen. I don't dare even try to read it. Overwhelmed, I bury my face in my arms.

I can't decide which is worse. The constant phone calls or her not calling at all. If she suddenly stopped calling, I'd know exactly what that meant—that she'd blacked out again. No matter which way I look at the situation, I still end up miserable. I haven't even cried yet. I haven't let myself. I'm afraid that once I start, I'll never stop.

It's ironic to me that she's the one thought of as the victim when I'm the one who deals with the damage and consequences of her addiction every single moment. I'm the one who pays. She gets to drink and disappear while I am clear-minded and sober and have to watch her destroy all of us with every swallow.

Another message comes through. Tormented, I hid my phone in the nightstand drawer and shut it tight. It doesn't really make me feel safer, but I can't take it anymore. Everywhere I look, I can see and hear her. I'm constantly reminded that I left her, that she's completely alone, and I'm too far away now to do anything about it. The panic seems to creep along the walls, waiting to trap me.

I push the sheet back and get out of bed. I need some air. I need to escape. The worn wooden floor creaks under my bare feet, and I make an effort to walk quietly as I pick up my guitar and go downstairs.

The front door isn't locked. We're in the middle of nowhere out here. The nearest neighbor is at least two miles away. It's such a foreign concept to me. Back in California, we have high-tech alarms and gates so high no one can see in. Here we've got horses and fireflies and an old yellow lab guarding the land.

Pushing open the screen, I step out onto the porch. It's not much cooler outside than in the house, but the summer air is warm and fragrant, and the open space helps clear my head a little. The swarming hum of cicadas and crickets, and the croak of frogs are the only sounds.

I walk over to the porch swing and sit down. Cradling my guitar in my lap, I sway lazily back and forth and look out over the land. It's so peaceful out here. I wonder if my mom used to sit in this same spot and look out over the trees and acres of pasture like I am now.

I wish I could burn that place to the ground. Her voice echoes in my head, and I can still see the tears on her face. *Why?* I wonder desperately. What happened to her here?

I can't find any trace of her yet. I keep looking for some part of her, some small clue as to why she had to escape. I've searched in closets, under the bed, through the drawers of the dresser and vanity. The faded flowered wallpaper in her room is the same, and so is the handmade quilt on the bed.

But she's not here. It's like she never even existed, and I wonder if she wanted it that way. She left nothing behind except more secrets and questions. There's no proof of her anywhere. As if she erased herself completely the day she left.

She knows where I am, but I already know she won't come to the ranch to find me. I've run to the one place she's too afraid of returning to. I just wish I knew why.

I don't want to think anymore. It hurts too much. I have no answers and keep spinning in circles. I begin to strum on my guitar, the sweet, sad melody floating out into the starry night. As the lyrics thread together, I start to sing and feel the rush of relief music always brings me. I follow where the song wants to lead and gratefully disappear. And for the first time since leaving, I finally let myself cry.

Chapter Eight

NICK

The nightmare snuck up on me. It always starts out the same. The summer rain, the song on the radio, Megan laughing, me looking over at her because I never could help but stare.

Then everything blurs, and time freezes. Screeching tires, blinding headlights, glass shattering, my truck rolling and skidding over the wet pavement. And then nothing but that sickening silence when the impact is over, and I know I've just lost everything.

Shaking violently and drenched in sweat, I jolt awake with her face so close I swear I could touch and taste her.

It's the loneliest time of night for me. It's late and quiet, and I'm completely alone. This is when I miss Megan the most. The dark hides me, and I can remember her without anyone watching me and pressuring me to get over the loss of her.

It's hard to be around people all day and act like everything is normal. That I've moved on and am fine. When in reality, not one minute goes by when I don't beat myself up for letting her die instead of me.

I barely sleep anymore. The guilt won't let me. The few times I've managed to drift under, I dream of the crash, the driver coming out of nowhere, Megan screaming my name before the collision, and then her being terrifyingly quiet. I'd been pinned under chrome and steel and glass and hadn't been able to get to her. She'd died just inches from my reach. It's agony to open my eyes and have her still be gone.

The worst part is that the accident was no one's fault. The other driver wasn't drunk, he wasn't going too fast, and neither was I. It was just one of those freak things that happened, an act of God, a random glitch in the matrix. Even the courts had ruled it an involuntary occurrence. No one got punished or sent to jail, and no one was held responsible. There was no justice. No one paid. Which meant there was no one to blame except me.

I can't even find an actual reason or purpose for it. I can't make any sense of it. It seems I had lost the only girl I'd ever loved for nothing. I've wrestled against the futility of that for the last two years, six months, four days, and seven hours. I know when I lost her down to the last excruciating minute.

If I'd just turned one second earlier, if I hadn't looked down to turn up the radio for her favorite song, if I'd been paying more attention, if I'd been going slower. I constantly torment myself, trying desperately to figure out the moment I could have avoided the crash and saved her. It's become an obsession and is what tortures me and won't ever let me rest.

Megan had died on impact; I'd ended up in the hospital for eight weeks with cracked ribs, a broken shoulder and pelvis, and a concussion from bashing my head on the steering wheel.

The other guy walked away with just a few scrapes, bumps, and bruises. How do you begin coming to grips with something like that? How do I forgive myself for letting it happen? It follows me everywhere, waits for me, and haunts me at every turn. I don't even try to outrun it. I know I deserve it.

The counselor I'd seen for a few months after the accident told me I had PTSD. It always strikes me as odd how something so dark and overwhelming can be contained in four little letters. As if labeling and diagnosing it miraculously makes it smaller, more understandable, controlled.

Preventable.

I understand the need to somehow find a way to put your world back together after it's been shattered, a defense mechanism against tragedy and the fear that it could happen again. The events play out, rewind, and replay as if stuck on repeat in my traumatized brain. Over and over and over. As if I could have found a way to stop it, turn back time, and change the course of our lives. But it doesn't matter what you call it. She's still gone. And it's still my fault.

I need to get up. I have to move. The depression will suck me under if I don't. I almost didn't make it out of the pit a few years ago. Ben and Becca came in after me, brought me onto their land, and gave me a place to live and time to heal. I've stayed on ever since. They are all I have.

I'm grateful for the distraction of the work on the ranch. It helps me stay sane. It gives me a purpose and keeps me from sinking back down into the bottomless pit where there is nothing to do but drown.

The horses understand me, and I understand them. I need them. They've saved me. They are the one good thing left in my life.

Getting out of bed, I pull off my sweat-soaked shirt and toss it in the hamper. I put on a new one along with my jeans and boots and head out towards the stables.

Our new arrival, Glory, who had been a renowned racehorse on the circuit for the last seven years, just got brought in today. After she'd stopped winning, her trainers pushed her to keep going, taking her almost to the brink of needing to be put down. How people can be so cruel to animals still continues to shock and enrage me. They were so helpless and as starved for love as the rest of us.

Glory was given up on and neglected to the point that she now was skin and bones, had sores and abscesses along her backside, and had stopped trusting everyone.

We have her in her own independent stall in a separate stable, away from the other horses, where she can heal and we can begin the long process of gaining her trust again.

I've already been kicked and snapped at. She's charged me and reared up when I've gotten too close. I'm encouraged to see that she's still got the spirit and strength of a champion. I'd rather have her fight than not care. It means she hasn't completely given up. Now she just needs to see that we won't give up on her.

After checking her sores for infection and locking her back down for the night, I walk slowly towards the cottage. I'm in no hurry to go to sleep. I'm so lost in thought that the sound of singing doesn't register right away, and I absently dismiss it as a radio someone left on during the workday.

It isn't until I'm near the main house that I realize the voice is getting louder and sounds strangely familiar. When I walk around to the front, I see Lexy sitting on the porch swing, her eyes closed, cradling a guitar in her arms, singing one of the saddest and most haunting songs I've ever heard.

She's crying. From the glow of the porch light, I can see the tears on her cheeks as she passionately pours out her heart into the music. I've never seen someone do this before. Fascinated, all I can do is stand there and stare. It's such a fiercely private moment. I know I shouldn't be listening, but I can't make myself move.

I stand back in the shadows, feeling every ounce of pain inside of her. She pulls me into where she is, and I discover a world exactly like mine—one of loss and waiting and thousands of hopeless questions that never have any answers.

Her voice is beautiful; it's so pure and heartbroken I can almost see where her soul is bleeding. I can feel her anguish in every note, every word, every breath. I don't notice I'm holding my own. It's more than just a song, I realize. She's making a confession. It's one of the most honest moments I've experienced in years.

This is what devastation sounds like, completely understanding and responding to it. Aching and raw and gut-wrenching. How does she know pain like this? What happened to her for this kind of misery to come seeping out of her?

I can't hear anymore, but I need to. It's hurting me, but in a way, that is a relief because someone finally is saying what I can't. No one lets me say these things. They don't want to hear them anymore. Everyone wants me to be fine, to be over it.

But I'm not fine, nowhere near it, and it's in this one moment, with this one girl, I don't have to be. She knows; she gets it. I hadn't realized how badly I needed someone to simply say it all out loud. To give me permission to just feel what I'm feeling. I don't want to be fixed or saved. I just want to be allowed to miss her.

I take a step closer, and as I do, my shoulder bumps against the wind chimes dangling from the porch awning. I freeze as the sound gives me away. The music abruptly stops, and her eyes fly open. We stare at each other. I don't know if either of us even blinks.

She looks like a deer caught in headlights, frozen and frightened, not sure which way to run. It crosses my mind that we're the same, both exposed in the very place we don't want anyone finding out about or taking away from us. We're both in front of each other with all our pain laid bare.

I wish I could back up and pretend I hadn't heard her. But she's already seen me. She already knows I've seen her. I awkwardly grab the chimes to stop them from clinking.

"Sorry," I manage, and my voice sounds so loud in the stillness. "I didn't know anyone else was up."

"I couldn't sleep," she stammers, quickly wiping the tears away. The look she gives me is slightly accusing. "What are you doing out here?"

The question annoys me. I don't have to explain anything to her. She's a stranger on this land; I'm not. This ranch may be her inheritance, but I'm the one who knows it like I know my own voice. She's never worked on it a day in her life. She's never even come here. She never once tried.

The thoughts cross through my mind, but I say none of them. The sooner I'm away from her, the better. I keep my face carefully blank.

"I was checking on the horses." I don't tell her I couldn't sleep either. It doesn't seem to matter right now. I can still hear her voice in my head. I don't understand how she knows so much. When I glance again at her guitar, I notice how she instinctively pulls it closer to her body, as if protecting herself. Uncomfortable, I look over my shoulder towards the cottage, wishing I'd never come over to this side of the house. "Didn't mean to interrupt."

"How much did you hear?" she asks.

Too much, I think, but don't dare say it. I feel trapped. I don't want to talk about this. I still don't know how to explain my own reaction to what I heard. "Only a little bit." I watch her expression go wary and vulnerable. I wonder what she's afraid I'll say. "You're really good."

Her eyes widen as she stares at me, completely stunned, which surprises me. People must tell her that all the time. A train goes by in the distance, its whistle blowing the only sound between us. "Thank you," she finally says shyly, still looking amazed.

I don't know what to do, so I just nod. I finally ask the question I've been carrying around since breakfast that morning. "What did Becca tell you about me in her letters?"

She pauses as if she's remembering and shrugs. "Just that you grew up with Ben and lived on the ranch with them," she answers as she lifts the guitar strap over her head. "And that you help out with everything around here." She sets the guitar on the swing next to her. I notice she keeps her hand on it as if making sure it's never far out of her reach.

"And that's it?"

She looks confused. "Yeah, why?"

I don't want to say too much to find out what else she might have been told. It seems Becca kept her word. "No reason." I start to turn away.

"You're really important to her."

I glance back at her. "Yeah, she's important to me, too." I can hear the accusation in my voice, but I don't care. I want her to know she isn't fooling me. "They both are."

She gives me a wounded look. "I'm not here to hurt them."

I don't try to hide the fact that I don't believe or trust her. "Then why come here? Why even bother after all this time?"

She flinches, and I see the pain flash across her face. I refuse to let it make me feel guilty. Becca had waited years to hear from her family, for one of them to simply acknowledge her. But she'd gotten nothing but silence. Maybe she was ready to just let the past be the past, but I wasn't. I'd heard her cry too many times. "I didn't know she wanted to know me until now. I just found her letters a few days ago. My mom hid them and told me Becca wanted nothing to do with us."

I don't want to believe her. Not trusting her keeps her at a distance. I frown as I study her. She has to be lying. I don't know why I need her to be. But her words aren't matching up with the perception I've had in my mind all these years. "Why would she do that?"

"I don't know. That's what I'm trying to find out. My mom won't tell me anything. She never talks about her family or her past." She meets my eyes, and this time, I don't look away. I'm not sure I can. "Is it true what you said?"

Nothing is making sense. The pieces aren't adding up, and the ones that are make me feel sick. And the devastation in her eyes makes it all too clear she's telling the truth. "Is what true?" I ask, trying to keep up. I'm suddenly exhausted.

"That she's been waiting for me."

I hear the desperation and longing in her voice and wish I'd never come out here. I hadn't meant to get this involved. The judgment and anger I've held against her is beginning to crumble. She wasn't indifferent and cold like I had imagined. I can't figure out why it's making me nervous.

The porch light is shining right on her face. I've never seen eyes that sad. She looks plagued. What had happened to this girl? I don't want to feel sorry for her, but it's kind of too late for that. She's been pulling at me from the second I opened the front door and saw her. "Yeah, it is. You're her family. She's always wanted to know you."

For a terrifying minute, I think she's going to cry again, but to my relief, she holds it back. *People do that a lot,* I think absently. Hold everything back. "I still can't believe I'm here. It doesn't feel real yet," she murmurs, looking out down the dirt road as if watching for someone. "This place is so beautiful."

"What did you think it would be like?"

"I don't know. My mom made it sound so different."

"How'd she make it sound?"

"Like a nightmare," she answers so honestly, so plainly, that it makes me stare. I'm not sure what to say. I've heard enough about this place to know she's not wrong. She drags her hands through her hair. The movement catches my eye, and I watch as the dark waves settle over her shoulders. It seems soft. She's quiet for so long I wonder if now is my chance to leave. I start to move away, but then she speaks again, stopping me. I reluctantly turn back to her. "Did Becca ever tell you anything about my mom? Do you know why she left?"

Helplessly, I look at the upstairs window, praying Becca will miraculously wake up and come down, but the house stays dark. I warily look at Lexy, realizing I'm on my own. I'm completely out of my depth here. I take another step back, trying uselessly to get some distance. Her pain feels like it's surrounding me. I don't have room for both hers and mine. "You really should talk to Becca about this."

Her shoulders sag as she realizes I'm not going to give her anything. Wearily, she nods, looking lost and defeated. I sometimes catch Becca with that same look when she thinks no one is around. What are both of them waiting for? "I just want to understand what makes her do it," she whispers fiercely.

I'm so focused on her, it's as if we're the only two awake in the world. "Do what?" I ask because I can't help myself. Why am I letting her get to me like this?

She seems to catch herself, realizing she said too much. She shakes her head, and I feel her pulling herself back in, away from me. I'm on the outside again, just as I'd told myself I wanted to be. I'm surprised at how it makes me feel.

"Nothing," she answers, her voice dull and detached like someone dealing with the aftershock of war. Her eyes are dark and sad and heavy with pain.

It hurts me to look at her. She reminds me of the horses when they first come to us. Scared and battered, and just waiting for the next hand that rises up to hurt them. Against my will, I feel the need to protect and soothe her. I can't just leave her like this. "I'm not sure if this will help at all, but I think I remember seeing where they carved their names into one of these posts when they were little."

"Really?" Her face brightens at this little detail. "Where?"

I bend down and feel around until I find the right one. The names are hard to find, as if the carving was something the two sisters never wanted anyone else to see. "Over here."

She pushes herself off the swing and comes over, crouches down next to me. She reverently traces her fingertips over the jagged letters that spell out her mother's name in the old, worn wood. It's not much to go on, but it is proof that her mom was here. A secret message left behind for her to find. It's a tiny glimpse into a life she knows nothing about.

"How did they carve them all the way under here?" she asks. "It's totally hidden."

"I don't know," I answer, shrugging one shoulder. "I found them a couple of years ago when I was doing some repairs."

She turns her head and gives me a grateful smile that makes my gut tighten. "Thank you."

She's too close to me. Her hair smells like flowers, the sweet kind that are growing up the trellis. I feel guilty for even noticing and quickly get to my feet. "I need to get some sleep."

She straightens, and nods. "Yeah, I probably should too."

I doubt either of us will. I know I won't. I still can't figure out what just happened out here. She's standing on the bottom step. She's eye level with me, which forces me to look directly at her. She didn't just look at you, I realize, startled. She *absorbed* you. And with her back to the light, she's in the shadows, and I'm the one exposed.

Unnerved, I deliberately turn away before she finds another piece of me I don't want her to. "Night," I mumble, not caring if she hears me.

"Goodnight," she says softly, still standing on the porch step.

I can feel her watching me as I walk away. I don't turn around. I'm annoyed at how much I want to. My mind is racing with questions I know I won't ask. After the little I just heard, I'm pretty sure I couldn't handle the answers.

Even when I'm around the back of the house and inside the cottage with the door shut and locked, I still don't feel safe. I have a horrible feeling that absolutely nothing is going to be the same around here.

Chapter Nine
NICK

I'm the first one up. I usually am. Normally, by this time, I would have already downed two cups of coffee, fed and watered the horses, and then come back up to the main house for some breakfast. I've been up for more than an hour, and I'm still on my first cup of coffee, which is now cold. I keep finding myself staring out the window, losing my train of thought.

I can't stop thinking about finding Lexy on the porch last night. Her voice keeps playing over and over in my head. I can't seem to shake the loneliness and grief in the words of her song or the hopelessness in her eyes. What happened to her? Why is she so sad? I wish I didn't want to know. I don't like it. I barely know her and want to keep it that way.

I'm relieved when Becca comes into the kitchen. I've been waiting for her. I need her to take the weight of Lexy's pain from me.

"Morning." She brushes her hand over my shoulders as she passes on her way to the coffee pot. She's one of the few I'm comfortable with. "Rough night?" she asks.

She thinks it's about Megan, I realize. I wish it was and feel guilty that it's not. "Didn't sleep much." Turning away from the window, I lean back against the counter. "Was up a lot with Glory."

She stirs creamer and sugar into her coffee. "How's she doing?"

"Making progress. She's eating and drinking, which is a good sign. Still having a hard time letting people get close to her, though. Gotten kicked and charged at a couple of times." I have the bruises to prove it, too.

Becca smiles knowingly. She's worked with abused horses for years and knows what to expect. "That's normal, especially with all she's been through. Just be patient with her. She'll be eating out of your hand in no time."

"Yeah," I answer, distracted. I know I have to tell her about her niece and am not sure how she's going to take it. "When I was up last night, I ran into Lexy on the porch."

She turns to look at me, her expression worried. "Was she alright?"

"Not really." I can still see her tears but don't mention them. I wouldn't want someone talking about that kind of moment for me. It was so personal. I don't think anyone was supposed to ever know. "She has a lot of questions about her mom."

"I'll bet she does," she says sadly, shaking her head. "What did you tell her?"

"Not much. I figured it should come from you." Since my old cup of coffee is cold, I dump it out in the sink, glancing over my shoulder at her. "I showed her where you and your sister carved your names into the post under the porch."

The kitchen gets very quiet. Too quiet. The temperature seems to have dropped a few degrees as if all the air has been sucked out of the room. Feeling the abrupt shift, I turn and look at her and see she's gone very still, a dark, haunted expression on her face. She seems to be shrinking into herself. I have the thought that if she could hide in a corner, she would do it. Her eyes are dilated, unfocused, as if she's somewhere else, someone else. Someone she doesn't want to remember.

"We spent hours under there," she murmurs, staring painfully into the memory. "Sometimes days." Her skin has gone unnaturally pale. Even her voice sounds different, detached and hollow, making my stomach clench. She holds her coffee mug with both hands as if she's cold even though the day is already warm.

It hurts me to see Becca like this. She suddenly looks very small and scared. I didn't know that. She's never told me before. As close as we are, there were some parts of her life she rarely ever talked about. But now, with Lexy here, I have a feeling a lot more is going to come to the surface. "Will you be okay telling her everything that happened out here?"

"I'm going to have to be," she says, forcing herself to come back to the here and now. "She deserves to know the truth." She pulls her hand unsteadily through her hair. I notice it's trembling and stand a little closer to her. "I'm also hoping she can fill in the blanks about what my sister has been doing all these years."

I remember the devastation I saw in Lexy's eyes the night before. *I just want to understand what makes her do it.* I have a sick, sinking feeling this conversation is going to be much more painful than either of them was ready for. "Do you want me to stick around?"

She shakes her head and straightens her shoulders as if trying to gather strength. "No, I'll be alright, honey." She touches my cheek and gives me a weak smile that pierces my heart because I know how much she's hurting. "Thanks for being there for her last night."

I don't deserve her gratitude. I hadn't wanted to help Lexy and resented her needing me to. I don't have the strength to save us both from drowning. I can barely keep my own head above water. I can't tell Becca that, though. She has enough to deal with.

I nod, not quite able to meet her eyes. I feel like I should be careful of my movements. The air is brittle and much too sad. I'm quiet as I pour coffee into my thermos and then turn back and look at her. She's still standing in the same spot, deep in thought. I've never seen her look so broken and fragile, like a lost little girl.

"I'm going to get out to the horses," I say and move towards the back door. It's very crowded in here with old ghosts and painful memories.

Becca doesn't answer, but I don't expect her to. I leave her alone so she can go talk with a niece she just met about a past that is still very much alive and present in this house.

Chapter Ten
BECCA

My hands are shaking as I knock on Lexy's door. I thought I had dealt with my pain and made peace with his memory and my past. The flashbacks, nightmares, and terrifying sound of my father's voice don't haunt me every night like they used to.

But the emotions rising up in me are intensely primal and raw. Even after all this time, he still has the power to shrink me down until I'm nothing but a helpless, cowering child. I feel as if he is stalking me. Was he always here just waiting? Do ghosts ever actually die? I thought I had laid him to rest years ago.

I know this won't be an easy conversation. I very much understand the places I will have to go back to, the violence I will have to remember, and the tears and trauma I will have to speak of. I will have to tell my niece about the hell that happened here.

"Come in."

My chest tightens at the sound of Lexy's voice. Steeling my resolve, I open the door and poke my head inside. "Good morning, sweetheart." I manage to smile at her as I step into the room. It's still such a shock to see her, a happy, sweet shock. In my hand is a steaming mug, and under my arm are a couple of photo albums. "I brought you up some coffee. Cream and two sugars, right?"

Lexy smiles sleepily. "Right." She pushes herself up in bed, propping the pillows behind her. She'd left the window open, which is a necessity in the sweltering southern summers. The heat gets trapped up in these rooms, especially later in the day. I'll have to remember to bring a fan in for her.

The early morning air drifting in smells of everything I recognize and helps soothe my frazzled thoughts. Closing the door behind me, I walk over to the bed, handing her the mug.

"Thank you," she says, blowing on it a moment, waiting for it to cool before taking a sip. She smiles at me over the rim. "It's really good."

"Be sure and let Ben know. He's our coffee master around here." I sit on the edge of the bed, nervously smoothing my grandmother Rose's quilt. I keep the albums on my lap. I try to gauge her mood, her expression. She looks tired, pale. Lost. My heart aches for her. "I wanted to check and see how you were doing. You were exhausted yesterday, so we didn't get much time to talk."

She looks at me with eyes that remind me painfully of my sister. "I'm okay," she murmurs, pulling her hand through her hair. "Just still trying to believe I'm actually here." She searches my face as if worried about me. "How are you? I know it was a surprise to have me show up like this." She says it as if she's apologizing.

"A very nice surprise," I reassure her. I smile as she does, feeling more comfortable.

She sips again and looks at me. I feel as if her eyes are trying to penetrate my every thought, and I pray we are both ready for what she will find. "Can I ask you something?"

"Of course," I answer, even as I feel myself bracing.

"You've been writing to us for years. How did you even know where we were if you and my mom didn't talk?"

I place the two photo albums on the bed between us. "It took a while. Your mama wasn't easy to find. I'm pretty sure she planned it that way. But a few months after she left, I received a blank postcard with a picture of the Hollywood sign on the front. I knew it was from her. I started with the yellow pages but didn't have much luck since she wasn't listed. It wasn't until she married your dad that I was able to track her down. I found her through his law firm. When he made partner, it was published in the monthly newsletter, along with a picture of the two of them. I looked up your dad and finally got their home address. I started writing to her that very day. I never knew if she was getting the letters, but none of them ever got returned to me, so all I could do was hope they were reaching her."

"They did. She saved every single one you've ever written to her."

My throat tightens as tears burn behind my eyes. "I'm so glad to hear that."

"How did you know about me?"

"I didn't know much about you when you were younger, but these days you can find out anything you want about pretty much anybody. Especially with social media. I found you on Facebook a few years ago."

She smiles. "I looked for you on there, too," she admits.

"You did?" I ask, surprised and pleased.

She nods. "After I found the letters. I also looked up your rescue foundation for the horses. I think it's great what you and Ben do out here."

"Thanks. We're pretty proud of it." Realizing all I've told her, I let out a nervous laugh. "I can only imagine what you think of me." Embarrassed, I shake my head. "I must sound crazy."

"I don't think you do," she says earnestly. "I'm glad you didn't give up on us. You sound like you really miss her."

"I do. All the time. Not one day has gone by that I haven't thought about her and wondered how she is, how her life has turned out. If she's happy." I notice that Lexy falls quiet and won't look at me. The skin on the back of my neck prickles as my fears are confirmed. I'm not the only one carrying dark secrets. "I know you must have a lot of questions for me. Nick told me about finding you on the porch last night." I pick up one of the photo albums. "I thought you might like to see some pictures of our family and your mama and me growing up."

Her eyes are instantly razor-sharp and aware. It was more than just curiosity, I realize. The girl was on a mission.

I open up the front cover. Lexy sets her coffee cup on the nightstand and then leans forward, searching intently for answers.

The first photo is a yellowed tintype of a young man, no more than twenty years of age, stoic and unsmiling, in old worn overalls, the brass buttons glinting in the sun. He's in an open, empty field where the barn now stands. A wooden wagon loaded up with lumber and supplies is next to him. "This is your great-great-grandfather, Beau Montgomery. And this," I point to the photo of a woman with her hair wrapped up in a neat bun, wearing a high-collared blouse and full skirt standing on the same porch where Lexy had been the night before, "is your great-great-grandmother, Adelaide Montgomery. Beau married Adelaide after the war ended, and they settled on this land. Built this very house with their own two hands."

We flip through black and white images of the land as it was being settled on and built into the ranch it was today. Not much had changed over the years. I point to a grainy photo of a man wearing a crisp, white linen shirt and chaps, pointy cowboy boots with spurs sticking proudly out of the sides, a huge, ornately-decorated belt buckle at his waist, and a large-brimmed cowboy hat on top of his head. He was standing under an oak tree holding the reins to a beautiful stallion.

"This is your great grandfather, Cade Montgomery. He was the local horse whisperer and was a legend around these parts. Everyone knew about him. Was even in the papers. Could make a horse dance simply with a nod of his head."

Lexy seems fascinated. "Really?"

"Yes. People would come for miles around to watch him work with the horses."

On the next page is a photo of Rose Montgomery wearing a glamorous fringed dress and standing in front of a microphone, her head thrown back, eyes closed, arms flung wide, as she performed on a stage. I notice how Lexy stares at the photo a little longer than the others. "Your great Grandmother Rose was a blues singer out in Memphis back in the twenties. We still have some recordings of her up in the attic. I'll try to find them for you." I glance over at Lexy's guitar on the bed. "Do you sing?"

She blushes, nodding shyly. "A little."

"I'd love to hear you sometime. Maybe you get it from her."

Lexy seems to like that. I notice her eyes light up as she smiles down at the photo. "Maybe."

"Your mama also has a beautiful voice. She used to sing to me all the time when we were little." She'd held my hand and sang softly under the covers to make my nightmares go away.

"She doesn't sing anymore," Lexy says sadly.

My brow creases as I look over at her. "I'm very surprised to hear that. Music was her whole world."

Lexy doesn't answer, and I notice how carefully she avoids my gaze. Is it my imagination, or did she flinch? My heart sinks even further into my stomach. A million questions spring to mind, but I swallow them back. The tension around my niece is thick and palpable, and I decide it's best to let it be for a bit longer.

The photos begin to come into color as the years go by and times change. When I turn the page, I feel Lexy go still and hear her quiet gasp as she sees my parent's wedding photo. She stares intently down into the faces of Ray and Lily Mason, searching for connection, revelation, and answers. "You look a lot like your mom," she says, glancing up at me.

"I've heard that," I say fondly. "Thank you." I have always felt honored to be compared to her. My mom was the most beautiful woman in the world to me.

"My mom looks like her dad." I notice how intensely Lexy studies her grandparents. "They seem so normal," she whispers, frowning. I can sense her confusion as she tries to make the puzzle pieces fit. I have no doubt that if she could reach through the photo and time itself, she would do it.

Lexy changes her focus to the photo on the next page, one of Victoria and I perched on the fence near the barn wearing our Sunday dresses. I was six, Victoria nine. Our clothes were handmade as we didn't have the money for store-bought ones.

Lexy gently traces her fingertip over her mother's face, and I realize how much she loves and misses her. "She was sad even back then," she says, as she studies Victoria's vacant, dull expression.

"Neither of you are smiling in any of these pictures. It's like you're not even there. Like you're both trying to be invisible." Her frustration continues to build as she flips through the album. I feel it vibrating in the air around her. The photos tell a story, but not the whole truth.

"We were," I murmur, wincing at how true that statement is.

"But why?" She looks at me, her eyes dark and full of questions. "What happened to her here? Why did she leave?"

How do I do this? I wonder helplessly. I'm not ready. My throat feels choked and hot. It's hard to push the words out. "She had to, sweetheart." My voice sounds hoarse, strained. "It wasn't safe for her. Daddy was an alcoholic, and he was mean when he was drunk. He was mean when he wasn't, too. Took out most of his anger on our mama and Victoria. He left me alone; I was young enough that he ignored me most of the time. But something about Victoria ate at him wrong. I don't know what it was, but he came at her just for waking up in the morning."

Lexy has gone very still and pale, her eyes wide and dark and glazed with shock. I can't tell if she's fully breathing. I'm not even sure I still am. "He would hit her?" The question comes out as a raspy whisper.

Hit her. Beat her until she was bloody and bruised all over. Kicked her so hard she threw up. I can't say it. I can't tell this innocent girl how her mama was dragged across the floor by her hair in this very room while I cowered in the corner, sobbing and begging him to stop.

I clench my hands tightly in my lap, so tight my nails are digging into my palms. Strange how the pain helps. "Yes," is all I manage to get out. It's such a small word for the gravity of what happened. I can't feel my lips moving. My entire body is on high alert. Why

83

does remembering have to hurt this much? It's as if I'm four years old all over again. "Anything would set him off. The television being on too loud, the screen door banging, his dinner not being warm enough. When he would get into one of his rages, we would run and hide under the bed or in the closet. Under the porch. We'd stay under there for hours waiting for him to pass out."

She stares at me as realization dawns. "That's why your names are carved on the post."

I wince. It feels like I'm still there. Sweaty and starving and so scared. All I can do is nod.

"Why didn't your mom take you both and leave?"

"She couldn't. We had nowhere to go. We had no money. He was the one who worked when he could keep a job long enough to bring home a paycheck. He'd either hide it or spend it all on whiskey and gambling. The little allowance he did give her, she spent to buy us food and clothes. And back in those days, you just didn't leave, no matter how bad it was."

"So, how did my mom finally get out?"

"She waited until she was old enough for him to not be able to stop her. The day she turned eighteen, she ran. He blacked out, and she was gone. It was just in time, too. Their fights had been getting worse; a couple of times, I had to call the police. It was at the point that if one of them didn't leave, they were going to kill each other."

"What happened to you after she was gone? Did he hurt you?"

"Not in the same way. He didn't pay much attention to me at all, would look right through me. He hardly ever spoke to me." I stare dully at the floor, remembering those lonely, indifferent silences, the blank expression in his eyes as if I didn't even exist and was insignificant. I guess to him, I was. "I can't even remember the last words he said to me. He died about fifteen years ago from cancer."

"Why didn't you leave, too?"

I feel myself sinking, the suffocating weight of my past trying to pull me down. He's gone, I remind myself. He can't hurt me anymore. But it feels as if he's still here, staggering up the stairs towards our bedroom. I swear there are nights I can hear his boots thudding over the floor as if he still haunts this place.

Fighting the urge to hide, to run for cover, I keep my eyes on Lexy, needing something to anchor me in the present. "I couldn't leave my mama. She still needed help with this place, and daddy was barely around, and when he was, he was so drunk he couldn't get up off the couch. So to help make ends meet, I got a job over at the local feed store. That's where I met Ben. His family owned it, and we started dating. Been together ever since."

"You seem really happy together."

I smile tenderly. "We are. He's a good man. I wouldn't have made it without him."

"You don't have any kids?"

My smile fades. Even after all this time, my heart still breaks at the question. It never gets easier to answer. "No honey, we don't. I've had two miscarriages. One at six weeks, the other at fourteen." I still think of how old they would be now, wonder what they would have looked like, what they would have become, what it would have felt like to hold them. I'll never know. "We've been trying, but so far..." I trail off, shrugging helplessly.

She takes my hand. "I'm so sorry, Becca."

"This is just how it is," I say. "It doesn't ever really go away, but it helps to have this ranch and the horses. And Nick is like family to us." I reach over and brush her hair off her shoulder, managing a sad smile. "And now, you're here."

She leaves her hand in mine to comfort both of us. "Is it hard for you to stay here with everything that's happened?"

"Some days are harder than others," I admit, sighing. "There's so much of him still in this house. But I knew if I left, I wouldn't ever be able to face what he did to us. This land has been in our family for over a hundred and fifty years. Before our mama died and left us the ranch, she made me promise I would make this place a home again. He can't ever take away what Ben and I have built here. I won't let him."

Lexy looks at me, her eyes clear and level on mine. "You're still waiting for my mom to come back, aren't you?"

She's the kind of person you tell things like this to, I realize. She has an unusual empathy for someone so young. And you don't dare lie to her. She'd see right through you. Victoria used to look at me the same way.

"Yes," I say plainly, knowing I can, that she'll accept and understand it. "I have always hoped she will." I look back to the photo of Victoria and me sitting on the fence, tracing my finger over the two little girls that we used to be. We'd told each other everything back then. All our secrets were whispered only to one another. "You're the same age she was when she left," I murmur, absorbing the ironic, sad reality of that. We've come full circle, I realize. "I haven't seen her in twenty-five years." Victoria's deliberate silence, the total abandonment of it, still continues to haunt me. "How is she?" I finally let myself ask because I can't hold it in any longer.

When I look back at Lexy, I'm shocked at how dead and dark her eyes are.

"She's drunk," she says, her voice dull and hopeless.

I feel all the breath and strength leave my body. "What?"

"She drinks all the time. I can't get her to stop." Her words spill out fast, like a tidal wave, and I wonder if it's so she doesn't change her mind. I can feel her relief that she is finally able to let the truth be known. "She blacks out for days, and then when she finally wakes up, she just does it all over again. I've begged her to get help, but she won't. I'm so scared she's going to kill herself." Her breath is coming in short, hysterical gasps. "I didn't know you wanted us in your life. When I found your letters, when I found out she'd lied to me this whole time, I had to come find you. I needed to know the truth."

I can't seem to get air in. My lungs burn as if I've been running and running for miles. "Oh honey, I'm so sorry." I instinctively grip her hand tighter. "Please believe me when I tell you that I have always wanted to know you. I never once gave up hope that one of you would come find me."

Lexy's eyes fill with tears, her face crumpling. "She wouldn't let me ask about you. She said you wanted nothing to do with us. Anytime I brought up anything to do with her past or her family, it would just make things so much worse." She clumsily wipes at her cheeks with the back of her hand, but more tears keep coming. "She would totally lose control, and so I stopped asking." Her eyes meet mine, desperate and devastated. Her pain is like a physical punch to the gut. "I'm so sorry that I believed her. I'm sorry I didn't come before now. I was terrified of what she would do to herself. I don't even know if she's alive right now. And it's all my fault."

"Oh, sweetheart. None of this is your fault." I pull her into my arms, her body trembling as she finally lets herself fall apart.

She clings tight to me, as a frightened child would. I wonder the last time someone held her like this. I feel the heat of her sobs and ragged breath against my neck. "I don't blame you, Lexy. I grew up in it. I understand all too well doing what you have to so you can survive." I stroke her hair, rocking her slowly back and forth. "You did the only thing you could do. You're safe now."

I continue to murmur softly, whispering promises and reassurance, as she cries. This has been coming for years, I realize, so much fear and pain pent up inside this poor, young girl. Her tears pour out from that shattered place inside her broken heart and soak my shirt and skin but I don't mind. I've waited her whole life to have her here.

After a long while, she falls quiet and stops shuddering. Her breathing gradually begins to steady and match mine.

When she pulls back, I gently move the curls back from her damp face. Her eyes are drenched and gut-wrenchingly hopeless as they meet mine. Her lips are swollen, cheeks flushed. "I'm really scared," she whispers.

"I know you are, honey. I am, too." I hand her a Kleenex. "Where's your dad? How does he deal with everything?"

"He doesn't," she answers. She says it with the weary resignation of someone used to being let down. "He works all the time and is barely home." She wipes at her tears. "When he is there, they get into these horrible fights, and my mom locks herself back in her room and won't come out."

Swallowing the hot rush of anger, I make myself hold back bitter words. It won't do Lexy any good. "So you were on your own out there?"

Lexy nods, looking lost and vulnerable and so much like her mother that it makes me want to weep.

I squeeze her hand. "You don't have to be alone anymore." Neither of us does.

As Lexy wipes the last of the tears from her cheeks, she notices the locket around my neck, reaching out to look at it more closely. "My mom has the other half of this heart."

Managing a bittersweet smile, I protectively wrap my fingers around the necklace. "Your great grandmother Rose gave us each one when we were little."

"I knew I recognized it yesterday. She still wears it."

Stunned, I stare at her. "She does?"

Lexy nods. "She never takes it off."

Lexy could have given me no greater gift. My sister has never forgotten. She's remembered me, all our promises, our secret pacts, our whispered, frightened pinky swears. Maybe she even misses me, needs me. I know how much I still miss her. I allow myself to hope in a way I haven't in years. "Thank you for telling me that," I say, my voice breathless and trembling with emotion. "It means a lot to me."

Lexy looks down at the photo album again. She picks it up, and as she does, a folded-up newspaper article flutters out from the back cover onto the bed. When she unfolds it, her eyes widen in surprise as she stares at Nick and a pretty blonde smiling on the front page. She looks up at me. "Becca, what is this?"

My heart sinks as Nick's pain, a pain he never, ever talks about, is laid bare right in front of us with no way to hide it. "I'd forgotten I'd put that in there." I try to pull it from her reach, but she's already reading it.

Next to their Senior Ball photo is a grotesque image of the car Nick and Megan had been driving that horrible night. It was demolished beyond recognition. I'm silent as Lexy reads more, her body going completely still as she finishes the story. I know every word of it. High school sweethearts ripped apart by a tragic car accident. They had just graduated and were planning on going off to college together in the fall. But on the night of Megan's eighteenth birthday, on their way back from the family celebration, the unthinkable happened.

Lexy's eyes are wide and full of horror as they meet mine. "She died? Nick's girlfriend died?"

As my breath constricts, I can only nod. "They hit a tree. It was raining, and the roads were too wet for either driver to stop. Nick tried to get out of the way of the other car but swerved out of control. Megan was killed instantly."

"She was only eighteen. That's my age." Lexy looked closer at the girl in the photo. "She was beautiful."

"Yes, she was. And so sweet. You would've liked her. Nick adored her. They met when they were freshmen in high school. They were together for four years."

Lexy shifts her gaze to Nick. He's young and handsome and smiling straight at the camera. "He was so happy back then. He looks totally different now."

"He's very different," I agree, trying to remember the last time I saw him smile, much less laugh. It's been years. He's almost unrecognizable. "Losing her has completely changed him."

"How could it not?" Lexy shakes her head with sorrow and grief in her eyes. "You never get over something like that. Poor Nick." She notices the date on the article. "This was almost three years ago. That's not very long. No wonder he's so sad all the time." She looks up at me. "How did he end up here?"

"Ben and Nick have been friends since they were kids. They grew up across the road from each other. Their families go way back. Nick is like a younger brother to him. When we found out about the accident, we asked Nick to come stay with us. He was depressed, and we were worried about him. We needed the help, and Nick needed somewhere to fall apart and start healing. The local news also wouldn't leave him alone, and this ranch was a good place to hide out. He's been here ever since. I honestly don't know what we would do without him."

Lexy pulls her knees up and wraps her arms around them. "It seems like he wouldn't know what to do without you guys either." She rests her chin on her knees as she watches me. "I guess this ranch is what you wanted it to be after all."

"What do you mean?"

"It's a safe place for everyone who comes here."

I stare at her as the truth of what she said sinks in. I think about the hundreds of abandoned, abused horses we've rescued, of Nick seeking solace and privacy, and now of Lexy looking for answers and a quiet place to rest and heal. "I hope so," I murmur, smiling thoughtfully.

Out of respect, Lexy carefully folds the article and holds it out to me. "I won't say anything."

I smile, touched by how thoughtful and sensitive she is. I'm amazed she's been able to hold onto a shred of goodness in an environment where she's surrounded by fear and addiction. I glance around my childhood bedroom, the four walls still holding a past I feel helpless to change. So many ghosts still live here, and none of them are at peace. I look back to my niece, who is expecting me to know the answers. "I'm sorry I can't do more for you."

"You've already done everything," Lexy reassures me. "Thank you for telling me the truth and for waiting for me."

Feeling tender and maternal towards her, I lightly touch her cheek. "I'm really glad you're here, Lexy."

"Me, too."

I drop my hand back into my lap. "Would you like to come down and see the horses? I'd love to show you around this place."

She picks up the other album I'd left on the bed. "Do you mind if I just look at some more pictures for a little while?"

"Not at all. I've got plenty more where those came from. I'll bring them down from the attic for you." I get to my feet, sensing she wants to be alone. She needs some time to process all I've told her, to let it sink in. I look down at this precious, young girl who I've never known but have loved simply because she was my sister's daughter. "I'm right downstairs if you need me."

I clutch the newspaper article close to my heart as I walk out of the room. It isn't until I close the door behind me that I finally let my tears fall. For my sister, for me, for Lexy, for Nick. We've all lost too much here, a long history of tragedy and heartache. Pressing my hand against my mouth to hold back the sobs, I quietly go up the stairs to the attic, so no one will hear me shatter.

Chapter Eleven
BECCA

I need aspirin.

My head is pounding, and the pain is radiating along my scalp, gripping my temples. Even my eyes are throbbing. I wept until I was empty and drained and exhausted. I hadn't realized it would be this traumatic to remember the past, but the force of it had rushed up and surrounded me so quickly, so violently, I hadn't had time to prepare for the blow.

Bleary-eyed from the tears, I barely notice Ben and Nick sitting at the kitchen table finishing up lunch as I come back downstairs from the attic. I feel like a walking zombie as I go to the cupboard, pull out the plastic bottle, open it, and pour two into my hand. I don't realize until that moment that I'm shaking as I numbly shuffle to the sink and fill a glass with water.

My movements are robotic, as if I'm outside of my own body. Swallowing down the aspirin seems to take the last of my strength out of me as I set the glass clumsily back on the counter. I can't seem to make myself move anymore and stare dully out the window. Nick and Ben are talking behind me, their voices muted and far away as if I'm underwater.

"Becca, will you please tell Nick he's got it all wrong? There's no way he—" Ben's laughter quickly fades when he looks over and sees my face. "Becca?" His chair scrapes back, and he's instantly on his feet, next to me in two strides. He grips my shoulders, turning me towards him. "What is it? What happened?"

"I was right," I manage to push the words out past the devastation. My throat hurts as if I swallowed shards of glass. "I was right about her."

"Who?" He frantically searches my face for something, an injury, a scratch, or a sign of what could be making me fall apart like this. "Right about who?"

I can barely focus on him. My eyes feel glassy, my head full of fog. "Victoria. She's an alcoholic, just like him. Lexy has been living with it for years." I'm surprised at how matter of fact my voice sounds, how clear. Especially since there is chaos churning inside of me, clawing my sanity to shreds. I can't feel my face or my lips. My skin is cold and clammy. "She said Victoria drinks all the time and then blacks out for days. Lexy has grown up the same way we did." I'm seeing spots, shifting colors of red and blue dance in front of me. Ben's face looks wavy and distorted. The air is too thin.

Alarmed, Ben holds me up so I won't slip out of his grasp. His hands are too tight, but I barely feel them. "Sit down," he urges, leading me to a chair.

I collapse in on myself as my legs buckle from beneath me. My entire body feels limp and weak, as if I'm boneless. "That poor girl," I murmur, shaking my head. "She's too young to have all this on her."

"What're you going to do?" Nick asks me. I notice how worried he looks. No wonder he wanted to stay close to me this morning.

His conversation with Lexy last night must have given him a hint of the storm that was coming.

I shrug helplessly. "There's nothing I can do. Victoria won't let me. I've tried for years to reach out to her, and she's shut me out at every turn." I look at Ben, fresh tears welling up and spilling over. I thought I'd cried everything out up in the attic, but there was so much pain inside of me. Decades of it. When does the cycle end? "Victoria left here to get free of him. Now she's exactly like him and is doing the same thing to her own daughter. She even told Lexy we wanted nothing to do with her. Why would she do that?" I look desperately at the one person I always thought would have the answers, my face streaked with betrayal and heartbreak.

Anger and grief flash over Ben's face, darkening his eyes. "I don't know. I wish I did. Where is Lexy now?"

"Upstairs. She's looking at more photo albums. She needs some time to process it all." I wince as I remember how she sobbed in my arms after she revealed the secrets she's been carrying all these years. "She has no one back home to help her. Richard is gone all the time with work. He just avoids everything and leaves his daughter to clean up the mess. She can't tell anyone. She's totally alone."

"She can stay here as long as she wants." He cups my face in his hands. "We'll figure it out. I promise."

Completely worn out, I look at him, at the face I fell in love with when I was sixteen. He's protected me from so many things; the nightmares, the flashbacks, the loneliness. He's seen me at my absolute worst and has never left. I'd trust him with my life.

But this is bigger than him. He's not strong enough to block the past from breaking down the door. He can't erase our childhood or prevent the poison of it from tearing apart all we've built out here. He can't keep the lies and abuse from swallowing us whole.

"How?" I ask hopelessly. "It's never going to be over." Burying my face in his shoulder, I start to cry again, but not because of Lexy. It's because, for the first time, I don't believe him. We've all been lying to ourselves. My father has never been gone, I realize, and he's still taking my sister away from me. And I'm a terrified little girl again, hiding under the porch with no one around to save me.

Chapter Twelve
LEXY

For the last two days, I've barely come out of my room. I've poured over any small detail I could get on the Montgomery family line, devouring photos, birth certificates, census records, report cards, and wedding announcements. Becca had saved every memento in dusty trunks up in the attic.

The last photo album has been scoured, and I still am not satisfied. My mind is racing with curiosity and more questions. I had no idea my mom's childhood had been so violent and horrible. I'd had my suspicions, and I've wondered, but without proof, without any answers, I had nothing to go on.

A gentle breeze drifts in from the window, rustling papers, and I look out at the acres of green spreading out for miles. I can't remember the last time I felt sunlight and fresh air. I need to get out of the house. I can't think anymore. I've been inside too long. I've been in my head too long. I've needed time to sort through the devastation.

Pushing myself off the bed, I arch backwards, stretching and rubbing the sore muscles in my neck. I'm stiff from sitting in the same position for hours. After days of spending so much time with people from the past, I am ready to explore the land and life they left behind. I quickly shower, get dressed, and head downstairs.

As I push open the screen door and step out onto the porch, I have to squint and shade my eyes as they adjust to the afternoon light. The summer air is humid and warm, bringing up the scents of irrigated pastures, the sweetness of honeysuckle, and moss and timber from the heavy, drooping oak trees that shelter and shade the land.

Off towards the back of the house, I hear the horses whinnying and turn towards the sound. A man's voice, Ben's, I think, is calling out commands to trot and then slow down and come back to center. His voice is soothing but firm, and I like the sound of it. I can see why Becca feels safe with him.

I remember the way he smiled at her across the table at breakfast the other morning. I've never seen my dad look at my mom like that. I wonder if he used to and if my mom would blush the way my aunt did when she caught Ben staring. I wish I knew what it was like when my parents first fell in love, or if they ever did. After all this time, is there anything left in them for each other?

How is everything so normal out here? The world has kept spinning; time has kept going forward. The sky and sun seem foreign, unreal, and tilted. I don't know what to do with myself now. I have no idea who I am without her addiction telling me how long I have to hold my breath before I can let it out again. I am so used to the stress and chaos of taking care of her, I don't know how to function without the fear hanging over me.

Time is so different on the ranch, slow and unhurried and easy. If I were back home, I would be anxiously waiting, worrying, and listening for her to finally wake up. I would be getting her breakfast ready, moving quietly and carefully through the house because her hangover was always so intense. The slightest noise would cause her to get sick and completely unravel her. I was constantly trying to outrun the monsters that made her drink in the first place. My sole purpose was to try and hide her from the next time they snuck up and grabbed her away from me. Only I could never find them in time and could never figure out how to save her.

My mom had been wrong, I think, wrapping my arms around myself as I look out over the pastures. I don't hate her now that I know. If anything, finding out the truth helps me to understand her better, the fear that drives her, and why she does what she does. Part of me desperately wants to run back to her, to tell her how sorry I am and that we will do whatever we can to fix it.

I wonder how she's doing. I haven't talked to her in four days. I'm still obsessively counting down the time. Her texts and calls have stopped. Every second, I have to fight against the panic of what I fear is happening to her. I know all too well what her silence means. She's disappeared into her room and blacked out.

I haven't heard from my dad. He must know I found the letters. Is he home, or is he still hiding out at his office? Who is taking care of her if I'm not? Does he know if she's alive? Still breathing? Has he even checked?

The anxiety is so familiar, thrumming through me like an electric charge under my skin. The guilt tears me up to the point where I can barely breathe past the vicious knots in my stomach. I feel so helpless. I've tried for years to rescue her and have failed at every turn. How do I help her when she doesn't want to be saved? How do I get someone to stop doing something they want and need to do? How do you put someone back together when you are shattered too?

Humpty Dumpty sat on a wall. Humpty Dumpty had a great fall. All the King's horses and all the King's men, couldn't put Humpty together again.

I don't know where the sudden memory came from. I haven't heard that nursery rhyme in years. My mom had read it to me in one of my storybooks once. It feels like forever ago, almost as if I imagined it. I don't know how to put her back together. I never have. Being here is the only way I know how to finally change things. There are more secrets here, more truths to uncover. I have to find them. I have to know. And maybe when I do, I will find all of us.

There is nothing but wide-open space in front of me. I could run for as long as I want and still not reach the end of the horizon. I go down the steps and walk to the back of the house towards the stables.

It's so quiet. That's the hardest thing to get used to out here. I've never liked silence. It always meant something was wrong. But here, the quiet is hushed and still and safe. I'm in the middle of nowhere, completely tucked away. I have the odd sensation of being able to hide in plain sight and wonder if that's also how my mom felt out here.

There's a narrow dirt path in the grass, one made by the generations of those who have walked here before me. The history of this land is all around me in every creaking board, the rippled window panes, and each ancient, gnarled tree. I feel the centuries brush up against me everywhere I look.

My great-great-grandparents settled on this land and built a life here, leaving a legacy for those of us who followed after them. I think of Beau and Adelaide Montgomery, of Cade and Rose, of Ray and Lily Mason, of Becca and my mom, walking on this same land. These fields have seen war and weddings, tears and laughter, fear and addiction, hell and heaven. And each person who lived and died here left some part of themselves behind to help me discover my place in our family line.

It's the first time in my life I've felt like I belonged to anyone, anywhere. I wish I could have experienced what life was like back then and known the people who came here before me.

The path leads towards the barn and stables. The barn looks exactly like what I always pictured one to look like. I've only seen them in books or movies. It's big and red with a hayloft up top, with wide, thick doors on the front. A rusted iron weathervane in the shape of a running stallion is perched on the roof. A rickety wooden windmill turns lazily nearby. The outbuildings have all been painted a clean, colonial white, the same as the main house.

Reaching the door to the stable, I slip in. The pungent smell of grain, hay, and manure is strong. Large overhead fans keep the air constantly moving. I hear someone talking in a low, patient voice. When I get closer, I realize it's Nick. He's with one of the horses in the last stall towards the back. I stand a few feet down and watch him, guessing it is one that arrived a few days ago. I remember overhearing Ben mentioning the arrival of a new mare. Nick is talking quietly so as not to startle or scare her.

The horse used to be beautiful; its coat is a deep rich mahogany but is now mangy with lack of care. I can see sores along her side and her back leg. A deep jagged scar is across her nose, and I wonder what happened to her. As Nick moves around her stall, he gets too close to her wounded side. Without warning, the horse cries out and rears up, trying to pull away from him, its eyes so wide and frightened, I can see the white around them. Startled, I gasp and back up against the wall, afraid of getting trampled.

Hearing my gasp, Nick looks over sharply, and I see his expression cloud over when he realizes it's me. "Stay back," he orders. He doesn't take his hand off the horse, continuing to stroke her neck and talk low and soft. She snorts noisily as a warning, stomping her hooves on the ground, challenging him. I wonder if she will hurt him. After a tense minute, she reluctantly settles, although her tail swishes irritably back and forth. Nick waits a few more moments until he's sure she won't charge and then moves a few steps closer and bends to examine her again. "Good girl," he murmurs, gently stroking her hindquarters. "You're alright."

I watch Nick, fascinated by how gentle he is, how patient. I hadn't expected this tender side of him. He's so closed off and guarded around people. I can feel the horse gradually getting used to him being in her space. The angry, primal fear has left her eyes. Now they are just cautious and aware and taking everything in.

From where I'm standing, I can see how skinny she is, her rib cage protruding painfully, her belly bulging out, every bone in her spine. I feel something stir deep in me. I want to cry. I'm drawn to her and step closer.

Nick sends me a dark look, annoyed at having his process invaded. "You shouldn't be in here," he says gruffly, trying to relay the danger of the situation.

I know I should listen, but I can't seem to make myself leave. The battered horse is watching me, her eyes defeated, desperate and devastated. It's like looking in a mirror. I see my mom. I see me. I feel a rush of compassion and keep my eyes on her as I take another step towards the stall. "What happened to her?"

Nick doesn't look over at me, but I can feel his frustration that I hadn't left. "She was pushed too far." There's a shelf next to me on the wall. He reaches past me and picks up a bottle of saline. I can smell the saddle oil and leather on him, the sweat, the musk of the horse. Heat radiates off his skin. I don't get out of his way. I don't seem to be able to move. We've barely seen each other over the last few days, only once at dinner. I haven't had much of an appetite. The last time we talked was the night on the porch when he heard me sing. I hadn't realized until now how much I had thought about him and wondered what he was thinking. He's the only one who knows my secret. "If you're going to be in here, you better stay back."

"I'll be careful," I promise. I'm close enough that I have to look up to meet the horse's eyes. "Why would someone do this to her?"

"Winning was more important, I guess," he mutters, and I can hear the disgust and anger in his voice. He opens the bottle of saline. "Don't get too close. She's not going to like this."

Obediently, I move away from the stall door in case she breaks free or charges, and watch as he washes out her sores. The horse whips her head around and snaps, snorting. "I know. I know," Nick soothes. "We're almost done."

I notice a bucket of apples next to the supplies on the shelf. They are cut into bite-size pieces. I want to do something to help her not have to feel what is happening to her, to make one thing easier for her, even if it's only for a second.

I reach in and pick one up. The horse tracks my movements and tentatively leans her head towards me. I carefully hold the apple out for her, palm up. She hesitates, and sniffs. Holding very still, I don't take my hand back, and she bends her head. I can't help smiling as she licks my hand and swallows the apples. Her tongue is surprisingly smooth. I hadn't thought it would be.

I don't back away and stand quietly where I am, letting her get used to me. We gauge each other. She's enormous and intimidating. She towers over me, and I can tell that at one point, she must have been a gorgeous racehorse. I'm in awe of her size, strength, and power. A few heartbeats pass with neither of us moving, and then the horse slowly lowers her head, thrilling me. I reach up and let her smell my hand, and she presses her nose against my palm for me to stroke her. "Hi, sweet girl," I whisper.

"What're you doing?" Nick snaps at me, his hand on the horse's side just in case. "I told you to stay—" he trails off as he realizes the horse is letting me pet her. He looks both stunned and amazed. He moves closer. "Be careful," he warns, watching to make sure he doesn't need to step between us. "Go slow with her."

I keep my movements gentle, being mindful of her gashes. "What's her name?"

"Glory," Nick answers, keeping a hawk-eye on us as he begins to gently work out the knots in the horse's matted mane. "Not that she looks much like it right now."

I look up into Glory's soulful, sad eyes. They seem to be pleading with me to help her. "Poor girl. I'm so sorry you were hurt." This isn't at all what she wanted her life to be. "She just wants to know she's safe." I understand the need painfully well. Nick doesn't say anything to that. "Will she make it?"

It takes Nick a while to answer as if he's in his own world and reluctantly has to pull himself out. "Hopefully. Still too soon to tell."

Glory pushes at my shoulder with her nose, searching for more apples. I can't help laughing when she nuzzles my hair. When I turn to get another piece, I catch Nick watching me with a frustrated scowl. I feel my face go hot. "Is it okay to give her these?"

He catches himself staring and frowns at me as if it's my fault, looks away. "Yeah," he mutters, and moves around to the other side of the horse, so I can't see him as well. I can't tell if it was on purpose. "Not too many, though. Don't want her getting sick."

I stay quiet and watch him, trying to understand him. He's different when he's with the horses, I notice. Patient and protective and kind. He feels safe with them. He trusts them. Even as Glory tests him, pushes his limits, and charges at him, he just takes it and keeps working on breaking through to her. He won't ever give up on them.

"You're so good with her," I tell him. "She'll believe it's not her fault soon."

He pauses then and glances over the top of Glory's back at me, an odd expression on his face. He seems surprised and looks like he's about to ask me something, but then changes his mind. Instead, he ducks his head back down where I can't see him and says, "I've got to take her out and walk her so that back leg doesn't freeze up."

He comes up to the stall door and reaches across me for the bridle and reigns. He's close enough that I notice the scar above his right eyebrow and think of the car crash, of Megan, of the tragic and terrible way he lost her. *Becca was right,* I think, picturing him young and smiling and in love in the newspaper article. He's completely different now. His grief has made him a stranger. Does he even remember who he used to be anymore?

I want to ask him how he deals with it every day, if he's ever managed to forgive himself, if there's ever one second that the guilt doesn't hunt him down. The words burn in the back of my throat. I'm so desperate for someone who understands, who knows what it's like to carry this kind of devastation and fear all the time. Where is it all supposed to go?

He catches me looking at him, and everything I'm thinking must be written all over my face because he suddenly goes very still. His eyes narrow, and I notice a muscle in his jaw clench. He knows I know.

"You need to step back," he finally says, and I blink, shocked by the cold sound of his voice.

I realize I'm just standing there staring at him. I flush and look away, embarrassed. I hear the warning in his voice, understanding completely that he means to step away from him, his past, his pain. Her.

I move to the side so he can get out of the stall and let him put the wall back between us. As he leads Glory into the daylight, I wonder if he knows the barriers he's put around him aren't hiding him at all.

Chapter Thirteen
NICK

I lead Glory into the training ring and then close the gate. Leaning against the rail, I observe and monitor her progress and natural behaviors. I'd made the round metal pen smaller to help her feel safer. As she gets more comfortable, I'll expand it, but for now, gaining her trust is the most important goal.

She's still weak and skittish and hesitant in her steps. I know she needs time to adjust to her new environment, so I won't keep her out here long. Too much too soon could overwhelm her, causing her to shut down and retreat back into her shell. I don't want to wear her out. I just want her to get some exercise and, at the same time, get used to her surroundings. We're working on respecting each other's space. After being hurt, neglected, and abused for so long, letting someone else in, is painfully difficult for her. Each day gets a little easier. She's beginning to slowly let down her guard with me.

I still can't believe how easily she'd let Lexy get close to her. The connection between them had been almost immediate as if they had some secret language no one else could hear or understand.

She'll believe it's not her fault soon. Where in the world did Lexy get that from? I wonder, glancing back towards the stables. How would she even know something like that? As far as I could tell, she's never been around horses in her life. She kept saying the oddest things and making me think. I don't like it.

The heat swelters and radiates up from the ground around me, up through the heavy denim of my black jeans, into my skin, but I barely notice. Some things you just get used to out here. Getting used to Lexy didn't seem like something I would be able to do anytime soon.

She knows about Megan. I could see it all over her face. Becca must have told her. But, Lexy finding out isn't what has me churned up. It was the recognition I saw in her eyes, as if she'd finally found the one person exactly like her. I want to tell her she's wrong but I'm not sure I can.

She knows things I need someone to understand. I felt the connection the instant I opened the front door and saw her. I experienced it again the night I found her singing on the porch. A strange relief came over me that I haven't been able to shake.

I haven't seen her in a few days. She's been hiding out in her room. I've watched for her. I've wondered about her. I've even worried about her. I scowl, annoyed that I've got Lexy in my head. I don't want her there. I haven't thought about anyone but Megan for so long. It makes me feel guilty as if I'm cheating, which I know doesn't make any sense, but nothing has been the same since Lexy showed up. I want things to go back to the way they were.

Discovering the truth about her doesn't change anything. It can't. Her life is still none of my business, and mine isn't any of hers. We're not friends. We don't even know each other. Neither one of us owe each other anything.

But I can't get rid of this simmering tension, as if you sense something is coming, but you don't know what it is yet. Like when you can smell a storm brewing in the air, or how the sky changes colors when a tornado is about to hit. My whole body is on high alert, but I have no idea what I'm supposed to be watching or waiting for.

I don't want Lexy messing with the way things are. I like remembering Megan. I like that she's still a part of everything I do, every breath I take. I even like the grief; it's all I have left of her. I don't want Lexy interrupting that. I don't want her voice in my head or her face in my mind. She isn't who I want to think about. But she keeps slipping through.

The guilt is never gone, not for one single moment. The heat of it fills my belly, seeps out, and flushes over my skin. To think of someone other than Megan is the worst betrayal for me.

I'm so distracted that I don't even see Becca until she's practically standing next to me.

"She seems to be settling in," she says, nodding towards Glory. When I say nothing, she looks over at me. Noticing my expression and silence, she frowns. "You okay?"

I'm quiet for a minute and don't look at her. I want to be careful not to say something I'll regret. "Does Lexy know?" I don't say Megan's name. It hurts too much. But, with Becca, I know I don't have to. She'll understand.

She does, instantly, and realization makes her eyes fill with regret. "Yes," she admits apologetically. "I'm so sorry. I meant to talk to you about it. She found the newspaper article about the car accident when we were going through photo albums. It fell out." She puts her hand on my arm. "I really am sorry, Nick. I know it's yours to tell."

I just nod. I know Becca wouldn't deliberately expose my pain to anyone. "She was bound to find out sooner or later," I say, with weary resignation. I don't even get angry about it anymore. What good would it do? Everyone around here knows already anyway. I'm a sad legend in these parts. "I just wish you would have let me know you told her." It hurts me more to be caught off guard. I'm not prepared and have no warning that my grief is about to be suddenly invaded.

"I know. I meant to. The last few days have been a blur. Did she say something to you about it?"

I shake my head. "No. Not exactly," I murmur, remembering the wreckage in Lexy's eyes when she looked at me a few minutes ago. "I just saw her up at the stable. I could tell she knew." I always can.

"You saw her?" Worry in her eyes, she glances towards the outbuildings. "She's barely been out of her room the last few days. How was she?"

She looked lost and wounded and much too sad, but I don't want to tell Becca that. I shrug. "Seems alright. A little tired, maybe. She came in while I was working with Glory." I nod my head towards the mare. "She let Lexy walk right up to her." I'm still amazed by it.

"Really?" She watches Glory figure out her territory in the ring. "I guess I shouldn't be surprised. She's such a sensitive girl. Horses recognize that. Glory obviously does. And maybe she's inherited the gift her Great Grandaddy Cade had with them."

"She's inherited something," I mutter wryly. Wild horses don't just bend to people like that.

Hearing the exhaustion in Becca's voice, I look at her and notice how worn down she is. I see the strain and the shadows under her eyes, the heaviness in the slight slouch of her shoulders. Having her past brought back so unexpectedly was taking a toll on her. She's strong, but there's only so much pain a person can stand. I know that all too well. I want to help her feel better and step closer so she can lean on me if she needs to. "Are you doing alright?"

She sighs. "It's been a rough couple of days. I haven't slept much. But, I doubt she has either." She looks towards the house, eyes troubled. "I'm worried about her. She's been so quiet and withdrawn. Finding out the truth about her mama was pretty traumatic. I hope it's not hurting her more to be here. I want this to be a safe place for her."

"You're here. She seems to feel pretty safe with you."

"I hope so," she murmurs, looking over at me. "She seems to like being around you, too. Thanks for letting her hang around with you. I know you prefer to work with the horses alone. I understand it's been an adjustment. You're used to things being a certain way. But I appreciate you letting her help out with some things. You, of all people, can understand what she's going through."

Panic makes my stomach clench. Shaking my head, I take a step back. I don't want this expectation on me. We're not the same. We can't be. I wish I felt more convinced. "How would I know what she's feeling? I don't even know her."

"But you do know what it's like to have your whole world turned upside down and to not know if it's ever going to be made right again."

"Mine hasn't been made right," I snap out. I hear the bitterness in my voice, feeling as if I am rotting from the inside out. A sour taste poisons my tongue. The loss is still so raw, so close, as if it is just happening now instead of three years ago.

"Neither has hers."

She says it so calmly, so quietly, I have no words to fight back. I feel the mad go out of me, like dark clouds breaking and blowing away after a storm, opening up the blue. I can't look at her. I feel too miserable. "What do you want me to do?" I ask wearily.

"Just help keep an eye on her." A light breeze has her hair skimming across her cheek. She brushes it back as she studies me. "She's going through a lot."

I finally look over at her. Lexy and Becca have the same eyes, I notice—beautiful, green, and heartbreaking. This is probably the reason I can't seem to resist either of them. "One of these days I'm going to figure out how to say 'no' to you."

She rests her chin on her hand, holding my gaze. "Is that day today?"

I feel myself softening. I've known her for years. I owe her and Ben everything. They're my family. Resigned, I let out my breath. We both already know what my answer is. Because it's her, I give in and smile a little. "No."

She smiles back, a real one this time, and my world settles back into place. "You're a good guy, Nick. You just can't help yourself." She leans over and kisses me on the cheek. "Keep her safe," she says over her shoulder as she heads back up towards the house.

I frown as I watch her go. I can't tell if she's talking about Glory or her niece. But it doesn't matter, I realize, shaking my head. Either way, I already know I'm going to have my hands full.

Chapter Fourteen
LEXY

The late-night air is fragrant and warm as I make my way towards the stables. I can't sleep. I still can't get used to the quiet. I'm scared to be alone. I don't want to dream and see my mother staring at me, pleading with me not to leave her, tears and betrayal and fear in her eyes.

The house is dark behind me, with only the glow from the porch light shining out like a beacon to guide me back. Everyone went to sleep hours ago. The night feels sultry, as if I'm walking underwater. Stars glitter through the gnarled, mossy branches of the trees. I've never seen this many before. They seem so close I could reach up and grab a handful of them.

Fireflies flash and wink and dance around me. Cicadas whir and click, crickets sing, frogs croak, their chatter and buzz calling out from their hiding places within the wild grass. Silver glowing moonlight helps me find the path that leads out towards the barn and stables. The weight of my guitar is familiar and reassuring on my shoulder.

I want to see Glory. I remember how I felt the first time I looked at her today, that pull I couldn't explain—some sort of kinship. I know what it's like to hurt like her. I understand her desperation to find someone out there she can trust. She's so strong, so valiant, and somehow, so fragile. I don't want to be alone in my fear, and I want her to know she's not alone in hers.

As I pass the cottage where Nick lives, I try not to look over, but my curiosity is too strong. A light is on in the small house, and it doesn't surprise me he's still up. I wouldn't be able to sleep either if I were him. I remember the night he found me on the porch, how late it had been. I wonder if the same guilt that haunts me also chases him. Even though I know he can't hear me, I walk a little lighter, trying not to be found.

The stables are only a few feet away now, its silhouette jutting up large against the night sky. Glory is in her own building, away from the other horses, until she is ready to be integrated with the herd. I know it's dangerous for me to be here by myself, but I worry about her being alone. What if she's hurting? Sliding open the heavy door, I quietly slip inside.

It's dim and still except for the few overhead lights that are left on and the moonlight coming in from the windows. The large ceiling fans are kept on day and night. She instantly looks over at me, her eyes wide and alert and wary. I'm not sure if she recognizes me, and I move carefully so I don't scare her.

"Hi girl," I murmur, staying near the far wall. Even weak and battered, I'm very aware of her strength and the reality that she could suddenly rear up and charge if threatened or frightened. I don't want either of us to get hurt.

She continues to stare at me, measuring me and gauging her safety. I completely understand the survival instinct. I've been doing it my entire life.

Leaning my guitar against the wall, I stand back, waiting to see if she'll let me get close. As I watch her, I immediately absorb her fear and sadness, the heavy helplessness and confusion that comes with being used and mistreated. I experience that same rush of connection and tenderness towards this broken, beautiful animal.

I remember Becca mentioning that horses can hear your heartbeat from four feet away. I wonder if Glory hears mine, if she feels how alike we are.

She must sense it; she must know because she presses up against the stall door and bobs her head as if trying to reach me. Smiling, I slowly walk up to her, feeling honored she's letting me in.

I reach out my hand for her to smell me, and she bends her head granting me permission to pet her. "Did you miss me, beautiful girl?" I can feel the indentation of the scars and trace them gently. "I won't hurt you. I promise." I stroke her neck, feeling the tense muscles and her matted coat, wishing I could wipe away every ounce of pain she's ever known. She allows me to stay close, and I lean against her, letting us both absorb the strength we need.

After a while, I move back and pick up my guitar. "I thought you might like me to sing for you." Glory continues to track my every move as I pull a wooden stool over and sit down near her stall. Closing my eyes, I begin to strum, not really playing anything in particular, just letting the music drift up. A hush falls over us.

The words come to life then, all my secrets I don't ever dare say out loud. I sing of a yearning search for more and trying to find something I can never hold onto, of not wanting to be afraid to close my eyes because of what I might see. And the hope for a love that won't destroy me simply for wanting it returned. It's the only way to get this bleeding pain out. The music lets me finally feel my own heartbeat and find my way through this unbearable, never-ending darkness. I pour all my anguish, despair, and loneliness into every feverish note.

There's nothing but melody surrounding me, helping me forget for one blissful moment that I'm an alcoholic's daughter. I crave it like my own breath. I'm alive in a way I can't be when the song ends, and I have to go back to being me.

I don't realize I'm crying until I open my eyes and notice my cheeks are damp. As I wipe the tears away, I look up to see Nick standing a few feet away. I gasp, jolting. How long has he been there? He keeps finding me like this. Neither of us speaks as we stare at each other. I can't tell what he's thinking and wonder if I'll ever be able to.

I feel vulnerable and exposed, just as I did the other night when he found me on the porch. He's the only person who has ever heard me sing and who knows what's really inside of me. Why won't he say something? A flush rises hotly over my neck, face, into my hair. Quickly, I make myself stand up, feeling clumsy and awkward and unsure of what to do. I wish he wouldn't look at me like that.

"I didn't want her to be alone," I stammer, looking towards Glory. I know I'm not supposed to be in here. I wait for him to say it.

But he doesn't. He doesn't say anything as he walks toward Glory's stall. He goes over to the stock shelf where supplies are kept and pulls out a jar of ointment, bandages, and gauze. "I've got to check her sores," he tells me, his voice detached and indifferent. "Now is when she's most prone to infection."

Unable to make myself move, I stand where I am and watch him approach Glory, murmuring soothing words like he did that afternoon. It still startles me how someone so closed off can be so unexpectedly tender. It's as if the horses find some part of him none of us get to see. He pulls sugar cubes out of his pocket, and she eagerly licks them up. Glory doesn't back away, doesn't paw or stomp, and he knows he can enter her space. He's careful to keep his body between the horse and the stall door in case she rears up or tries to bolt. He strokes her neck and back, and moves to where he can examine her leg. Even weak and wounded, she still manages to stand defiantly regal and stoic, as if she knows she'll always be a champion thoroughbred. She only flinches once as he gets near where the worst of the sores are.

"Good girl," he soothes. "Just be still a second. This'll be over in a minute." Crouching down, he removes the bandage and examines her. He presses gently around the wound for swelling and knotting abscesses and uses a betadine solution to flush out the cuts. I wince, wondering if it stings her and hope Nick doesn't get kicked. She grunts and tries to step away, but he gently reassures her and hangs back, waiting until she goes still again.

He continues to speak low and soft as he applies more ointment and wraps fresh gauze and bandages over her sores. Standing, he comes back around to the front of the stall and holds out more sugar cubes to her. "Here you go, girl." Nick rubs her nose, steps out of the stall, and closes the door, making sure it's firmly locked.

"How is she doing?"

He tossed the old bandages into the trash. "About the same." He pulls a rag out of his jeans pocket and wipes his hands. "There is still a lot of swelling on her backside, so we're going to have to keep a close eye on her. Don't want her to reopen those sores."

We stand there, neither of us knowing what to do. I realize I'm still holding my guitar. It feels strangely heavy and somehow bigger than I remember. There's no way I can hide it without him noticing. I wait for him to tell me to leave. I'm surprised he hasn't yet. I figure he'd want to.

"How do you do that?" he suddenly asks, confusing me.

"Do what?"

"Sing like that."

He'd heard me. Unnerved, I feel my face go hot again. Singing is so personal for me. I'm still not sure how to talk about it. With as closed off as he is, I can't figure out why he is even asking me about it. "I don't know." Embarrassed, I fidget with the guitar strap. I need something to do with my hands. "I just sing whatever I'm feeling in the moment."

He seems to think about that. He glances back to my guitar, looking like he wants to ask me something more. I wait, but he says nothing. That intense silence comes between us again. I wonder if I'm the only one feeling it.

He starts to walk towards the door. He has to move past me to get out, and I try not to stare at him. He's a foot away when he stops. "Look, I know Becca told you what happened." He doesn't say Megan's name. He doesn't have to. I already know who he means. "I don't talk about it, and I don't want you asking me about it." He looks right at me, one of the few times he ever has. My entire body goes still. "I just want that clear between us."

All I can do is nod. I can barely breathe and can't figure out why I get so nervous whenever I'm near him. His pain is heavy and thick around us, like body heat. He again looks at my guitar and hesitates, about to say something. Instead, he reaches into his pocket and pulls out some sugar cubes. "These are her favorite." He holds them out to me. His fingers brush mine as I take them, and I blush, praying he can't tell how embarrassed and aware of him I am. I notice he quickly pulls his hand away and doesn't look at me.

"Thanks," I say, flustered.

"Don't go into her stall. You'll get hurt." He doesn't wait for me to respond and doesn't say anything else as he walks out of the stable. I stay where I am and watch him go, wondering what he would have asked me if he'd said the question out loud.

Chapter Fifteen
BEN

The most important thing to know when dealing with an abused horse is that you've got to keep showing up. You've got to keep trying. You've got to let them know they can kick you in the ribs, buck you off, toss you into the dirt, but at the end of the day, you'll come right back and still care about them.

They've been taught not to trust the hand that feeds them, and so yours needs to be full of kindness. You've got to be gentle and reassuring. People don't realize how much horses know, how sensitive, smart, and sweet they are. They want to be loved just as much as anyone, and when they get hurt, they feel it deep. They are naturally tender animals, and experiencing pain and abuse is extremely traumatic for them. Some horses never make it back from that kind of hurt. But the ones that do, reveal a strength, resilience, and beauty that takes your breath away.

You've never experienced freedom until you've seen a horse that was once beaten down, scared, and shut down, running wild and joyfully, its hooves pounding over the earth, with a power, unlike anything.

I whistle as I make my way out of my office in the barn. It's been a good morning so far; I got some bills paid and made arrangements for two more horses to be brought in. Every one we rescue means one more that stands a chance.

I walk out into the early morning light. The air is rich and fragrant as it usually is when the sun begins warming and waking up our land. As I walk past the stable where we are housing Glory, I notice the door is partly open. Concerned that an animal had somehow gotten in, I step inside and then come to a stop when I see my niece fast asleep on the ground, wrapped in one of the saddle blankets. Abraham is curled up against her side as if protecting her.

"Well, what do you know?" I murmur, unable to stop smiling. She looks just as fragile and vulnerable as the horse she's sleeping near. I wonder what she's doing out here. Her guitar is on the ground near her head, her hand still resting on it. Crouching down next to her, I gently touch her shoulder. "Lexy?"

She stirs as I lightly shake her. Her eyes flutter open, looking blearily up at me. I don't think she's awake enough to recognize who I am.

I grin down at her. "Morning."

Suddenly alert, Lexy quickly sits up and looks around, clearly trying to remember where she is. "Morning," she says, her voice raspy, as she clumsily tries to untangle herself from the blanket. Abraham reluctantly rolls over and stretches, ambling sleepily to his feet. His collar jangles as he shakes out. "I must have fallen asleep out here."

"Looks like it. Didn't mean to give you a scare." I hold my hand out and help her stand up.

Still a little groggy, she straightens her clothes and brushes herself off. Looking confused, she bends down and picks up the blanket. "Did you cover me up last night?"

I shake my head. "No, I didn't even know you were out here. Why?"

A strange expression crosses her face as she looks towards the stable door. "No reason," she says, folding up the blanket. "I wanted to check on Glory." She puts the blanket back on the shelf. "I was worried about her being by herself."

I smile, touched by how sweet she is. Nick had told me how Glory had responded to Lexy the day before, how she'd broken through. Being around the horses would be good for her. They'll take care of each other.

I'm pleased with Glory's progress and how well she's settling in. Her wounds are still extremely raw, and she needs a lot of time and care, but she'd already bonded with both Lexy and Nick, which was encouraging. We just need to give her a safe place for healing and let her get used to her new life here. This ranch and land offer a good place to start over.

"I'm sure she appreciated the company."

She yawns, pulling her hands through her tousled hair. "What time is it?"

"A little after six. Becca should have breakfast ready soon. I was just heading back up to the house to help her." Lexy has been here about a week now. She's spending a lot of time with Becca and Nick. She seems comfortable enough around me. I'd like to get to know her. "Why don't I walk back with you?" She nods and goes to pick up her guitar.

We walk together back out into the daylight. Abraham bounds happily ahead of us, knowing Becca will have a bowl of buttermilk waiting for him.

I glance at Lexy, who is quiet as she walks next to me. "How are you holding up?" I ask her.

"I'm okay." She didn't sound that convincing. I doubt she even believes herself. "It all still doesn't feel real yet." When she meets my gaze, I see Becca staring back at me. Wounded, bruised—a generation of lost, broken little girls. And now, all that pain and loss had come full circle. "Thank you for letting me stay."

"We're happy to finally have you here. You can stay as long as you like." I nod towards the guitar strapped over her shoulder. "That's a nice Gibson. You sing?"

She seems embarrassed, flustered. I notice her blush. "Yeah, I do," she admits.

"I'd love to hear you sometime."

Brow creasing, Lexy watches me, trying to figure me out. "I thought you'd be mad at me," she says quietly.

I can feel her bracing, putting an inch more of distance between us, as if expecting disapproval from me. Becca was right, I realize. She's the saddest girl I've ever seen. No wonder Nick keeps getting tripped up around her. "Seems to me you've had enough of that," I answer. "Besides, what good would it do? I don't blame you for what you didn't know and couldn't change."

Her eyes fall from mine, guilt radiating from her, like an aura. The poor thing is suffocating under it. "I just wish I would have known everything sooner."

"You know now. And you're here." I decide to make one decision simple for her. "How about we start from there? Deal?"

She looks back at me almost as if she's afraid to hope it could be that easy. She's used to the struggle and has lost too much. She's silent for a few moments and then I hear her slowly let out her breath. I can tell how hard she's trying to put the pieces together and her frustration that she doesn't have them all yet. But, she needs to be for so many reasons she's just beginning to understand. And she wants to know us as much as we want to get to know her. "Deal," she finally says.

"Good." We reach the house and walk up the back steps. With his tail wagging, Abraham is already excitedly waiting; I smile at him as I hold the screen door open. I follow both him and Lexy into the kitchen.

"Look who I found in one of the stables," I say, taking my hat off and setting it on the hook near the door. "She fell asleep keeping watch over Glory."

Becca glances over as we walk in, beaming when she sees her niece. The look on Becca's face is another reason I want Lexy here. It's been a long time since I've seen her smile like that. "You slept out in the stable last night?"

"Yeah, I guess so," she answered, laughing shyly. She still has a few strands of hay in her hair. She motions over her shoulder. "I'll be back in a minute." She goes out of the kitchen, and we hear her footsteps running up the stairs, the click and latch of her bedroom door closing.

"That's really where you found her?" Becca asks as she puts the bowl of buttermilk down for Abraham, who eagerly laps it up.

Laughing, I walk over to the sink to wash my hands. "Sure was." Becca tosses me the towel so I don't drip water on her clean floor. "Did you know she sings?"

Becca nodded. "She's mentioned it. I'm so curious to hear her. She's pretty private about it. I wonder if she's any good."

"Very," Nick says, drinking his coffee at the table.

Both Becca and I turn to look at him. "You've heard her sing?" I ask.

Caught, his brows come up, and his mug freezes mid-air. "Accidentally," he admits, clearing his throat. I notice he seems embarrassed and doesn't fully meet our eyes. "I ran into her once on the porch and then again last night in the stable. She's really good. Better than good, actually. I've never heard anyone sing like that."

There was more that he wasn't saying. The fact that he'd even mentioned anything about it was telling in its own way. He normally keeps his thoughts and feelings to himself. Something about her was clearly affecting him. I wonder what else has happened between them. I exchange a secret look with Becca, who I can tell is thinking the same thing.

"I guess I shouldn't be surprised," Becca says. "Her mama has a gorgeous voice. Probably got it from her." She hands Nick the pitcher of orange juice. "You knew Lexy was out there?"

He shrugs as he sets the pitcher down next to the syrup. "I went to check on Glory and found her. She was playing a song for her when I walked in."

Becca smiles, her expression tender. "How sweet," she murmurs, shaking her head. She walks back over to the griddle and scoops pancakes onto a plate.

We all look over when Lexy comes back into the kitchen. She'd cleaned up and changed her clothes, brushed her hair, and pulled it back. I catch Nick staring at her. I haven't missed the way he watches her; he's curious, fascinated, and protective of her. He's letting her get closer than most, and I can't figure out if he's moving towards her or if it's the other way around. Lexy seems just as fascinated and drawn to him. They are a lot alike, and I think Nick knows it. He doesn't seem too happy about it.

He realizes I'm watching him and frowns, quickly glancing away. I think I know who covered Lexy up with the blanket last night. I notice how careful he is not to look at her as she sits down next to him.

Becca hands me the plate of sausage, and I carry it to the table and then sit in my usual spot. Becca brings the plate piled high with pancakes and sets them in front of us. "Breakfast is served," she says as she sits down next to me, completing our little circle.

After saying the blessing, I open my eyes and look around at all the people who have found their way to this land and think that even with all our broken pieces, maybe we can somehow help make each other whole.

Chapter Sixteen
LEXY

D ust stirs up into small whirlwinds, evaporating into the air as Glory breaks from Nick's hold and bolts across the training pen. The force of it knocks him back a few steps, and he stumbles to the ground.

Nick let out a growl of frustration. He'd been working with her for almost an hour. It was the fourth time she'd broken free from him that morning. He quickly scrambles to his feet before he gets trampled and brushes himself off, being mindful never to have his back to her. Dirt coats his black denim jeans, streaking across his face and arms and hands.

Glory stands stubbornly on the other side of the pen, looking like a sulking child.

I had been helping Ben and Becca unload supplies into the storehouse when Nick brought Glory out to walk her. After the sacks of grain and feed were stacked, we wandered over to the pen just in time to watch Nick fall face-first into the dirt, his hat tumbling off his head.

"Rough day?" Ben asks, leaning his arms on the rail.

"Yeah, you could say that," Nick answers. "She's in a mood." Picking up his hat from the ground, he bats it against his palm to clear off the dust and plops it back on his head. "Won't stay on the reins."

"Why don't you let Lexy try?" Becca suggests, nodding towards me.

Shocked, I look over at her. "What?" I can already guess what Nick's answer will be. He doesn't disappoint me.

"Why would I let her do that?" he asks, annoyed, not taking his eyes from Glory. "She doesn't know anything about working with horses."

Already backing up, I shake my head at my aunt. "He's right. I've never trained one before."

Becca looks at me. "It's not about training as much as it is about building trust. You get her to trust you, and she'll do anything you want her to. And you've already got a bond with her."

"No. It's not a good idea," Nick argues.

"You won't let anything happen to her," Becca told him. I glance warily at Nick, who scowls in response.

"She shouldn't be in here, Becca," Nick repeats, and I can tell he's trying to keep his voice low and even, so the horse doesn't get more agitated. "Glory's pretty unpredictable right now."

"The most important thing for Glory is that she feels safe," Becca says. "We've all seen how she responds to Lexy. She needs to know no one will hurt her, and right now, she doesn't believe that. I don't want that for her, and I know you don't either." She looks back at me. "Trust me on this. Nick will stay in the ring with you."

Seeing she's not going to give up on the idea, Nick reluctantly agrees. "Fine," he mutters.

Ben opens the latch, offering words of encouragement and reassurance. I don't believe him, but don't say it.

The gate clicks shut behind me, locking me in, and I glance warily over my shoulder, wondering if this is a huge mistake. I have no idea what to do. Glory instantly looks over, watching me with her dark eyes that are volatile and full of mistrust. Her breath snorts out, her tail swishes angrily, and frustration vibrates from her. I feel a rush of fear and wonder if she'll suddenly charge me. Nick must be thinking the same thing because he positions himself in between us.

"Just stay near the edge for a bit," Becca instructs me. "You don't want her to feel cornered. Let her get used to you being in her space."

Glory and I gauge each other. My heart aches for her. She looks trapped and much too large for the pen. She used to compete on the most famous race tracks in the world and won the Triple Crown three years straight, but now is scarred, scared, and sad.

I understand why she's so angry. This isn't what she was supposed to be or how her life was supposed to end up. Her beauty and strength have been used against her, and it's broken her. All she ever wanted was for someone to love and care for her. But, instead, she'd been run into the ground and then given up on and forgotten. Now she doesn't trust anyone.

I can feel her exhaustion and weariness. She just wants to be left alone and for everyone to stop pushing at her. She doesn't want the weight of the expectation. It's too much, too painfully hard. She's been let down too many times and no longer has faith in even the kindest touch.

I instinctively fall completely silent. I'll wait for her. She needs to know I'm not going anywhere more than anything else right now.

131

The only sounds are the latch of the gate clinking and bumping against the metal bars of the pen, the slight breeze moving through the trees and pastures, the swarming buzz of insects and distant birdsong. Her breath, mine, and the crunch of her hooves in the dirt as she shifts under her weight in the shimmering heat.

Glory continues to defiantly hold her ground on the far side of the ring, almost as if daring me to try and catch her. Nick is a few feet away. It makes me feel safe having him close by. Still challenging us, she jerks her head and stomps but doesn't bolt or rear up. I understand her enough to know not to force her to trust me. I don't try to coax her. I don't speak or move towards her, or demand she listen and obey. I want her to be the one who chooses and invites me in.

The silence stretches out, one minute... three... we stay that way, quietly watching each other, waiting, letting the frustration and tension simmer and ease from the air. I block everything else out until there's nothing but the two of us on this small piece of land underneath the great big blue sky.

And then, just when I think nothing will happen, suddenly, miraculously, she takes a tentative step toward me. Stunned, I catch my breath but try not to react so I don't startle her. I can feel Nick watching me, straining against his own instincts, wondering what I'm going to do, silently willing me to sneak around her to get the reins. But I keep my eyes firmly focused on Glory, unwilling to risk breaking the fragile connection between us.

I slowly take a few steps and then wait to see how she responds. She doesn't back up, shy away, or run. She continues to stare at me, trying to figure out my motives and intentions. Where her safety is. If I'll hurt her and take away her last bit of power like the people who abandoned her before. She remembers what they did to her; every bruised bone in her body reminds her. How can I help her believe I'm different?

As she gradually begins to relent, we move toward each other, inch by slow inch, until she's within my reach. I'm now close enough that I can feel the heat radiating off her body, her muscles trembling, her loneliness, her need. Not wanting to spook her, I don't grab for her and continue to stay still.

In an act of trust and submission, she bows her head, pressing it against my shoulder. My heart feels as if it's going to burst in my chest as I reach up to pet her. Her coat is warm and musky, and I can feel where the mangy patches have begun to grow in. She's gained a little of her weight back. I've never experienced anything like this. The sweet gift of her letting me in leaves me breathless.

"Hi, beautiful girl," I whisper and stroke her neck. She nuzzles my hair and leans into me, almost as if searching for somewhere to hide.

"Wow," Becca says, astonished. There are tears in her eyes. "That was amazing. You're a natural, Lexy. I knew you two needed each other. Your Great-Granddaddy Cade would be real proud of you."

I smile at her, struck at how much I need that to be true. I can't remember the last time someone was proud of me for anything.

"Why don't you see if you can try walking her?" Nick says, and I realize he's standing next to us.

I look over at him. "What do I do?"

"Take the reins and stay by her shoulder. Tell her to walk on and then move forward around the ring."

"What if she doesn't follow me?"

"She will," he says, with no trace of doubt in his voice.

Nick walks ahead of us, and I let him lead me as I lead Glory. I offer her praise and encouragement as we walk around the pen, once, then twice. When I pass Ben, he winks at me, and I grin at him, feeling more alive than I have in years. Being with Glory is healing in its own way. I hadn't realized I needed something like this.

"We'd better give her a break," Nick finally says after we've rounded the pen three more times. "Don't want to wear her out. She's still healing." He decides not to take the reins as he watches the way Glory stands close to me, almost as if we are protecting each other. He doesn't want the horse to see him as a threat. "You want to walk her back up to the stable?"

"Are you sure?"

Nick nods. "She trusts you."

I look up into Glory's brown eyes. "I trust you, too," I murmur. Nick watches us, a look crossing his face I can't read. Before I can figure him out, he turns away and opens up the pen gate, and I lead Glory out of the ring.

"Good job, Lexy," Becca says, beaming at me as I walk Glory past her. "I'm going to go get lunch ready. Y'all meet us up at the house when you're done."

Ben follows Becca, and I notice the sweet way he takes her hand as they walk up the path together, still fascinated by how affectionate they are with each other. I'm not used to it yet.

Looking back towards Nick, I'm suddenly very aware that we are alone together. He doesn't look at me or say anything as I lead Glory out onto the path back up to the barn. It's easier to be with him while Becca and Ben are around.

The wall is back up between us. He's walking right next to me, but it feels as if he's somewhere else. He always keeps me on the outside. He's so quiet and lost in thought. I wonder if I'll ever understand him.

We reach the stables. Glory is still in her own building while she gets used to being in her new home. He removes the halter, bridle, and bit from her before she gets put back in the stall. I had already figured out it was to prevent her from getting tangled.

She doesn't fight or resist him, and he murmurs praises to her, feeding her a few bites of apple, which she licks up. "Go on in, girl," Nick says, patting her on her hindquarters, and she ambles into her stall. He closes and latches the door behind her. We stand side by side, leaning against the wall, watching Glory. The fans keep the warm air moving around us. "You did good today," he finally says.

Surprised, I glance over at him. I know the words weren't easy for him to give me. "Thanks. I'm glad you were in there with me."

He nods towards Glory. "She'll follow you anywhere now."

I feel both protective and tender as I look over at her. "I hope so," I say, smiling as I gently rub her scarred nose. "I want her to know she's safe with me."

My easy smile fades when I meet Nick's eyes and notice his expression. I see his loneliness, his weariness, his grief. I expect him to look away, to step back like he always does, but for some reason, he doesn't.

The intensity and awareness I feel whenever I'm around him is like a live wire surging and sparking beneath our feet. I know what he's thinking. I wonder if he's finally going to tell me about Megan, if he's going to let me into the one place so few really know about him, if he'll just once say her name out loud to me. I never dare ask and walk on eggshells to avoid the subject, the slightest idea, the smallest memory of her. I couldn't stand to see the pain it would cause him.

The desperation to know what he's thinking and break through his walls is quickly turning into an obsession. He keeps me up at night. I've even dreamt about him.

"Do you ever wish you could just—" he begins quietly.

I hold my breath and wait, wondering what he's going to do, if he's going to finish his sentence, if he'll go all the way. "Do I ever wish I could what?" I whisper, trying to keep him with me.

The space between us feels thin and fragile and seems to burn with all the things he wants to say. I'm so absorbed and focused on him that I see the exact moment he changes his mind, noticing his eyes darken as they become guilty, guarded, and distant. His breathing is heavy as if he caught himself just in time before his feet slipped off the ledge. "Nothing," he mutters hopelessly. "Forget it."

"Nick—" I stop when he shakes his head, a warning in his eyes. I can't tell if he thinks he's protecting me or himself.

"It doesn't matter." He abruptly steps back and starts walking out of the stable. "We better get up to the main house."

I'm not ready to move yet. I realize my legs are unsteady and have to force myself to come back from where we just were. I look once more at Glory, murmuring that I'll be back soon, and then turn and follow wherever Nick leads.

Chapter Seventeen
LEXY

My days here are quickly falling into a routine. Early to bed, early to rise is the farmer's motto, and now I understand why.

Ranch life is so different from what I knew back in California. We're up before dawn, which definitely has taken some getting used to. There's a lot to do. The horses need to be fed and watered, brushed down, their hooves, teeth, and ears checked. We walk and train them in the pens, muck out the stalls, stock grain and hay, and clean out the water troughs.

The land heats up fast, so the sooner the work is done, the better. There's a consistency and stability here that I've never known, and I am learning to depend on the chores and responsibilities. I don't mind dust on my skin, dirt under my fingernails, or my muscles being sore and strained from hard work. It makes me feel normal and useful for a little while.

Breakfast is another routine Becca and Ben are firm about never missing together. We eat at seven sharp every morning. All four of us, no matter where we are or what we are doing on the far corners of the ranch, are to be in the kitchen, sitting at the table and ready to eat.

The conversation revolves around what the work is that day and who will be taking care of what. Which is how Becca's suggestion came up about me helping Nick fix the perimeter fence on the south side of the ranch.

Nick sends Becca a dark glance over a spoonful of grits, and I feel the lurch in the air as if I can actually hear his stomach drop. "She doesn't know the first thing about working on the fences," he says, and I sense a flicker of panic and resistance—the fear of me in his voice.

I think of the other afternoon in the stable; it's all I've been able to think about, when he almost told me about his grief and let me in. He'd been on the verge of breaking, but then had changed his mind and shut me out again.

He's been more distant than usual the last few days, off on the far ends of the land, quiet and safely out of my reach, evading me and the risk of any conversation. I understand his withdrawal, but it still hurts.

"Well, how else will she learn unless she does it?" Becca asks as she bites into her toast. "You're a good teacher. You know everything about this land. I have no doubt you can show her."

"I can do something else," I offer, trying to keep the peace, to ease the tension and static between us. It's so strong, thick, and loud that I don't know how anything normal is happening around us.

"Don't be silly, sweetheart," Becca says. "You're just as much a part of this place as the rest of us." She looks pointedly at Nick. "And Nick needs the help even if he is too proud to admit it."

Annoyed, Nick shakes his head. "It's not about needing help," he argues. "It's just not a good idea. What if she gets hurt?"

Unfazed, Becca smears more blackberry jam on her toast. "You'll take care of her out there," she says and just smiles when he frowns at her.

"I don't have time to keep an eye on her, Becca," he says, and I again feel that same undercurrent, the avoidant push from him. What is he afraid I will get him to do? "I've got a lot of work to do today. And besides, I doubt she even wants to."

Nick is sitting right next to me, close enough that I could touch him if one of us moves wrong. I notice both of us have been careful never to let that happen. I glance over at him. I think he wants me to give him an out, but I can't. I don't want him far away anymore.

"Yes, I do," I quietly interrupt, pulling him back towards me. He's too lost and lonely on his own. We both are. *Come here.*

He pauses mid-argument, looks over at me, and I instantly feel the fight drain away, as if he's stopped running and came to a breathless standstill.

I see the same ragged look in his eyes from the other day and wonder if he's struggled to stay away from me, if he thinks about me when I'm not around, if he wishes he would have let me into his pain. I haven't been able to get him out of my mind for a single second.

Neither of us notices the secret smile Becca gives Ben as if this is what she wanted all along.

"It's hard work," he warns me. "You might get bored."

I'll be with him, so I didn't think that would happen but don't dare say it. "I don't mind. I want to help." I need to do something to fill up the time here. I don't want to give myself too much space to think. I want to stay busy and stay ahead of the guilt. I'm not ever fully able to do it. My mom is never far from my thoughts. She's a lurking shadow stalking my every step. But the work is a good distraction. He must sense my aimlessness. He must understand it because he gives in.

"Okay fine," he mutters, letting out a defeated sigh. But his armor is still tight around him as he shovels in a mouthful of eggs. "We're driving out in ten minutes."

Nodding, I quickly finish the rest of my breakfast. He is already up and heading for the door by the time I swallow my last bite. Becca just winks at me and hands me a thermos of water as I run out after him.

Almost an hour later, I found myself walking the fence line, looking for gaps, sags, or loose nails that could injure the horses and cause infection. Nick's idea of letting me help is telling me not to touch anything as I follow behind him, watching him work. The only thing he's trusted me with so far is carrying the shovel.

I jolt as he bangs a nail into place. "Why do you need to check the fences all the time?"

He straightens. "The horses push up against them," he answers, wiggling the board to make sure it's secure. "Don't want them breaking out and walking too near the road." He tucks the hammer into the slot of his tool belt. "It also keeps horses and cattle from other ranches from getting in."

The fence is a bright, clean white. Nick explains they have to paint them every couple of years to make sure the horses can still see them and won't try to jump over and risk their hooves and legs getting caught.

Music carries over from the radio Nick leaves on in the back of his truck. It's an old classic country song I haven't heard in a while, but one I've always liked. I wonder if I could learn to play it. As quiet and flat as the land is, I can hear the strain of it perfectly and lean toward the sound as if it said my name. Lulled by the melody, I hum quietly, finding the harmony, and blend my voice in with it.

The air is hot and muggy. The morning light is a golden shimmer around us, and the song is slow and pretty. I'm drawn in and drift with it, letting the lazy rhythm wrap around me. I sing to myself as the sun shines down, and I follow after Nick. For one single moment, everything seems so simple and easy, and I think this must be what a perfect day would feel like. I've never had one before.

When the song ends, a commercial comes on, bringing me back. I go still, my smile fading, as I meet Nick's gaze. For an instant, he seems fascinated and curious. What is he thinking? And why do I feel like this every time he looks at me? "Sorry if it bothers you," I say, blushing. "It's one of my favorite songs."

He catches himself staring and quickly looks away. "Didn't say it did," he answers, again leaving me wondering as he moves on.

We walk the fence line in silence for a few moments. My tension grows, straining and rippling in the air around me with every step. I have never met someone who can say so much with barely saying anything at all.

"You ever think about doing something with it?" he asks, and I'm embarrassed that I jump a little at the sound of his voice. I notice he doesn't look at me. He seems to be concentrating really hard on the posts.

"With what?"

"Singing." He says it with his back to me as he runs his fingers over the nails to see if any are jutting out or loose. "You obviously love it, and you're good at it."

My stomach knots up at the possibility. "What would I do?"

"Anything," he murmurs under his breath. I don't think he meant for me to hear him. I stare at him, but he's not facing me, so he doesn't notice. He shifts, shrugs. "You could always post a video of you singing on Instagram or Facebook. People get discovered that way all the time." He's the picture of indifference as he pulls out a rusted, bent nail and replaces it with a screw, tightens it into the fence board. "Or you could try open mic nights. I've also heard of some music schools that are pretty good."

"Yeah, I know. Vanderbilt School of Music is here." I excitedly blurt it out without thinking. He turns and looks over at me then, his brows raised in surprise. Flustered, I fumble, feeling my face flush. When he holds my gaze, I give in and tell him. I am dying to share it with someone. The secret has been burning inside of me. "I have an application," I finally admit. I've been holding onto it for months, like a lifejacket on a sinking ship. I still had it, hidden in a pocket of my suitcase. "I filled it out and recorded a demo but haven't sent them in yet."

I feel so guilty about it. I had printed out more than twenty applications, all to different music schools around the country. I had done it out of the desperation that there had to be something more than what I knew. I'd needed to have something to hold on to, some small shred of hope in the middle of so much darkness and devastation. If the only thing I had for the rest of my life was the disappointment of my mom's broken promises, I knew I wouldn't make it.

He put his screwdriver back in his tool belt, retrieving his thermos of water from where he'd set it on one of the posts. "How come you haven't sent them in?"

Feeling overwhelmed, I just shake my head. I'm not sure where to begin. "Everything is such a mess right now. I don't even know how I would deal with it. And I know how much it would hurt her." Just talking about it makes me feel like I'm betraying her. I helplessly look away, wrapping my arms around myself. "Besides, I'm not sure if I'm even good enough to get in. I haven't had any training, and you have to audition if they accept your application. I've never sung in front of anyone before." I falter and blush again as I realize he's the exception. "You're the only one who has heard me."

"Why?"

Since I can't think of a reason not to, I tell him the blunt truth. "I didn't want her to take it away from me."

He doesn't tell me he understands. He doesn't have to. It's the same reason he doesn't want to talk about Megan. He continues to watch me a moment longer and then slowly nods. He's quiet as he brings his thermos up to his lips and drinks, lowers it, screws the top back on. Because he's still watching me, I catch the questions, the pity. Awareness crackles between us, like the sound a match makes when it's just lit. I wonder if he'll risk asking me, but all he says is, "You better drink up, too. You'll get dehydrated real quick out here."

Breaking his gaze, I shakily let out my breath as I turn to get my thermos. Opening it, I drink greedily. The heat is sweltering and drains me. At least I tell myself it's the heat. I pull my gloves off and pour water into my hand, rubbing it over my face and the back of my neck. It trickles down, soaking into the collar of my shirt, dampening it. With no breeze, it brings little relief.

He'd waited for me before moving on down the line, and I wonder if he's getting used to me. I walk up to him, and we continue our inspection of the perimeter. I decide it's safe to talk to him again. "Can you please do me a favor and not say anything to Becca yet about what I told you? I'll tell her," I say quickly. "I just have to figure it out first."

Noncommittal, Nick kicked his boot against the bottom of a fence post. "It's none of my business what you do." His brow creases as he notices the beam gives a few inches. He bends to inspect the ground. "Can you hand me the shovel?"

Not safe enough yet, I think, wincing. I keep running into walls. I'm grateful he's not looking at me to see the hurt. I'm quiet as I pass the shovel to him. I know he's right, but his words still pierce me. We're not friends, and we don't know each other. Expecting him to care is unrealistic and unfair, but I didn't know until this moment how badly I needed someone to tell my secrets to. Singing has been all I've had. When there was nothing but my parents' arguments or the horrible silence of the blackouts, music kept me from drowning. I've kept the love for it to myself all this time. I've had to. He's the only one who knows. For the first time, I want to let someone in to be a part of this dream with me. But he doesn't want to.

Out of sheer survival instinct, I quickly shut down the need. I'm used to the disappointment. I've been on my own for as long as I can remember. But I wasn't prepared for how lonely it would make me feel. I guess I should be used to that too, but the ache of it is somehow more painful after losing the hope of maybe, finally, being able to trust someone with the one thing that is most important to me.

I change the subject. I need something easy to talk about, something that doesn't require anything out of either of us and will level the ground between us again. "Why is there an old boot hanging on the front gate?"

"It was your Great-Great-Granddaddy Beau's. Hold this rail."

Surprised he actually let me do more than just stand there, I turn and look down at him. "What?"

He sighs, resting his arm on his knee, and squints up at me. Even under the shade of the brim of his hat, I can see the impatience in his eyes. "You want to help or not?"

"Yeah," I say quickly.

He jerks his head. "Then come here." Holding back my annoyance, I walk over to him. Before I can ask what I'm supposed to do, he says, "Just keep it still a second."

I'm not sure what changed his mind. I figure he probably wouldn't tell me anyway. Wanting to prove I can be useful, I brace my body against the rail, gripping the top to hold it in place. "Like this?"

"Yeah, that's good." He's close enough to me that his arm brushes against my leg as he sifts through the dirt, using a spade to weed out rocks and roots that are growing near the base. Everything about him is too close, even with so much space around us. To distract myself, I glance back towards the front gate of the ranch. The tall, broad posts can be seen from miles around.

"Why did my grandfather hang his boot on the fence?"

"It's a tradition that's been around forever." I keep the rail in place as he fills in the hole and packs dirt around the post. "You can let go now." I step aside so he can test the beam. When it holds firm, he gets to his feet, tucking the spade in with the rest of his tools.

"What's the tradition?"

He removes his gloves, takes off his hat, and runs his hands through his hair. The heat and humidity have made it damp, darker. I smell the faint scent of his shampoo. "Back in the days before there was electricity, ranchers would hang a boot on the gate to let neighbors know they were home and they were done working, and that people could come over to visit."

"Really?" I ask, delighted. "Did all ranchers used to do it?"

He shrugs. "I imagine they did." He uses the backside of his sleeve to wipe the sweat off his brow, sets the hat back on his head, and glances past me to the road. "That boot has been on the fence for I don't know how long. Over a hundred years at least."

I could listen to him tell me about the history of this ranch all day. I like the sound of his voice, the lazy, low southern drawl of it. It's soothing and makes me think of cool porches and weeping willows and old westerns on slow Sunday afternoons.

"Over a hundred years," I murmur, letting my family line tie itself to me, securing my feet where I stand. I've been blowing untethered in the wind for so long, with no one and nothing to hold onto. Would anyone notice if I flew away and disappeared into thin air?

Maybe I had originally run to this ranch looking for my mom, but the longer I'm here, I realize I'm also looking for myself, for a home and family. To find somewhere safe and someone to belong to.

I think of the yellowed, grainy photographs Becca had shown me. I can see the tintype of Beau Montgomery looking serious and strong in his worn overalls, his young face weathered from the sun. He'd settled on this land with his wife, Adelaide, and they built the very fence we are working on with their own two hands. And now, I'm here, continuing to preserve the life and legacy they left behind for all of us who followed after them. I feel something quietly and perfectly fit into place inside of me.

"What a great tradition. I wish I had known him." Nick is facing me as I smile brilliantly up at him, thrilled to be given another link to my family and our past. It seems to startle him. Disarmed, his guard is momentarily down, and he allows himself to smile too, not fully or completely, but enough that his face changes, softening as his eyes lighten.

Fascinated by the transformation, all I can do is stare at him. He looks like he used to; the way he did in the photograph I saw of him in the newspaper. Open, painfully tender, and vulnerable. He breaks my heart.

There you are, I think, mesmerized. I don't notice I've stepped closer, but the movement makes him suddenly back up, his smile instantly disappearing as the guilt takes over. His expression is carefully hooded again, shielded and closed from me. Confused by the abrupt shift, I can't figure out why he seems so frustrated. What do I keep doing wrong? I wonder, my own smile fading, as I watch him turn away.

We don't say much over the next few hours. It's just easier. Talking to him keeps confusing me and leaves me feeling like I'm in his way. He finally relents enough to let me do more than just carry supplies. I pay attention and try to learn quickly. I want to be a part of life out here. I do what he tells me and help him test the posts and prune out rocks from the fences so they don't get caught in the horses' hooves, handing him the hammer and holding the nails when he needs them.

I don't know how much time has passed. The sun is up in the middle of the sky now, blazing down upon us. It barely was a hint between the trees when we'd started out earlier that morning. The days here stretch out long and wide along with the land. Only the shadows shifting farther across the pastures tell of the hours going by.

We finish another section. Nick tosses a rock over the fence and then turns to look at me. "You hungry?"

I nod. My stomach has been grumbling for the last hour. "Yeah."

"We better eat something. Don't want you passing out on me." He walks over to the back of his truck, where the cooler is. *Becca was right,* I realize, as I follow him. He will take care of me out here.

He takes off his tool belt and lays it down. Picking up the cooler Becca had packed for us, he brings it over to a spot in the shade. Opening the lid, he hands me a pastrami sandwich, getting one for himself. He sits down, takes his hat off, and sets it down on the ground beside him. Stretching out his legs, he leans back against the large trunk of an old oak.

I sit cross-legged down next to him. The shelter from the canopy of the branches drapes above our heads. The air is heavy and humid, and the hum of insects is constantly around us. I let out a content sigh as I absorb the simple, rustic beauty. The song on the radio has changed, I notice. I always do. I listen for music everywhere. LeAnn Rimes was singing about being blue. I let her rich, lilting voice wash over and soothe me as I look out over the land. Even the light seems magical and dreamy.

"This place is so beautiful," I murmur. "I could sit out here for hours."

Nick just nods the way someone does when they are used to seeing this kind of beauty all the time. He keeps eating. He must have been hungry because the first half of his sandwich is completely gone in less than two minutes.

"How many acres are here?" I ask, licking mayonnaise from my finger.

"About five hundred, give or take," he answers with his mouth full.

My eyes widen with astonishment, and my jaw drops. "That many?"

Unimpressed, he shrugs. "It's a big ranch." He reaches into the cooler, pulls out a bowl of potato salad and two forks, and hands me one. "And it's all yours."

Awed by the thought, I look across the sprawling miles of sun-drenched pastures. I can't see the end of them. They go all the way to the skyline. This ranch has been in my family for a hundred and fifty years, passed down from generation to generation. It's been waiting for me all this time. I feel the weight of the inheritance settle over me.

Nick hands me the mason jar of lemonade Becca had made from scratch. I take it and drink. The taste is cool and tangy and a little bit sweet. I watch him over the rim. I know he needs this place as much as I do.

I hand the jar back. "This ranch is yours, too. You've been here a lot longer than me."

He shakes his head, putting the lemonade between us to share. "This land doesn't belong to me." He holds out the salad, and I scoop out a bite.

"But you feel like it does," I say, swallowing. He looks at me and holds my gaze longer than I thought he would. He doesn't deny what I've said. "You take really good care of this place. It seems like you wouldn't know what to do without it. I can see why." I scan the horizon, taking in the old Victorian farmhouse, the scattered outbuildings, the horses peacefully grazing under the afternoon sun. "I'd love to live here."

"You would?"

"Yeah." Does he look worried? I recognize the same frozen look in his eyes from breakfast that morning. "I've never had a home like this. Isn't it strange how somewhere you've never been can feel so familiar? As if you've been here your whole life?"

Nick doesn't answer. He seems distracted and tense. I can't tell what he's thinking.

A few moments pass by while we eat. I need to fill the space between us. I have a feeling Nick could go days and not say a word, but his silence is making me edgy. "Does your family still live around here? Becca said you grew up near Ben."

Lost in thought, it takes a minute for his gaze to come back to mine. His expression is unfocused. I wonder where he's just been. "What?"

"I was just asking where your family was."

"Oh," he answered absently, his mind obviously somewhere else. "Yeah. They live about thirty minutes away from here. Out in Franklin." Almost as an afterthought, he hands me the rest of the potato salad.

I take the Tupperware from him. "That close?"

"Where'd you think they were?"

"I don't know. You never talk about them. Do you have any sisters or brothers?"

His eyes are wary, as if he doesn't trust how far I'm going to ask him to go. Or maybe he doesn't trust himself not to let me take him back to the place we were a few days ago. "You ask a lot of questions."

What I don't know is that ever since Megan died, he barely spoke to his family. He'd pushed them away as he'd done with so many other people he'd known back then. Resigned, I give up. He doesn't want to talk, and he doesn't want to let me in. He doesn't even want me out here with him.

"Sorry," I mutter, feeling wounded. I keep eating and keep my mouth shut.

We sit in awkward silence for what seems like hours. I don't have to look over to know he's watching me. I can feel the intensity of his eyes penetrating through my skin and fight the urge to squirm. Even the daylight seems to be full of him; his body heat, his smell, his sweat, his pain.

"I have an older brother," he finally says. Surprised, I raise my head and meet his gaze. I can't tell if he answered out of guilt or if he actually wants to share a part himself with me. My guess is the first one. "Before you ask me, his name is Jake, and he and his wife live over in Valley Grove."

"Are you guys close?" I ask, finishing the last bite.

"Close enough," he answers, and I wonder why there seems to be a double meaning behind his words.

"It must be nice," I sigh, and I can hear the wistfulness in my voice, the loneliness. "I don't have any sisters or brothers."

He doesn't say anything to that. A look comes over his face, one that makes me feel unexplainably sad. I only catch it because I'm watching him, but I see the regret and grief flash and then fade away. I'm guessing it has to do with Megan. Everything about him leads back to her.

He unconsciously rubs at the scar above his eyebrow, old wounds still raw, before wearily turning away from me. He's finished eating and busies himself with gathering our containers and silverware, and puts them in the cooler, shuts the lid. Picking up his hat, he gets to his feet and looks down at me. "Break's over."

I don't want him to see that I feel sorry for him and am thankful for the sun in my eyes. I shade them with my hand as I squint up at him and nod. He walks away to put the cooler in the truck. I stare after him, more fascinated than ever. Standing, I brush myself off and walk over to him.

He hands me his thermos. "Will you fill these back up for us?"

"Sure." I take his along with mine and go over to the spigot. Bending down, I turn it on, holding my hand under the stream until the warm water cools. I fill both and then meet up with him a few feet down. I hold his out for him.

"Thanks," he says, taking it. He straps his tool belt around his waist and puts his hat back on. He hands me the shovel as he carries our other supplies. "Let's go."

We get back to walking the line. Mending the fence is tedious and time-consuming work. It doesn't take long for my muscles to get sore and strained from the exertion. My skin and clothes are damp from the heat and humidity, but I don't mind. I like the work and the purpose it brings me. Nick's experience makes him a good teacher, and I catch on enough that I can anticipate what he'll need for each task.

As the hours pass, I no longer have to ask and can spot a sagging beam or a nail that needs to be removed and replaced.

We don't say much as we trade off tools and make the necessary repairs. With the fence between us, the silence is easier and more comfortable.

When we reach the end of the perimeter, Nick stops and turns. He stretches his neck and rubs his shoulder as he stands back to inspect our progress. I've stopped, too, and wipe the sweat from under my hair. I can tell from his expression that he's satisfied, and I'm quietly pleased. I want him to be proud of me. I watch as his eyes follow the fence back towards where we're standing and then slowly focus on me as I come into his line of vision. "We're done for today."

I nod and take a step forward, expecting to follow him back to the truck. But he doesn't move, and I end up just stepping closer before quickly catching myself. My breath hitches as I look up at him. He doesn't back up and is closer to me than I thought he'd let himself be. He doesn't look away this time, and I feel my body instantly tense. How does he do that? My palms are damp.

"You should submit your application," he says, his deep drawl seeming to float on the breeze between us. Everything inside of me leans toward him as if he's telling me a secret. "You'll get in."

I blink as it registers that he's talking about applying to the music school. I hadn't known he'd been thinking about it or even listening. I'm so stunned I don't know what to say and can only stare stupidly up at him.

He doesn't wait for an answer or even acknowledge what he just gave me. Instead, he completely changes the subject. "We better get back. Still have a lot to do today." He takes the shovel from me and swings it up onto his shoulder. It isn't until he finally looks away that I'm able to breathe normally.

I fall into step beside him. I like being close to him and am struck by how natural it feels. I'm not sure if he notices. I definitely wasn't bored. We walk down the fence we repaired towards his truck. It brings me a great sense of accomplishment to see what I helped work on. I desperately want to contribute in some way.

It's a small thing, but I want to succeed at just one thing after years of being slapped in the face with the constant failure of not being able to save my mother. I don't want my life to be a waste. I don't want to feel helpless anymore. Maybe, out here, I can be given a second chance to be something more. To be someone better and to make up for all the things I never knew how to change.

I sneak a glance at Nick. What does he wait for, need, dream about? I don't have the courage to ask him but quietly wonder if he's hoping for the same thing I am. For the proof that all this pain and loss has to be for something. That somehow, if we ever make it out of this struggle alive, everything will finally make sense, and we'll find the answers we've desperately searched for.

As I stay close to his side, I also hope, for both our sakes, that we're not waiting in vain.

Chapter Eighteen
NICK

C losing my eyes, I step under the spray of the shower and let the hot water wash away the gruel, sweat, and grime of the day. The heat and steam seep into me, and my tense, sore muscles gradually ease and relax. But my thoughts are still spinning and churning.

I missed dinner. I'm not very hungry. And when I'm asked—and I know I will be—that's exactly what I'm going to say. Truth is, I'm not ready to be around her yet.

We spent the whole day together working on the fence. I figured she would either get bored or hurt herself and then give up and go back inside. I certainly hadn't expected her to like it, and I definitely hadn't expected her to be any help.

But she surprised me by stepping up and digging in right alongside me. She hadn't even complained. Not once. And she worked hard. She understands the commitment and responsibility this land asks of you, and what it takes to keep it carrying on long after we are gone.

She wasn't wrong in what she said today. This ranch does matter to me as if it's my own, and I wouldn't know what to do without it. It seems Lexy wouldn't either. She needs it as much as I do, and probably for a lot of the same reasons.

I thought Lexy being here was temporary. I thought she'd stay a few weeks until things settled down with her family, then she'd leave, and life could get back to normal. It never occurred to me that she'd want to make this ranch her home. The possibility that she might live here permanently has got me more than a little worried.

It's getting harder to stay away from her, which is why I had fought against her helping me today. It isn't that I don't want to spend time with her. It's because I do. She's too easy to talk to and be around. It's dangerous. I don't want to trust her and am not sure how to deal with the fact that maybe I already do.

She has the same effect on Glory. I thought Becca was crazy for putting Lexy in with her. She could have easily been hurt or trampled. But, Becca always had the instinct, as she likes to call it, about who a horse needs. And, she hasn't been wrong yet.

I stood in the ring, breathless and watching, as Lexy brought an angry, broken-down horse back from the brink. She hadn't done a thing except stay silent and still and patiently wait her out. She has an innate understanding of Glory's wounds and fear. I think it's because they are so similar to her own. There's a strange, secret, kindred connection between them. I'd been just as shocked as she was when Glory had taken the step towards her.

I've heard the stories about her Great-Granddaddy Cade; the legend of him still lives large in these parts. He'd believed compassion and gentleness were the way to earn the trust of a horse. Not discipline or rods or ropes. Just kindness and a soft touch. He'd had them so wrapped around his finger; they'd roll over at his feet simply with a wave of his hand. It seems Lexy has inherited his heart and gift with them.

I see why Glory gave in and followed her so easily. There's something about Lexy's pain that pulls you in. It's accepting and comforting, not harsh and jagged like mine. It's an odd relief to be around her and not have to explain or apologize or sidestep the stares—no judgment, reminders, pressure. I haven't had that kind of ease and quiet with someone in years.

Even the way she looks at me is different. As if she senses what I need before I do and catches it before I even realize I'm handing it over to her, just like the other afternoon in the stables.

I was on the edge of telling her everything. I almost gave in after we'd walked Glory and were alone.

I'd been so close to confessing the whole horrible, tangled-up mess to her. All my secrets. My grief. Megan. I could have. I wanted to, and Lexy would have let me.

But then the guilt had come in, gritty and hot, that I would dare share her with someone else. The grief is too personal, too raw, too mine. I can't let someone else into our space. No one is allowed in there but us. What I can't forgive myself for is that one split second when I had wished to find relief from the agony of remembering her. I hate that I almost betrayed her like that.

I don't like how much I'm thinking about Lexy, how I can't seem to help it, how I can't make myself stay away. Megan's memory has been so deeply branded into me that it's jarring to have someone else breaking through. I keep trying to avoid her and hold her at arm's length. But, when she smiled at me today, I had completely lost my train of thought. A guy didn't stand a chance against sweetness like that.

Frustrated at where my thoughts have ended up, I roughly turn off the tap, the water trickling down to a drip. The tarnished brass appliances are pretty ancient and never worked right, but that's just part of the charm of this place.

Pushing back the shower curtain, I grab a towel off the hook and scrub it over my face, through my hair, and down my chest. Still dripping, I step out of the clawfoot tub. The scents of shampoo and soap swirl around me in the small, muggy bathroom, and I open the door to let the steam out.

I walk into my bedroom and dry off, toss the towel into the hamper, and dress in faded jeans and a gray T-shirt. Leaving my feet bare, I run my hands through my damp hair, not bothering to comb it. I don't care enough, and it'll dry on its own.

Opening up my screen door, I step out onto the small porch. The evening has fallen; the air is warm and hushed and smells of the land. The sun is beginning to set behind the trees, and the sky is streaked in glowing shades of violet, pink, and orange. It's my favorite time of day. The whole world seems to slow down. I sit on the steps, giving myself a minute to soak in my own little piece of heaven. I want to be off the grid for a bit.

Something Lexy said is gnawing at me. I keep thinking about the fact that she has never let anyone else hear her sing. I wish I didn't already understand why she had to hide it. I can only imagine what would have happened if she had tried to have something of her own in an environment where everything revolved around keeping her mom alive.

She's beautiful when she sings. I'm fascinated by how she loses herself inside a song. I envy her for it, that she's figured out a way to disappear and escape. I have nowhere I can go to get away from myself. My pain is everywhere.

I meant what I'd said. She would get into the music school. I want her to have a chance at something more, even if I no longer do. But she shouldn't be trusting me with her secrets. I don't deserve it. I don't want her to give so much of herself to me, and I'm frustrated that she thought she could. I know it's just a matter of time before I disappoint her.

I hear Abraham before I see Ben. He's barking, the sound echoing over the wide, open pastures as he runs through the grass towards the cottage steps. I find it funny how he always seems to seek out the person who's hurting the most, as if he's got a sixth sense about it. He's never been wrong. He bounds up to me, and I scratch his ears. "Hi there, boy," I murmur and manage to smile a little when he licks my face as if trying to comfort me. It does help some.

Ben walks around the corner off the path. He's whistling, and I tense up as he comes into view. I knew sooner or later Becca would send him to come find me. I just wish I'd had more time to get my head straight.

"Hey," he says. He's carrying a plate wrapped in foil and has a mason jar tucked under his arm. "You missed dinner."

"I wasn't hungry." I test the lie out, and the words feel flat and fake on my tongue.

I can feel him reading me and don't meet his eyes as I watch Abraham wander off to explore, sniffing through the pastures. He never strays too far, always keeping an ear cocked towards us in case we need him.

Ben quietly hangs back, as if he's got all the time in the world. He's always been able to do that. Wait things out. I don't have his patience. We've spent hours on these porch steps, talking, or watching the land change and come to life, saying nothing at all. He

159

treads carefully, giving me room. He holds out the plate. "Brought you some meatloaf and mashed potatoes. Becca also thought you'd like some sweet tea."

"Thanks." Taking both from him, I set them down next to me. I don't bother trying to make small talk, knowing he'll get around to what he came to say soon enough.

Ben looks out over the pastures, the shifting, darkening, glowing sky. "It's a nice night."

I just nod, following his gaze, watching the lavender twilight hover and dissolve into the acres of green. It's breathtaking, but I can't make myself focus. Annoyance simmers low in my belly. I wish he'd stop stalling and spill it.

Noticing my silence, he looks back at me. "Everything okay?"

"Yeah." I nod, shrugging. "Just tired."

"I'm not surprised." He already knows that's not the real reason but lets it drop. He leans against the porch rail. "You and Lexy got a lot done today," he says casually, tucking his hands into his pockets. "You two are spending a lot of time together."

The mouth-watering smell of the meatloaf makes my stomach growl, betraying my lies. I'm not sure if he hears it. I don't meet his eyes as I pick up the mason jar, screwing off the lid. "Yeah. So?" I challenge him, resenting that he brought her up.

"Just making an observation," he says innocently.

"Right." I've known him for years and can tell when I'm being set up. I look square at him. "Did Becca send you out here?"

He doesn't even try to cover. He gives me a half-smile and shrugs. "She was worried. You don't usually miss dinner."

I let out a frustrated breath. I wish he'd leave me alone. I wish everyone would. "She doesn't need to worry. I'm fine," I lie again, even though I know it won't get past him. I drink the sweet tea, wiping my mouth with the back of my hand. "It's just crowded in there."

"A lot has changed over the past few weeks."

"Tell me about it," I mutter. Without warning, Lexy's smile comes back into my mind and sets my teeth on edge. The building tension makes it hard to keep in check what I'm thinking, and I decide to lay it all out. "You know, I'd be so mad at Lexy if I were you. How can she just show up like this after all this time? Who does something like that? It makes no sense."

"No, it doesn't," Ben answers, seemingly unaffected by my outburst, almost as if he's been expecting it. It only makes me angrier. "Why a mother would lie to her own daughter her whole life makes no sense at all. Why Victoria would ignore her own sister for the last twenty years makes even less sense. It does make me mad, but not at Lexy. It's not her fault for what she didn't know."

"She didn't try to know, Ben. She knew Becca was here. She never once reached out." I want to push at her, to punish her. I want all this need and confusion and guilt to be her fault. It isn't fair. Deep down, I know that, but for right now, blaming her is easier than admitting the real reason I'm so upset.

"Lexy did what she had to survive. Just like Victoria and Becca did with their family. Sometimes people don't have choices. But the second she did find the letters, she was on the first plane out here." He lets the moment sit for a minute and then quietly asks, "Why are you so mad at her?"

The question stops me, knocking some of the wind out of my lungs. I want to keep arguing but no longer have anything solid to stand on. "I don't know," I answer bleakly, looking away. I can't take the sympathy in his eyes. I wish I could figure out a way to fall off the face of the earth and completely disappear. "She's just..." I trail off, not knowing how to get the words out.

Ben waits for a beat. "She's what?"

I helplessly shake my head, words failing me. All this time, her family's silence had built up this negative perception in my mind about them. I'd had Lexy pegged as someone selfish, cold, uncaring. But the lost, scared girl who had knocked on the front door was nothing like I imagined.

She lives in constant fear of making that one wrong move that could bring her entire world crashing down. She has tried for years to save her mother, to the point that it had completely worn her out and broken her. When she'd finally found her way to the ranch, it didn't take much to realize that one more blow could have knocked her down for good. She's brave, although I don't think she knows it yet. What she did, coming out here like this, took guts. She's far more courageous than I could ever be. I still can barely get out of bed in the morning.

"She's just not who I thought she was," I finish wearily. I'm suddenly unbearably tired and wipe my hands over my face—every muscle in my body aches.

"No, she's not." Ben agrees, shaking his head thoughtfully. "She's going to be around a while." He says it like he's warning me. "She has nowhere else to go."

I don't either, I realize, sighing heavily. "I know." The fight is draining from me. I feel myself giving up. And it's at that moment I finally admit to myself why I'm so angry. Somewhere in the last couple of weeks since she'd shown up here, I had started to feel something for her. I hadn't meant to. I certainly hadn't wanted to. But she'd somehow broken through. I feel my stomach sink as I realize I'm running out of reasons to push her away. What do I do when I get to the point where I no longer can? "She's making everything different."

"I know she is."

"I just want things to go back to the way they were."

"What if they don't?" Ben asks, and I glance at him, wondering how he's always able to read my thoughts.

My eyes fall away from his, and I stare helplessly out into the night. The sky is a deep cobalt blue now, but I barely notice the beauty. I don't answer him. I can't. Because my worst fear is that I would let things change, and let myself move on. Let Megan actually really be gone.

And how will I ever live with myself then?

Chapter Nineteen
BEN

The light is still on in the bedroom as I come upstairs. Becca had waited up, and just because I like the view, I stand in the doorway and take a minute to stare at her.

I met her the summer we both turned sixteen when she started working at my family's feed store after school. I knew of her and her sister, and had heard the gossip and rumors around town about their drunk of a father. I had seen her in the halls in between classes, and her locker was a few down from mine, but I could never muster up the courage to talk to her.

She was hard to get to know, and there was a sadness about her that made me wonder all the more. She was withdrawn, wounded, and mysterious. She didn't say much and kept to herself and constantly left me wanting to find out what she was thinking. I carried around the foolish, adolescent fantasy of being the one she'd let rescue her.

My mama had taught me that the best things in life are always the ones worth waiting for. I was more than willing to wait as long as it took for Becca.

I'd tried to play it cool and strike up a conversation with her as we stocked shelves and counted inventory. Nothing too personal at first, just small talk. Easy and harmless. I'd sneak in questions here and there, trying to draw her out. We'd talk about our favorite music, the annoyance and stress of homework, and our love of horses. I'd tell her silly jokes to help ease the haunted look in her eyes. The first time I ever made her laugh is still one of the best days I have spent on this earth. It was the sweetest sound I'd ever heard.

I thought I'd never get the chance to go on a date with her. She was always just out of my reach. Earning her trust was slow progress, like waiting for molasses to pour from the bottle. A few times, she let me drive her home but always made me drop her off before we got near the gate to her ranch, as if she didn't want me to come inside or see where she was from. Or maybe she was afraid of what would happen to me if I got too close.

I felt like I'd take two steps forward and five back. I could barely eat. I lost sleep over her. I was starting to lose hope.

And then, on one of the hottest summer days on record, where even the flies panted and fainted from the heat, my luck finally changed.

My palms had been clammy, and my heart had pounded so loud I'd swore she could hear it, but I'd worked up the nerve to ask her to the movies. When she'd said yes, I could only stare at her for a second in shock. She'd looked up at me with her shy smile and lonely, beautiful eyes, and I knew my life would never be the same.

We saw *Forrest Gump*. Becca loved it, and to this day, it's still her favorite movie of all time. Afterward, we went to the Sonic for milkshakes and then drove out behind old farmer Larson's field, where we sat on blankets in the back of my truck and looked up at the stars.

All throughout the night, I'd reached for her hand, holding it as long as she'd let me. I didn't even try to kiss her. I didn't want to scare her off. As we searched the heavens for constellations, she leaned a little closer and finally let herself reach for mine. And that was the second I knew I loved her.

We spent every waking minute of that endless summer together and haven't been apart since.

She looks up from her book and gives me the same smile that had turned me upside down at sixteen. "Hey, you."

I smile back. Even after all this time, she still makes my heart do a sweet, slow flip in my chest. She's the prettiest woman in the world to me. "Hey." I push myself off the door jamb.

"How's he doing?" To cool herself in the heat, she pulls her hair back off her neck, tying it up in that effortlessly feminine way women do. "Did you get a chance to talk to him?"

"Yeah, I did." Since my niece is in the bedroom right down the hall, I close the door and then come over and sit on the edge of the bed. I look over my shoulder at her, a knowing smile on my face. "Lexy's got him pretty tangled up."

She grins, flashing the dimple in her right cheek. "I knew it." She folds down the page, and closes the book, keeping her palm on the cover. Her smile turns wistful and dreamy. "I could tell he was falling for her. He needs her. And it's so sweet how she looks at him like he's her hero. She's fascinated by him."

"Unfortunately for him, I think the feeling is mutual." I unlace and remove my work boots, setting them on the floor by the bed.

"They've both been through so much." Putting her book on the nightstand, she picks up her lotion. She flips the cap up and squeezes it out into her palm. Her nightly routine has always intrigued me, and I watch as she slathers moisturizer on her hands and up over her sun-kissed arms. I recognize the scent of lavender. "They'll be good for each other."

Standing, I walk into the bathroom. "He's struggling with it." I open the medicine cabinet and pull out the dental floss, toothpaste, and my toothbrush. "He's feeling guilty for caring about her. It's hard for him after losing Megan the way he did." Turning around, I lean against the sink as I floss. "You're going to let this happen on its own, right? You know he doesn't like to be pushed."

"I know." She sets the lotion back on the nightstand while she waits for me to finish brushing my teeth. "I'll stay out of it." When I raise my brows at her, she laughs and rolls her eyes. She innocently holds up her hands. "I will. I promise." I know her too well to believe her but wisely say nothing as I turn back to the sink. "I just want him to be happy again."

I rinse out my mouth with Scope, spit it out, and wash it down the drain. "I know you do." Pulling a towel from the rung, I wipe my face. "He'll get there. He's already let her in more than most people." Since I know Becca is watching, I fold the towel and hang it back up instead of leaving it crumpled on the sink and come back into the room. "Any word yet from Richard or Victoria?"

"No, nothing." Becca sighs sadly, shakes her head as she flips the sheet up to create a breeze, and lets it billow back down. The humidity makes even the dust cling to the skin. "I don't know how someone does this to their own daughter, Ben."

"I don't know either." I strip off my socks and jeans, tossing them into the hamper. "But you can't make someone want to get help."

"I wish there was a way we could," she says helplessly. "At least Lexy is here and away from the drinking. Do you think she's doing alright?"

My white T-shirt follows the rest of my clothes into the pile of laundry until I'm wearing only blue boxers. "I think she's doing the best she can, considering what she's dealing with." Going to the window, I push the lace curtains aside so more air can circulate through. The old, metal fan tiredly groans as it rotates back and forth, uselessly trying to get ahead of the sweltering summer heat. I feel its pain.

Becca takes a sip of water from the glass she leaves next to the bed. "I hope she knows she's safe with us." She sets the glass back down and turns off her light. "I want this to be a place where she can heal."

"It will be. She's just figuring it all out right now. A lot has changed for her over the last few weeks." I climb in beside her, the antique wooden bed creaking under my weight. I turn out my bedside light, the room settling into the muggy, moonlit dark. Adjusting my pillow, I lay back, sighing as my body relaxes, my sore muscles easing into the comfort of the mattress. "We just need to let her get used to everything. She seems to like it here and is starting to settle in." When I lift my arm, Becca nestles into the crook, fitting perfectly, and I turn my head so I can breathe in the scent of her hair. It's too hot to be this close, our skin is already damp and sticking, but I don't mind.

She tilts her head to look up at me. "Did I tell you she called me 'Aunt Becca' this morning?"

"She did?"

She smiles, and even in the shadows, I can see her eyes light up. "While she was helping me with breakfast. She was asking me where the cinnamon was and just said it as if it was the most natural thing on earth. As if she's always been calling me that."

I know all too well how huge and important the moment was. Becca has dreamt for years of having her family back. She's never stopped needing or missing them. I kiss her forehead. "See? She's finding her way."

"I hope so. I don't want her to be hurt anymore."

"Try not to worry so much," I soothe as I trace my fingers lightly up and down her arm. "We won't let anything happen to her."

She catches my hand and links her fingers with mine, just like she did that starry summer night so long ago. I've held on tight to her ever since. "I love you."

There's not one man on this earth as lucky as me. I'd bet my life on it. Propping myself up on my elbow, I smile down at her. "Have I ever told you how much I like the way you look at me?"

"You're my hero," she murmurs, tenderly touching my cheek.

I keep my eyes on hers as I lean down to kiss her. I'd save her every day to hear those words.

Chapter Twenty
VICTORIA

P eople get asked all the time what they want to be when they grow up. Astronauts, doctors, firefighters, baseball players. Young children with big dreams. You have so much hope when you're young, so much promise. A whole life waiting ahead.

But all I ever wanted was to figure out a way not to be me.

I find it ironic that my mama named me after Victoria Woodhull, who was the first woman to run for President of the United States back in 1872. She didn't win the election, but went on to do great and astounding things and was a force to be reckoned with back in her day.

"Sometimes people aren't ready for things to change," mama had told me, "but that just means you have to find a different door."

She had such big plans for me. I still don't know what she saw in me. She thought I was going to make an impact, start a movement, stop a war. Be a revolutionary. She believed I was someone who knew how. She was convinced there was something good in me, something more, better. Worthy. That I was a person who knew how to fight and win and survive. She made it sound as if I had a purpose and a future. Or maybe she wanted me to become everything she didn't have the courage to be.

If she could only see me now.

I had my first drink at twelve. I'd found daddy's bottle of Wild Turkey hidden behind sacks of grain in the storehouse on the ranch. He had bottles of it stashed everywhere. Under the saddle blankets in the stable, behind the couch, on the shelf in the hall closet. I guess he wanted to make sure he never ran out.

I drank until I couldn't see or feel anymore, drank until the world spun, drank until I threw it all up. I didn't want to stop. I couldn't. I had a taste for it even then. The burn of it going through my system felt as if it was scorching all the bad out of me.

Becca found me in the pastures behind the house, delirious, shaking and green, crying and curled into a ball. Daddy was off on one of his drinking binges and had been gone for two days doing God only knows what. Becca carried me back inside, climbed into the shower with me and cleaned me up, put me to bed, and stayed up all night with me while I writhed and mumbled incoherently. Mama knew I was drunk but was so worried about how sick I was, she never yelled at me for it.

I recovered and vowed never to drink again. And, for years, I didn't. But I never forgot how every swallow made my pain disappear and turned me into someone strong and brave and invincible and somehow beautiful.

I never wanted to be like him. I had left home to make sure I wouldn't end up the same way he did. But some things can't be outrun or prevented. I wonder if it was already in my blood to become an alcoholic, to end up a failure exactly like him. You can't reverse genetics and biology. It was a dark passenger I could never throw off my trail. I'd dreamt of being someone else, something else, anyone else. I had wanted to be a singer since before I had ever spoken my first word.

But I never stood a chance at being anything other than a drunk. I could never escape the curse of being my father's daughter.

I knew I had to get out. I'd die if I didn't. I managed to stash up exactly $1842 from odd jobs helping out Callie Simmons, who was a widow that lived on the next farm over. I worked on her land, watered and fed her horses, went into town for her groceries, and picked up supplies. She was one of the few who was kind to me, and every afternoon after school, she'd feed me sugar cookies and sweet tea before I'd go out to the barn.

I had spent the last few years secretly stashing items from our home I figured I'd need on the road and stuffed them into a faded blue duffel bag I hid under the floorboards of our bedroom closet. Old socks, a few pairs of underwear, band-aids, tampons, toothbrush and toothpaste, deodorant, a few shirts I barely wore so mama wouldn't notice they were missing from the wash. Becca knew and would keep watch while I tucked a few more dollars under the floor.

On the day of my eighteenth birthday, I was ready to run. I think daddy knew it and spent the morning swearing and slapping and shoving me into walls. As if to remind me he could still do whatever he wanted, no matter how old I was. He didn't care. I took it because it never did any good to fight back. I would just get hit more. But this time was different because, in a matter of hours, I'd be gone, and he could never, ever touch me again.

Once he finally passed out, snoring loudly and drooling like a fat, old slobbering dog into the cushions on the couch, I gathered up the duffel bag and my grandmother Rose's guitar. I wrapped some biscuits, and sausage mama made for my special breakfast that morning into a napkin and tucked them in with my other belongings.

My lip was swollen, and my nose was bleeding, and the pain and rage made me more determined to leave. Becca clung to me, and we both sobbed, but we knew if I stayed, I might not make it to my next birthday. I swore I'd write to her as soon as I could to let her know I made it safely to California. I left a note for mama while she was out in the stables and asked Becca to give it to her. I couldn't bear to say goodbye. I left the ranch, vowing I would die before I ever returned.

I rode the Greyhound as far as I could afford to, rationing the corn nuts, granola bars, and beef jerky I'd gotten from vending machines and gas stations. I hitched rides the rest of the way. I slept in bathroom stalls, rest stops, and bus terminals along the interstate. I didn't care where I was as long as I was gone. I'd wanted to get as far from Tennessee as I could, and moving clear across the United States seemed like enough space to put in between me and my past.

I had seen pictures and postcards of Los Angeles with its palm trees, Hollywood sign, and glamorous movie stars. It seemed like a completely different world than the flat, dusty pastures of the ranch. I counted every marker of all the miles we passed, feeling relief that the farther I got, the harder it would be for him to find me. I made it to California four days later. When I finally crossed the state line, it was the first and only time I ever felt something I'm guessing was safety. I've never known how it felt. I've never been safe in my life.

I planned on auditioning for anything I could find as soon as I got settled. I had thousands of songs I had written that I knew would be hits if I could just get the right person to listen. I was going to bang on as many doors as I could. But first, I needed a job and a place to live.

Searching through the classifieds, I found work as a waitress at a hamburger joint in West Hollywood. I was still young, pretty, and southern enough to charm the owner, and he hired me that very day. It didn't pay much, but the tips helped me rent a small studio above the liquor store across the street. Rats and roaches crawled along the floors, and the heat and plumbing never worked right, but I would have been willing to live in a cardboard box to avoid going back home.

The diner is where I met Richard. My first thought when I saw him was there would be a day when he wished he'd never met me. He was twenty and was going to law school. He was smart and serious and quiet, and much too good for me. He reminded me of the movie stars on the billboards on the strip with his clear blue eyes and dark wavy hair. His smile was brilliant and breathtaking. He always sat in my station. And he paid attention to me, which was an addiction in itself for me.

He'd come in every afternoon to study for the bar exam and stayed until the place emptied, and we'd talk while I cleaned tables, refilled the napkin holders and ketchup bottles, and counted out my tips. I let him hear a few of my songs, and he was fascinated by my voice and told me I was the best singer he'd ever heard. I greedily ate up every compliment like it was candy and was always starved for more.

I didn't tell him much else about me. I couldn't. I didn't want to ruin who he thought I was. When he would ask, I lied, setting in motion years of secrets. I told him both my parents were dead and my sister and I didn't speak anymore. My family was too far away to prove me wrong. And the lies I started telling became a new way of hiding.

I still don't know how or why, but he ended up falling in love with me. I wanted to warn him that he shouldn't, that he should run as far as he could from me. But I already couldn't live without him. I had never been in love before, and the feeling was an intoxicating drug I couldn't get enough of. I fell hard and fast and breathlessly raced into the new life he promised me. We were inseparable, a feverish, obsessive fix for each other. It all happened so quickly, a whirlwind romance that was intense and euphoric and the kind of rush I had only known at twelve when I found the Wild Turkey. I had been chasing that same kind of delirious high ever since. And Richard gave it to me. He made me feel alive and different and beautiful, and I never wanted to go back.

He passed the bar and proposed to me, and we were married by a Justice of the Peace at City Hall. We had Lexy a few years later. Richard got a job at a local law firm, and we moved into the suburbs, complete with a 30-year mortgage and a minivan in the drive. Our lives seemed to be on track.

I can't say what the trigger was. Maybe there wasn't one, and that was the problem. Maybe the normalcy of my life made me start to unravel. I couldn't handle how ordinary it was. I wasn't used to it. I had grown up hiding under beds and porches and running for my life. Anything other than violence and chaos felt abnormal and somehow wrong. It was the only thing I knew. I wasn't bored; I was terrified.

No one knew who I was or where I came from. They couldn't hear me screaming inside. I had completely reinvented myself. I was president of the PTA, put on luncheons for Richard's clients, and volunteered in the community. I perfected the performance as the ultimate southern belle with the pretty smile that covered up all my damage. I desperately wanted to be good, just like mama believed I was. I had the life I had always wanted but never could escape the dark, clammy panic of having everything taken away from me. I didn't deserve to be loved and knew it was a matter of time before everyone figured it out.

And then, Becca's first letter arrived in the mail. The rope I had been clinging to frayed and shredded even more, until I was holding onto nothing but a thin thread that spun me in circles and threatened to snap at any moment. I still don't know how she found me. I tried to completely disappear and erase myself off the map. I cut off all contact years before. I thought we were too far apart for her to reach me.

But the letters kept coming, each one reminding me over and over that the past would never die. It hunted me, crouching around every corner, waiting to grab me and drag me back to where I escaped from. I felt as if it laughed at me for even thinking I would be able to outrun it.

I bought my first bottle of vodka on a Thursday morning after I dropped Lexy off at school. I had to stop at the grocery store for a few things, and as I walked past the liquor aisle, I just picked it up. Milk, eggs, laundry detergent. Vodka. It was a surprisingly easy decision as if I had been searching for an answer, and it just opened right up to me. Like when you get lost and suddenly turn down the very street you were looking for and feel that flood of relief that you finally found your way. It made sense in a way nothing else did.

To calm the crippling anxiety, I secretly drank while Richard was at work and Lexy was at school. Not a lot at first, just enough to smooth out the edges and keep the fear from completely overtaking me. Daddy had taught me early how to hide and cover, and I tucked the bottle behind the storage boxes in the garage.

The nightmares were back, and they were disturbing and intense, and violent. I could no longer shut out the flashbacks. I would wake up screaming, convinced daddy was right outside the door coming to get me. Richard was terrified for me, but I was too ashamed to tell him what had happened. I tried sleeping pills, but they didn't protect me or stop my bad dreams. The post-traumatic stress was like a landmine I had to sidestep and tiptoe around, or I'd explode. Drinking was the only way to numb myself and keep me sane. The vodka created a glossy, hazy bubble around me where the fear couldn't break through.

I didn't know until it was too late that it would also not let me get out.

For a while, the drinking seemed to work. I thought I was functioning well, and my life was back in control. I didn't even notice the cracks and gaps starting to slip through. I overslept and became distracted and forgetful. I'd miss appointments, not go to the store, and the house stopped getting cleaned. I blanked out on dinner meetings. When Lexy was seven, the principal called to ask why she was waiting alone on the curb when school had been out for hours. It was the first time I ever drove her home drunk.

I started losing track of time. The days blurred one into the next. All I thought about was my next drink. I was detached, disorganized, and disoriented. I stopped looking over my shoulder. And I forgot to check the mail.

The day Richard brought Becca's letter to me, I completely shattered. I ended up sobbing hysterically and telling him everything about my childhood, the abuse, and the drinking. He cried with me, was enraged and devastated for me, and begged me to get help, to talk to my sister. I vehemently refused and said I wasn't ready. I made him swear not to tell Lexy and promised I would explain everything to her when she was older. I didn't want her to know monsters were real. I didn't realize then that I was the one she should have feared. He felt so sorry for me that he didn't push and let me keep my secrets. I think he hoped that him finding out the truth would make me stop drinking. But, in my mind, it just gave me permission and an excuse to do it more.

I'd thought Lexy was young enough that she wouldn't notice, but she started asking questions, ones I dreaded, ones I couldn't answer without opening up a past I had vowed never to speak of again. She would ask about our family, where we came from, and why no one ever came to visit. I tried putting her off, changing the subject, but as she got older, her curiosity became harder to avoid. She was far more perceptive and sensitive than I realized. She began to figure things out, and the questions became more probing, intrusive, and painful. What had happened to her grandparents? Why didn't I speak to my sister? Why didn't I want to ever go back to Tennessee? Why did I lock myself in my room all the time? Why was I always so sick? Why didn't I sing anymore?

I couldn't handle it and drank more and more as the years went by until I was doing it all the time, no longer having the restraint or control to hide it. I didn't want to be saved. I needed the vodka more than air, more than my own life, more than my family. I spent every moment of every day trying to get to the next drink. The craving was unbearable. I knew I'd sold my soul to have it, but I didn't care anymore. No one understood what would happen if I didn't have the bottle to hold onto. I was too wasted to notice that the more I chased oblivion, the more exposed I became.

As my drinking grew worse, Richard retreated further into his work. I would fall apart when he tried to convince me to get help, and our fights would cause me to have violent, furious meltdowns. I pushed him away and shut him out, and every day, I lived in the fear that what I dreaded most was happening. And I had no idea how to change it. I was already too far gone to stop. Maybe I always had been. So, I let the rope snap, and my world fell to pieces around me. Ironically, the breakdown felt like the most natural thing in the world.

And now my daughter is gone. Richard broke his promise and had given her the letters. I would have eventually told her, but how do you explain to your own child that her grandfather beat and kicked her mother until she was bruised and broken beyond recognition? There was never a right time or the right words or a right way to talk about something that was so horribly wrong.

She's run to the very place I had tried to keep her from, that I swore I'd never go back to, and have spent years trying to forget. My sister is there and by now has told my young, innocent daughter of the hell that happened to us. It should have all come from me, but I was never strong enough to do it. I wonder if Lexy will ever want to speak to me again. I haven't heard from her, and she won't respond to my texts or calls, which only confirms my fear that she has shut me out for good.

I meant what I'd told her the morning she left. I was trying to protect her. I didn't want her to have to know the abuse I experienced or realize fear like that existed. I couldn't face it for myself enough to even talk to her about it. It was too terrible and traumatic. She said she had to go so she could find out the truth. But I know she left to break free of me. Because all this time, I'm the one who is the real monster. I've turned into the very thing I've spent my whole life trying to avoid becoming.

That land also belongs to Lexy, every God-forsaken acre of it. I wonder if she'll want to be a part of it, if she'll want to carry on the legacy her great-great-grandparents left for all of us. If she'll find a home there. She doesn't have one here. I've taken that from her. I've ruined everything I've ever touched. Maybe Lexy leaving will somehow save her. Maybe being away from me is the best thing for her.

I know Richard is going to make me go into rehab. Ever since Lexy left, I have felt the pressure closing in, inching and backing me into a corner. Through the barrier of my wooden door, I've heard him quietly on the phone, making decisions, plans, and arrangements. For me. Because of me. Without me and despite me. He's going to force me to go, to give it all up. To get sober. Clean. Little does he know the real ugliness that's underneath. Rage fills me that he would dare take the thing I need most away from me. As if I could actually be rehabilitated. Doesn't he realize I'm beyond saving? It makes me laugh and laugh and laugh, delirious and insane, a crazed woman unhinged.

I'd left Tennessee more than twenty years ago, hoping for a new start, new beginning, new life. But, my past has followed me here, and I haven't ever been able to tear free from it, not for one single second. It feels like all the abuse just happened, as if my father is still standing over me, with his fist raised, sweating and sneering and swearing in my face. No matter how far I try to run, I will always be that scared little girl cowering under the porch with my sister. Daddy will never let me go.

Mama had been wrong about me. I have nothing good in me, and I will never change the world. I've never known how to fight. He will always win. Nothing is going to be different, and nothing will get better.

I found the other door mama told me to look for. I already know what I am going to do, what I have to do. Maybe I've always known, and my life has been leading up to this very moment since the day I was born.

I don't say goodbye, don't write a note, don't leave behind any last words.

No one will miss someone who is already no one.

Huddled in my bed, I hold on tight to the bottle of Xanax as if it's my salvation. I'm still feeling too much, the anxiety is ripping up my insides, and the panic, that horrible, vicious panic, won't ever die. The pressure in my chest is so tight I feel like my heart is going to burst through my skin.

I look absently at the alarm clock on the nightstand.

2:18.

I think it must be night. It's dark outside. Morning will be here soon, and I'll have to try and drag myself through another excruciating day. Even one minute seems too long to stay alive. I can't do it anymore.

My hands are trembling and sweaty as I open the lid and pour the blue pills into my palm. I stare down at them, thinking how dangerous and powerful something so small could be. They seem to make the decision for me as if they are doing me a favor.

I don't want to feel. I just want the fear to end. I thought I could get away from him. I thought I could find a way to reverse time.

But I realize now I can't. My life is a self-fulfilling prophecy. *Like father, like daughter,* I think bitterly, and I swear I hear him laughing, mocking, daring me to get away from him. I feel a resentful sense of defiance as I shove the handful of pills into my mouth and bring the bottle of vodka to my lips. I quickly swallow them down before I change my mind and wait for them to swallow me.

I keep drinking until the room tilts and sways, until I feel my heart rate slow, and my body goes limp and slumps over. The empty bottle slips from my fingers, rolling away from me, falling onto the laminate hardwood floor with a loud clanking thud. It's the first time I've let go of it in years.

I stare dully at the clock, which is inches from where my head has landed, the large red numbers glowing and blurring as the toxic combination seeps through me and poisons my blood.

3:00.

It only takes forty-two minutes to wait to die. That's not very long at all.

Freedom is so close; it's right there. I can taste it. I don't even fight. I'm weightless, nothing, and somehow powerful. I'm the one in control now. Not him. I'm now the one laughing. He can't find me when I've vanished into thin air. It's the perfect escape. I feel as if I'm about to be born again, even though I'm trying to end my life.

There's no more sound or thought. Blissful stillness. My mind shuts down, and my father's voice is finally silenced. There are no memories, no past, no him, no me. No more nightmares. And no more pain. It's almost over, and it was so easy.

I'm already passed out and don't realize my system is rejecting the toxic combination of pills and vodka. I'm not aware that I'm convulsing and throwing up and lying in my own vomit. I don't notice I've urinated myself. I don't hear my moans as my body fights against what I most want. And I don't hear the pounding on the bedroom door as I drift away into the black.

Chapter Twenty-One
RICHARD

Her coffee cup is the only way I've known she's still alive. Every few days, I will find it, along with dirty dishes, in the sink. I've counted on her routine, no matter how dysfunctional it is, to let me know she's survived her latest binge.

I've only seen her twice since Lexy left. She walks right past me as if I don't exist. I don't even think she does anymore. She's a thin, frail ghost of herself. Pale, withdrawn, invisible. I can see straight through her. Her eyes are blank and dull, and I feel her accusing me even though she never says a word.

She won't look at me, talk to me, acknowledge me at all as she shuffles in and out of reality and then locks herself back up away from the world. I'm still being punished for giving Lexy the letters, for letting her leave, and not trying to get her back. For believing our daughter needs to be saved from her own mother.

I think she thought Lexy would come home by now. It's almost been a month since she left. As the time and distance stretch out from days into weeks, Victoria has become more agitated, angry, panicked, and fearful. Paranoid. I've heard her up in the middle of the night pacing and rambling manically, inside the four walls of her room, like a madwoman. She's hanging on to sanity by a thin thread.

I've even heard her singing. She hasn't in years, and at first, I thought she had the television on and was watching one of those competition shows. The sound of her is still clear and ethereal, which is a surprise to me. Even with the addiction ravaging every part of her, the purity of her voice still breaks through. Her undeniable talent hasn't died or burned out, even though she slowly is.

I've missed hearing her. She was so passionate about music and used to have so many dreams. I don't know the song, and the words are slurred and jumbled, but I recognize her, the beautiful, fiercely determined girl I had met all those years ago at the diner. She's still in there somewhere, under all the layers and residue and years of abuse. I fell for her instantly, had never met anyone so gorgeously on fire, and haven't ever recovered. I'm still hooked and strung out on her.

When is enough finally enough? Something has to change, break, give. She's never going to stop on her own. I don't know how I ever thought she could. She's beyond the point where she can. The beast is too strong and has its claws too deeply embedded into her.

We can't go on like this anymore. I know I'm pathetically too late, but I can't keep living with the guilt of what I'm allowing her to do to herself, our daughter, our lives. I have to be the one to finally draw the line and have decided I'm going to make her go into rehab and get help. I'm forcing an intervention. I've made some calls and am going to tell her she has to go.

I know the fallout will be messy and violent and hysterical, and she may go through with her threats to kill herself. But, I have to try, for all of us. Lexy is safe and far enough away from any collateral damage. As soon as the arrangements are finalized, I'm getting her into treatment. I'll drag her there if I have to.

I didn't sleep well and have a headache, the pain nagging at the base of my skull. I thought I heard her laughing, or maybe I dreamt it, the sound eerie and deranged in the dark. A loud noise had startled me awake, and I shot up in bed, trying to figure out what was going on. It sounded like something falling or being dropped in Victoria's room.

Ever since Lexy has been gone, I've obsessively listened, checked, and watched for her, worried about her going over the edge. It's a little after three and still dark out. Something feels off, but I can't figure out what it is.

I don't like the silence. It feels different. Stale, stagnant, and unused. Abandoned and deserted somehow. The air is too still. The laughing stopped. I don't know how to explain the uneasiness in the pit of my stomach. I can't shake it. This isn't normal, whatever that is in our house.

I get out of bed and go down the hall and have the surreal sensation of entering the twilight zone. The walls feel as if they are expanding and breathing, warning me. The floor seems to narrow and get longer with every step I take, like I'm walking in slow motion.

I knock, already knowing she won't let me in. But I try anyway, hoping for a miracle. Something is wrong. It was only a matter of time before she broke under the pressure of losing control. There's no answer. I can't figure out what the noise was that jolted me awake. I'm worried she fell or hit her head. I rattle the knob.

"Victoria!" I call out. "Please open the door!" Nothing. No sound on the other side. I uselessly bang on the door, louder this time, but still no response.

I don't even have to imagine the worst. It's a reality I live with every day of my life. I have to get inside. A smell is wafting out into the hall, like food spoiling or rotting.

I throw myself up against the door, heaving the whole left side of my body into it. Pain radiates through my shoulder and my hip, knocking the wind out of me, but I can't feel anything through the panic. The force jars it, but it doesn't open.

I shove and lunge against it again and again with an unnatural strength that only comes with terror until I'm sweating through my clothes. My shoulder is throbbing and about to fracture, and then the wood finally splits around the frame.

Stumbling forward, I frantically push the door open and get inside. Her bedroom light is still on. The aroma of vomit and urine hits me, and I throw up my hand to block it, trying to find fresh air. But there isn't any. The stench is a film on the walls as if the whole room has been sealed up tight. The windows are never open, the blinds closed to the outside.

Gagging, I run toward the bed. My foot kicks the vodka bottle that had fallen, and it bounces and spins across the floor. I realize that must have been the sound I heard.

I know she's not sleeping. Her body is at too awkward of an angle, like a puppet whose strings have been clumsily dropped. It's then that I see the empty bottle of Xanax lying next to her hand.

"Oh, God." It's half prayer, half cry for help, half curse, as I move her hair away from her face searching for any sign of life. Her skin is still warm. Had she just taken the pills? Mucus, saliva, and vomit are drooling from her mouth, streaked along her skin, and there's a pool of fluid on the bed under her cheek. Had she choked? How long has she been under?

I lean close to her to see if I can feel air coming through her nose or her lips, but there's nothing. I don't know what to do. Do I perform CPR? Does that help if she's already dead? Am I supposed to move her? Everything I've ever been taught and told to do in a disaster completely blanks out of my mind. I thought I'd be more prepared. I've known this day has been coming for years.

"Please don't die. Please don't die." I'm begging, whispering, crying. "Please stay with me. I'm so sorry." This wasn't an accident. This was deliberate. She wanted to end her life, and I'm suddenly irrationally and intensely furious, which I know isn't fair. But nothing about this ever has been for any of us. Maybe she thought she could live without me, but I know I can't survive without her. I'm angry that she wants to leave us, that she's so selfish to take herself away.

And there's another sick part of me that is secretly relieved to have the nightmare over, that I won't have to constantly worry about her anymore, but I quickly shut down the thought. It makes me feel like a monster. It's a horrible, exquisite agony loving her. I know the weight of the blame is all mine. I'm the one who made her think she had no other choice. How am I going to tell our daughter?

I need help. I want to yell, but there's no one here. I'm alone. Lexy is gone. And I'm the one who sent her away. This overdose is my stinging, harsh reminder of why I'm in this situation. I caused it.

I clumsily pull my cell phone out of my sweatpants pocket. My hands are shaking so violently I can barely press 911 and misdial and drop the call and have to hang up twice. I growl and shake the phone in frustration and swear under my breath. Why are three numbers so hard?

I finally get through, and the operator answers, her voice slow and a little bored as if she's tired of having to deal with all of us and our problems. "Do you have an emergency?"

I almost laugh at the absurdity of the question. Why else would I be calling? I've always had one. I've been living in a war zone for decades.

"Yes," I manage. I don't take my eyes from Victoria, silently pleading with her to wake up, to breathe. An eyelash to flutter. Anything. "I think my wife is dead." I'm surprised it's taken me this long to have to say those words.

"Try to stay calm, sir. Can you tell me what happened?" She still sounds dismissive, and she says it like she's talking to a five-year-old. I don't think she believes me, as if I'm overreacting or being dramatic. I want to strangle her through the line.

I don't have time for this, I think, as impatience surges and makes my entire body tense and hot. We're wasting precious minutes that we need to save Victoria. My breathing is coming in short, shallow puffs. I feel lightheaded. I'm holding Victoria's limp hand in mine. I don't want to let go, as if hanging onto her will keep her from being gone. Is that a pulse? Or am I in total shock and denial?

"She's not breathing. She overdosed on Xanax and vodka." I'll have to find the bottle that was kicked across the room, I remind myself, feeling dazed. The paramedics might need to see it.

"What is your address?" She asks, and I can tell she's realized how urgent the situation is. Her voice sounds higher and more alert, and she's no longer telling me to calm down. I don't know why it scares me more.

I give her the information; she says the ambulance is on the way, and I weakly drop my phone onto the bed. I'm still holding Victoria's hand, my fingers closed at her wrist, and I feel the faint blip of her pulse again. I'm not imagining it. She's still alive. "Victoria! Can you hear me?" Hope fills me, and I jump up, carefully rolling her over.

Tilting her head back, I press my mouth to hers, trying not to think about the vile smell and taste of vomit, and breathe into her. Her chest rises. I check her airway again, listening for her heartbeat, but still nothing. She doesn't exhale. It occurs to me that Lexy has been the one breathing for her all this time. She's been her oxygen. But she's far away, and without the life support, Victoria finally ran out of air.

Straddling her, I start the compressions, praying I'm not doing it wrong and accidentally break her ribs. I cringe at how alive she feels beneath me, as if she's going to open her eyes any second and ask what I'm doing. Those plastic dummies do nothing to prepare you for the real thing. It's a much different experience when it's an actual person—your own wife. Nausea backs up in my throat, along with the hysteria. I can't lose her. I want to break down and sob, but there's no time. Was that a moan? I swear I'm hearing things. I go back and forth between breathing for her and trying desperately to get her heart to beat.

Somewhere off in a detached place in my mind, I hear the distant sound of sirens, indicating help has finally arrived. As I pump my locked fists into Victoria's chest, I can't help thinking they are years too late.

Chapter Twenty-Two
LEXY

I stand next to Nick, feeling anxious and excited as he opens up the pen gate. Patting Glory on her backside, he murmurs encouragement and lets her find her way.

She had already been moved into the main stables a few days before to see how she would handle being around the other horses. She'd adjusted well, and they had not become aggressive or territorial with her. Nick wanted to get her integrated with the herd. I helped him widen the pen to give the two mares enough room to get used to each other.

He'd put her in with the most gentle and calm of the horses. Ben and Becca had rescued Maddy, a glossy black quarter horse, from a temporary shelter about ten years ago. She'd been one of the thousands that had been a refugee from the hurricanes in Louisiana.

I'm fascinated to watch how they greet one another. I feel like we're eavesdropping on their conversation as they walk towards each other, round their necks, and bend their heads close as if telling each other secrets. My brows come up in surprise when they blow into each other's nostrils. "Why are they doing that?" I ask Nick.

He's close enough to me that our arms and shoulders touch as we watch their progress. Our hands could brush if one of us shifts. I'm not sure if he realizes it, but a few minutes have passed, and he hasn't moved away. I wonder if he's getting more comfortable and quietly let him lean on me as long as he allows himself to.

He's on the side nearest to the gate in case he needs to intervene and seems pleased to see it doesn't look like he'll need to. "They're exchanging scents," he tells me, not taking his eyes from the horses. "It's how they get to know each other."

I'm startled when Maddy suddenly lets out a shrieking neigh, the sound bellowing loudly and echoing over the land. Tossing her head, as if motioning for Glory to try and catch her, she turns and gallops across the length of the pen, dust billowing under her hooves. Glory watches for a moment as if she's trying to remember what to do, and if it's safe to, and then follows after her, her hesitant trot quickly turning to a prancing run. They remind me of children rushing out to play after being let out for recess. She almost seems to be smiling, her tail and mane swishing giddily as she matches Maddy's pace.

I'm laughing when my cell phone rings. Thoughtlessly, I pull it out of my back pocket, not even looking at the number. I'm thinking it's probably Becca, not realizing I never, ever should have stopped paying attention. I answer it, not remembering that sooner or later, my life would catch up with me and all the consequences I left behind in California. I had forgotten that nothing was really normal or typical about my life. I had forgotten that, for me, there is no such thing.

"Hello?" I say breathlessly, still laughing, as I watch the two horses chasing and teasing each other as best friends would. My heart is full seeing Glory this free.

"Lexy?" My dad's voice comes over the other end. I can barely hear him through the chaos and noise. A sound I don't recognize is blaring in the background. It sounds like carnival screams, but that doesn't make any sense.

I freeze. My laughter instantly dies and fades into thin air. The ground tilts sickeningly beneath me, and I have to clutch the rail for balance. "Dad?" Nick looks sharply over at me. We're both so still like marble statues. Even the birds overhead seem to go silent. I know why he is calling. She's dead. He's going to tell me my mom is dead. I start to tremble. "What's happened to her?"

"We're in the emergency room." I can hear the fear in his voice. I've never heard it before. It terrifies me. "I found her early this morning. She overdosed."

Sirens, I realize, panic curdling like bile in my throat. The sound I hear are sirens. "Is she alive?" My voice rises hysterically. My hand is clenched so tightly on the rail that my knuckles are white. There's a strange taste of copper in my mouth, and I vaguely realize I bit my cheek. I didn't even feel it. "Is she still alive?"

"Yes, but barely. She's not conscious. They are pumping her stomach. The next few hours are critical."

What have I done? What have I done? What have I done? The words beat through my brain like primal drums, loud and violent and accusing. I feel like I'm going to faint. My ears are ringing. My vision has dimmed and narrowed to where I can see nothing except shades of gray. Everything is spinning as if I have been sucked into a whirlpool and am going under and am about to drown. I close my eyes and try to breathe.

"I'll get on the next flight out there," I hear myself saying the words, but it doesn't even sound like me. The girl I was a minute ago is gone. I don't know why I'd been foolish enough to think my life could be different, that I could. "Let me know as soon as you hear something."

"I will."

"Okay. Dad, I—" If he were anyone else, I would have told him I loved him, but he isn't anyone else, and we've never said it. I don't dare say it now. I don't deserve to. Especially since this whole thing is my fault. "I'll get there as soon as I can."

He gives me the information for the hospital and hangs up, and even when the line is disconnected, I keep the phone pressed against my ear. I don't want to open my eyes. I don't know how to be in this moment even though I've been expecting it for years. It's finally here. My greatest fear has finally happened. And I caused it.

I thought I would know, that I would be able to tell that something was wrong. I was certain I'd have an overwhelming premonition of dread, some kind of sixth sense. A dream, nightmare, vision. Something. We'd always been so close. I made sure to match my every move with hers. But there had been nothing. While I was sleeping, she was trying to kill herself. And I had no idea.

I reluctantly open my eyes and stare dully at the horses. They seem so far away even though I haven't moved. I stand perfectly and completely still. If I move, I'll crumble. I'm suddenly so tired. I can't think. I can't seem to do anything. I just want to curl into a ball, close my eyes and go to sleep until all of this is over. I don't even register Nick stepping in front of me.

"Lexy," he says quietly. I don't dare blink or breathe. Keeping his eyes firmly fixed on me, he cautiously takes the phone from my hand, tucking it in his back pocket.

I try to think, to focus. I notice how Nick's face shimmers and ripples at the edges as if I'm looking at him from underwater. I realize I'm cold even though it's well over a hundred degrees outside. I'm shivering from the inside out. My teeth are chattering from fear and shock. "She's in the hospital," I finally manage. Why can't I feel anything? My entire body is numb. "She overdosed. I almost killed her."

Nick flinches. I think I hear him swear. "No, you didn't." He holds my arms to pull me out of the pit I'm sinking into to keep me afloat. "Don't say stuff like that. This isn't your fault."

"Yes, it is!" With a strength I didn't know I had, I threw his hands off. "You don't understand!" Adrenaline has kicked in, fueled by panic, fear, and anger. It's a lethal combination. I direct it all at him. A part of me is grateful to feel it. If I'm angry, I'm not afraid. If it's Nick's fault, then at least for this one split-second, it isn't mine. I need him to take it from me. "I'm the one that left her even though I knew this would happen. If I had stayed, she wouldn't have done this."

"Stop it." He shakes me a little. "You couldn't have saved her." I must look crazy because from some far-off place in my mind, I notice he looks scared for me. I have the delirious urge to burst out laughing. "She still would have gotten here. You didn't make her do anything."

Infuriated, I shove at him. "Yes, I did!" I shout, inches from his face. "I knew she couldn't make it on her own. I knew what it would do to her. I shouldn't have come here. Don't tell me it's not my fault!" I push at him again, harder this time, needing to feel some sort of power in this place of being so helpless. I wish he'd do something, yell at me, push back, anything to make this horrible pain stop. But he stands there and takes it, just like he does when the horses charge him, as if he knows that any minute I'm going to collapse.

There's a vicious ache spreading through my body. The reality is setting in. I feel like I'm being swallowed whole. I can't think. My breath is coming in fast, short gasps. I wish I could go back to feeling nothing. This is worse, so much worse. I had just wanted her to stop drinking. How could I have been so stupid to think that would happen without her falling apart or one of us going insane? Why hadn't I realized it would hurt this badly? How was I so naive to think there wouldn't be this much damage? How did I not know I would be the one who paid for it all?

I'm suddenly so angry that this has been what I've been expected to hide and put up with. I want to throw something, wail, scream, rage, rip my whole world down until there is nothing left. How can a mother tell her daughter she loves her and still destroy her? How could she ask me to watch as she poisons herself right in front of me? How can she expect me to carry this much pain? How am I the one who is thought of as selfish for not being more understanding? Why couldn't she ever just be my mom? And now, I'm being punished for not being able to save her and for trying to take the bottle away. I was never asked if I could survive hell. No one cared if I couldn't. I was just told I had to. I never once had a choice.

I had gotten what I wanted, I realize dully. She had finally reached her breaking point, but at the cost of what? What if she died, and I'm the one who pushed her off the edge? Breath heaving, I double over, clutching my stomach, frantically trying to somehow hold all the devastation in. I can't do this. It's too hard. It's too much. I'm not going to make it. *Nick had been right,* I think, as he blurs and disappears when the tears finally come. I was just about to crash.

"I'm sorry. I'm so sorry." I'm sobbing so hard, so uncontrollably, I don't know I'm repeating the words over and over and over. I don't notice when Nick pulls me up and wraps me tight in his arms. All I can do is bury myself against him and drown in the grief.

I cry for all the times I couldn't, for all the times I was forced to stay silent, for all the times I was told not to. I cry because I don't want to do this anymore. I cry because, deep down, there's a part of me that secretly hates her. I've hated that she chose the addiction over me, that I was just told I had to let it have her. That she let it. I cry out of sheer relief that our lives have finally shattered and for the guilt that I've wanted them to.

And I cry for her, for all the pain and suffering and a terrible, abusive past that made her believe her only way out was to die.

I sob until I'm numb and exhausted, and my mind shuts down. I don't know how long we stand there. Seconds, hours, days. It seems like such a short amount of time in comparison to the years and years of waiting. Tragedy doesn't take very long. Just a couple of minutes.

Slowly and painfully, I start to become aware of my surroundings again, as if waking from a coma. Resurfacing is traumatic. Somewhere in the distance, a train is going by. My head is buried against Nick's shoulder, my lips pressed into the warmth of his neck. The horses are still standing side by side as if nothing is wrong and the world hasn't fallen apart. I hear the jagged gasps of my breath. I feel the cotton material of Nick's shirt still gripped in my hands and the smell of soap and woodsy scent of the aftershave he uses. He's rubbing my back, my shoulders, my hair. I burrow closer and can feel his heartbeat against mine, constant and steady. It's reassuring and comforting.

I'm breathless, dazed, and disoriented. My head hurts from crying so hard. I pull back a little, so I can see his face. I need to find something I recognize, something I know. His expression is dark but gentle and reminds me of how he looks at the horses when he's trying to get them to know they can trust him. I stare blearily up at him as he moves my hair back from my tear-streaked face. He's so close I can feel his breath on my skin, see the light flecks of gold glimmering through the brown in his eyes, the jagged white line of his scar above his brow. I hold his gaze. I don't dare look away. I don't want to see anything beyond where he is. He's the only thing I have left that is safe and makes any sense. His body heat, the scent, and the feel of him radiate around me, protecting me from the disaster that waits just outside to surround me.

"Don't let go of me yet," I whisper.

His arms instinctively tighten around me, and he shakes his head. "I won't."

Sighing, I close my eyes and lean weakly into him, resting my cheek against his. His skin is rough and warm. I let him breathe for me, in and out, deep and slow. I'm not ready to do it on my own. Rays of sunlight dapple hypnotically over my face, making the darkness feel surreal and dreamlike. I drift, weightless and detached, blocking everything out but this one moment.

I don't know who moves first, if he shifts or if I do, but I hazily feel the corner of his mouth brush and skim over mine, and I turn my head, finding his, and let him seal us together. The relief is intense, instant. I melt into him, dissolving as if I'm made of water, and my lips part blissfully under his. Our tongues meet, and he makes a sound deep in his throat, his breath rushing unsteadily out and into me. I absorb every piece he gives me, letting them fill my empty, broken places. I feel him stagger slightly, and he grabs on tighter to me as if losing his balance. I cling to him, and we hold each other up, and I let him take me wherever he wants to, far away from here, from me, from her. I knew he'd know how. We're both searching and starving and so sad. He needs the same thing I do, and we desperately escape into each other. All I can feel is heat and heartbreak and him.

Everything I want to say and scream and sob is channeled into the kiss. I pour it all out, letting him take every ounce of my hurt. I've never experienced an understanding like this, where all our anguish and devastation are completely heard without having to say a word. I'm amazed at how perfectly my pain fits with his. It's so familiar and necessary and easy to rest in.

Finally. I can't tell if one of us said it, or if I only thought it as I mindlessly lose myself in him. I feel as if I've been waiting a lifetime for this. Maybe we both have.

He hears Becca coming before I do. Somewhere in the blind haze, I feel him pull back and let me go, the separation abrupt, the need interrupted. I wasn't prepared, and I'm suddenly holding onto nothing. I am still wanting more and sway towards him, but he's moved out of my reach. I stumble forward, but this time, he isn't holding me up, and I have to catch myself.

We stand just inches apart and stare at each other. Our breathing is ragged, our cheeks flushed. My lips are tender and damp from his. I can still taste him, and I press my fingers against my mouth. If it's to hold in words, needs, my heart, I'm not sure. My tears are on his shirt. It's the only proof I have that it had been real.

He looks stunned, as if it's just occurred to him what we did, and he can't figure out how it happened. Guilt radiates from him, as if he regrets going farther than he meant to and giving up so much of himself to me. I inwardly cringe. I can't hear it was a mistake. Not when I need him this much. Not when I'm this vulnerable to him. I want to ask him what's wrong, but then I see Becca walking up to us.

"Hey, you two." She's smiling as she watches Maddy and Glory nuzzling each other. "Looks like they—" Her smile fades as she gets closer and notices the tension, the distance, our expressions. Her brows come up as she glances back and forth between us. Can she tell I've been crying? Neither one of us can look her in the eye. "What's going on?"

For a second, I think she knows about the kiss. I don't know if she saw us. But then I remember, and all the pain Nick had temporarily protected me from comes rushing back. I flinch as if I just got punched in the stomach, and my breath whooshes out from the force of the impact.

It's such a beautiful morning, I think, dazed. How can something so horrible be happening? I feel as if it should be dark and stormy, with winds violently swirling and gusting. The light is too pretty for bad news. "My dad called." I have to force the words out as if the trauma made me forget how to speak. "My mom is in the hospital. He found her this morning."

From a completely separate and unreal place in my mind, I watch the shock, fear, and panic flit over her face, widen, and turn her eyes a bit wild. I have the surreal feeling that I'm looking at her from behind museum glass as if we're frozen in this horrible scene and not even alive. Shell-shocked, I feel her grab my hand and dully stare down at it. It's too tight, too desperate, and reminds me of the way my mom held onto me when I told her I was leaving California. I can't tell if it's to hold me up or her. "What happened?"

"She overdosed." The words scorch my throat, my tongue, my lips. I wonder if Becca will blame me, if she'll regret letting me come here now that she knows what I've done, what I'm capable of. "She's alive, but she's not conscious." My head is pounding. Even my eyes hurt. I press my palm against my forehead and look helplessly around as if I'll somehow find the way I'm supposed to do this. I can't seem to figure out where I am. I'm so far from where I need to be. "I have to get to the hospital."

"I'm going with you." She wraps her arm around my shoulders, tucking me close. I'm surprised, thinking she'd be angry with me, but all she says is, "Come on, we'll get packed and get to the airport. I'll ask Ben to book us a flight."

She leads me past Nick, who stays where he is. I try to meet his eyes to see what he's thinking, but he isn't looking at me. He still hasn't said anything. I don't want to leave him. I wasn't ready for goodbye yet. What if I never see him again? It's all happening so fast. My heart twists, and I hold my breath, praying he'll give me some sign that I mean something to him, that our kiss did. When he says my name, I almost cry from relief.

I turn back to him, hoping, needing.

But all he says is, "You forgot your phone." Face deliberately blank, he holds it out to me.

"Oh," the word comes out on my breath, and I feel my heart deflate. That's it? That's all I get? How can he let me go like this? As if everything we felt and experienced and found in each other wasn't real at all? Had I imagined it? I want to ask him, the questions push up against the back of my lips, but I don't dare speak them.

I can't have my heart broken again. It's already too fragile. I can't take one more blow.

My hand is shaking as I take the phone from him. I notice how careful he is not to touch me. I look up at him; I can't seem to help it, knowing he can see everything I don't want him to. But, I don't have the strength to pretend anymore. None of it will matter once I'm gone. At least not to him. "Thank you," I murmur, trying to figure out when I had fallen for him. I want to go back and undo it. This hurts too much.

I can feel him holding himself out of my reach, but I catch the flicker of yearning, of regret, and something more, something deeper, but it's too far down inside of him for me to grasp onto it. His eyes lower to my mouth and stay there longer than they should. Becca is still close by and waiting, and I wonder what he would do if she wasn't. His gaze lifts back to mine and holds for three heartbeats, and I see what I know he's feeling in that split-second before he blinks. He leans a little closer, and I foolishly wish he would tell me he doesn't want me to go, but all he says is, "I hope your mom is okay."

I can barely see him through the tears that well up. I think I manage to nod. I can't feel what my body is doing. He steps back, forcing me to have to do the same. There's nothing left to say. It's all over, just like that.

Tears slide down my cheeks as I make myself walk away from him, from the horses, from a life I was only pretending could be mine. I don't turn around. I'm too afraid I'll see that he's already turned his back on me. As if it's easy letting me leave. I can't figure out if I'm going as someone completely different or returning to the person I've always been. I wonder how I'll know either one when I don't even remember who I am anymore.

Chapter Twenty-Three
VICTORIA

I don't want to come back. I want to stay at the bottom of the sea, where everything is murky, silent, and dark, where there are no accusations, memories, or consequences of an addiction to face.

I thought I was dead. That's the last thing I remember—the relief of nothingness. I'm not sure how I got pulled out of the hole I tried to bury myself in. I hoped I had dug myself so deep down underneath the earth that my father could never find me again. But, he still won, even in death.

I drift in and out of consciousness. The sounds and images that seep through are a distorted blur of colors, shapes, and hushed voices, and I wonder if I'm hallucinating. Muted, secret conversations with words like *close call* and *lucky to be alive* hover above me in the atmosphere.

My husband, daughter, and sister flood my dreams. Even from so far below the surface, I feel their eyes boring down on me, never looking away, as they desperately watch, wait, and plead for me to come back to them. Their expectations are unbearably heavy, almost like another person in the room.

Memories and nightmares from childhood torment me, and I writhe and restlessly toss and turn as my body sweats and purges out the toxins from years of pouring poison into my blood. I even think I hear singing. The voice is pure and sweet, and strangely familiar. I let it wash over me and soothe away the bad dreams.

I desperately try to cling to the oblivion of sedation, but I keep drifting up towards the surface, my body resisting total surrender. Air blows into my nostrils from the oxygen tubes, forcing me to breathe whether I want to or not.

Beep. Beep. Beep.

The machines are a constant intrusion that penetrate through the fog and keep my heart beating. I hate the sound, resenting it for deciding for me that I'm going to live and that I want to.

Blearily, I squint at the wall, and through my lashes, I notice the clock reads 12:42. The time my new life will start. *The first day of the rest of my life,* I think bleakly, as if I still have a chance at redemption.

My skin hurts. Even the hairs on my arms seem to be screaming, itching, and burning as if the air itself is on fire. There are little purple bugs crawling up and down my body, biting, pinching, sucking, and devouring me. I want to shrug and swat them away, but more just keep coming. The cloth of the hospital gown feels like sandpaper, chafing against me with the slightest movement. My stomach shudders as if my tissues, muscles, and intestines have been twisted up and tied into a thousand knots.

I feel a sense of panic that with every drip of the IV seeping through me, I'm losing more and more of who I used to be. I'm being hollowed out against my will. How much have I lost already? Is the last drop already gone? Is the old me flushed away? No one even asked if I wanted to be saved.

I want to shout that it won't matter. I won't ever be clean. Even if every drop of vodka is drained from me, I will still be his daughter. How do I make everyone understand that the addiction wasn't what I was running from? He is still waiting for me, no matter how sober I am. And what's worse, is now I'll be forced to feel every scalding slap and scar he left on me without the protection of a bottle.

This whole thing is a joke. They think they'll be able to change me. Everyone thought being free from alcohol was the answer. They have no idea what I'm up against once I am bled dry.

The first thing I see when I fully open my eyes is my daughter asleep next to me on the bed, her head buried in her arms. Her hair looks so dark against the sterile white of the blankets. It's almost been a month since I've seen her. I stare at her, absorbing being near her again. The relief at having her close is like a drug itself.

Her hand is next to mine. Almost afraid to believe she's real, I slide my fingers over, gritting my teeth as hot coals erupt up my arms and scorch down my shoulder blades. But I have to get to her and push through the pain to finally reach where she is. I lightly brush her, and she stirs.

Lexy lifts her head and groggily blinks at me. Has she slept here the whole time? I brace myself for her resentment and anger, the blame and accusations I'm certain will come hurtling at me from a daughter I've lied to all her life. I watch her eyes widen and come into focus when she realizes I'm alive. I must look terrible because she looks much too worried. She sits up quickly, almost apologetically, as if feeling guilty for falling asleep.

"Mom," she says breathlessly, sounding painfully young and piercing my heart. I've never deserved for her to call me that. I've never been a mother to her. "You're awake." She pulls her chair closer to the bed. "How are you feeling?"

I fiercely want to feel nothing, but my entire system is on overdrive; revving and churning and vibrating, like an engine about to explode. Every inch of me is magnified as if I'm looking at myself from underneath a microscope. My pores seem too close in focus. All my flaws, mistakes, offenses, and sins are glaringly in the open under the harsh fluorescent lights. I have nothing to help hide me from the aftermath I now have to face.

It's the first time we've seen each other since she left, and I hungrily drink in every detail of her face. I don't know how I ever thought it wouldn't matter if I never saw her again. Can I change my mind after I've already jumped off the bridge and am in mid-air?

She looks too much like me, and I pray to God that is where our resemblance ends. How is it possible to love someone this intensely? How can I make her understand that everything I did was to protect her from my past?

She'd gotten some sun, I think absently, noticing how her cheeks and arms were brown and bronzed. Her eyes seemed to glow. The southern summers can be brutally hot out on the ranch. Even a breeze can barely whisper under it. I thought she might look different, that she'd be stained or tainted, bruised and beaten down. Ugly somehow. I know what that land did to me, how it destroyed everything good in me from the inside out.

But Lexy looks beautiful and healthy and strong and more alive than I have ever seen her. I wonder how she managed to survive there when that place almost killed me.

I guess I was right. Being away from me has been better for her.

"I'm thirsty." My insides are screaming from the vicious craving. My voice is raspy and hoarse. My lips feel cracked and chapped, my tongue too thick for my mouth. Every breath feels like thorns are stuck in my throat.

Lexy looks around and finds a Dixie cup of water on the bedside table. "Here." She brings the cup to my lips, and I drink through the straw. It's not the taste I wanted. My throat is raw and swollen from the tubes they had shoved down and intubated me with when they pumped my stomach. Swallowing is difficult and painful, and I am only able to take a small sip before violently coughing and choking, water spurting up and spattering over my chin. Pain screams through my abdomen, and I cry out as my entire body is wracked with agony.

Alarmed, Lexy starts to get to her feet. "I'll call the nurse."

"No," I wheeze out. I blindly reach for her, managing to grasp onto her wrist. I can't let her leave yet. I just got her back. I don't let go until she sits back down next to me. "Is Becca really here?"

"Yes. She went down to the cafeteria to get us some lunch. Dad is talking to the doctor. Do you want me to get them?" She starts to pull her phone out of her pocket.

Richard. My entire body jolts. He must have saved me. He was the only one there. I can't imagine how terrifying it must have been for him to find me. I'm stunned he's still here. Why? After all I've done to him. Guilt smothers me, and I shake my head. I can't face my sister or my husband yet.

It's afternoon, I think, dully. As if the hour made a difference. All I can see are the days stretching endlessly ahead of me, sober and unprotected to who I truly am.

I seem to have no control over my emotions, and my body flushes feverishly hot, making my skin clammy and damp. I can't stop shaking. My eyes flood with tears. I don't know if it's from seeing her, from the detox, or the trauma of almost dying. Or maybe it's from finally being able to tell my daughter the truth. My heartbeat sounds so loud in my ears. I'm surprised it's still beating. I thought I had finally figured out a way to stop it. Lexy looks panicked.

"I'm sorry," I manage. For everything, for yesterday and today and tomorrow, for all the years and years and years I've hurt her. It's not enough. How do I ever make it up to her? I hate that I'm aware enough to actually feel. The small cup of water is a worthless weapon against my shame. I feel naked and much too vulnerable. "I'm so sorry." I can't seem to say anything else.

"I know." Lexy holds my hand tight in hers. Her touch hurts me, prickles and singes, but I don't dare let her go. Tears are in her eyes. I've made her cry far more than I should have in her young life. "I'm sorry I left you. I wanted to know what happened."

"I couldn't tell you. I swear I was trying to protect you. I didn't know how to face it." My words come out in a rush, sloppy, stilted, and slurred, but I seem to have no control over anything anymore. I need to tell her everything before I can't, before the sedation sucks me back under. I need her to forgive me. I realize it's unfair and much too soon, and she probably won't believe me, but I have to make her understand. I feel a frantic urgency to everything.

"I never knew he hurt you so much."

"I just wanted to forget it all, but no matter what I do, I can't ever get away from him." The regret was searing and so familiar. Sometimes it felt like my past knew me better than I knew myself.

I stare dully up at the ceiling. I can feel the tears and sweat on my face trickling down and soaking into my hair, my ears, down my chin, and my neck. Is it possible to hate your own skin?

This wasn't even the hard part, I realize, swallowing down the urge to vomit. Once I am thrust back into real life, I will have to constantly face my demons without the bottle. I will have to face myself. I wish more than ever I had never woken up.

We both look over as a nurse comes in. Feeling intensely exposed, I weakly wipe my arm over my face trying to rub away the tears, but they won't stop falling, and I give up and can only lay there, blubbering pitifully. I can't help it. It's like I've broken something so deep within me that there is no end to it. Through the misty haze, I hear my daughter anxiously ask the nurse if I'm alright. I almost burst out laughing. When have I ever been?

"This is normal, sweetheart," the nurse reassures Lexy. "Her entire body is in a state of shock right now. We're giving her something to take the edge off the withdrawals and to help with her pain. She'll sleep soon."

I want Lexy to stay but can't open my mouth to speak. I'm so tired. All I can do is stare dully at the clock. 12:56. Only fourteen minutes have passed, I realize, wearily. Is this what it's always going to feel like to be alive? This is recovery? Is this the one day at a time they talk about? It's excruciating and awful.

The nurse fusses around me, watching the monitor, checking my heart rate and vitals. Her touch is soothing and competent. She doesn't wipe away my tears. I think it's because there are too many. Or maybe she's just used to seeing addicts fall apart. As she leans over me to adjust my oxygen tubes, I notice the ID tag clipped to the pocket of her blue scrubs and see that her name is Sarah. What a pretty name. I wonder if her mama is proud of her.

Beep. Beep. Beep.

I internally swear and want to throw something. That stupid machine is going to drive me mad. The sound is like nails on a chalkboard.

Nurse Sarah injects my veins with drugs that will somehow trick my body into thinking it's getting what it craves. A fake rush. The illusion of being drunk. Everything about me is pretend. Soon they will have stripped it all away until the real me is left. And then what?

Lexy blurs and shimmers out of focus. I don't want her to disappear again. I can't tell if she's holding my hand or if I just dreamt she's here. If this whole thing is a nightmare. Maybe I really am dead, and this is the purgatory I'm stuck in. I still have so much I want to tell her, but my mind has glazed over.

Beginning to float, I watch the drugs go through the tube of my IV. I notice some of the purple bugs that have been crawling on me have forged a trail across the floor and are climbing up the wall. I don't know how they got over there. Someone needs to get rid of them.

I feel the heat penetrate my skin and slowly trickle into my veins, taking me back under the surface, letting me escape myself, and everyone else, for a little while longer.

Chapter Twenty-Four
VICTORIA

The first thing I see when I open my eyes is the locket around Becca's neck. The half of a heart glints in the glow from the lamp that sits on the table next to my hospital bed. She's in a chair, reading a book while she waits for me to breathe, blink, and come back to life. Still heavily sedated, I stare in fascination at how beautifully the gold seems to gleam.

I'm surprised she's still wearing it. It's comforting to see it on her. I can't find mine, I realize, as I reach up for the chain that has never left my body since our Grandmother Rose gave us the lockets years before. My neck is bare for the first time since I was a little girl. I wonder if I lost it. I wouldn't have taken it off. I notice my wedding ring is also missing, and it occurs to me they were probably removed after my overdose. Precautions against using them as weapons to hurt myself. I'm a hazard risk. I always have been.

I didn't expect the intense rush of relief at seeing her. I thought I would feel her anger and resentment, my own panic, and of course, guilt. But all I feel is the fierce bond and love, and the pull towards her is so overwhelming and strong, that it completely overrides everything else. I didn't realize how much I had missed her. All the time and distance and fear instantly fall away the second I see her.

Sisters really do have their own language. She's the only one who knows me, the only one I've never had to lie to. She's been there since the beginning and is the only one who understands what it's like trying to survive hell. She was the one hiding under the porch with me. She's my safe place. She always was. Seeing her is breathlessly euphoric, and I break through the layers of dust and decades and debris to get back to her.

"Becca," I rasp, already crying. Or maybe I've never stopped. I'm tied to the bed by chords and wires and tubes. I'm not even breathing on my own, and it's an unwanted reminder that I'm still not trusted or allowed to. I want to rip them off. I can't get to her and desperately hold out my hand.

She instantly sits up, the book falling off her lap. I hear it clamber to the floor. But she doesn't bother picking it up and is already reaching for me, her expression worried. "Are you in pain?" she asks me, her voice sweet and southern, and so much like mine.

All the time, I think, as I breathe her in. She smells the same. Lavender and sunlight. "You're here."

She's so close that our foreheads touch. Her eyes are exactly the way I remember them. Pure and clear and green. Everything about her has always been lighter. I have too many iniquities. I flash back to a memory of looking at her in the dark under our bed while daddy threw things and mama cried downstairs. Her eyes were all I could see as we cowered on the hardwood floor, clinging to each other while his voice and the fear of him filled our whole house.

"Ssshhh. Yes, I'm here. Oh, honey, you're shivering." She gently tucks the blankets around me. I can't seem to get warm even though my body hasn't stopped sweating in days. My teeth are chattering. The sheets are damp beneath me. "Better?"

It wasn't, but I don't care. I feel so young all of a sudden. "Stay with me," I beg, still sobbing. I can't control myself. I have no right to need her like this, not after all I've done, but I don't want to let go of her. It's like survivors finding each other after something traumatic and catastrophic has happened.

"I will." She moves my hair back from my damp face. "It's alright," she soothes. Nothing is alright; it has never been, but my sister is here, and for now, I let myself fall apart in her hands.

Minutes tick by. Without realizing it, my breathing slows and matches with hers. Our hearts always somehow beat the same. I finally realize how quiet it is. We're alone in the room. "Where is everyone?"

"I made Lexy go get something to eat. She hasn't left your side since you got here. Richard went to get some coffee in the lounge."

"How long have I been here?"

"About eleven days." My hospital gown is slipping off my shoulder. Becca gently pulls it back up so it covers my skin. It reminds me of something our mama would do. But I still feel too exposed.

"What time is it?"

"Almost midnight."

It will be tomorrow soon. That will be twelve days without a drink. Another day to get through. And another and another and another. Hopelessness washes over me. I can't think about it yet and make myself focus on her. "I'm surprised you came."

She gives me a wounded look. "Of course I did," she says, her voice fierce and fervent. The intensity makes me go still. "You're my sister. Nothing can ever change that."

Nothing ever has, I realize. Not time or space or the unanswered letters. She kept each and every promise we made to each other. All this time, she's held on to me, even when I was so drunk I couldn't remember my own name. It's comforting that she's always known me no matter how lost I've been. "Does it look the same out on the ranch?"

"Pretty much." She adjusts my oxygen tubes, so they are not tangled over my arm, and I can't pull them out. "We painted the barn and the outbuildings a few years ago, but not much else has changed. Our tree is still standing."

I can picture the large, gnarled oak out front. We would take turns pushing each other on the tire swing. I would go higher and higher and higher until I thought I could almost touch the sky. I was free and out of his reach for a few seconds until I fell back to earth.

Every blade of grass on that land is branded into me. I can still smell it, the horses, the dust, the soil, the whiskey, his sweat. I don't want to remember that house and the fear that lived inside those walls. I tuck the blankets closer around me and hold tighter to Becca. I don't know how I lived without her for so long. "Why do you stay there?"

"How else would you know where to find me?"

Her words register, and the guilt floods hotly over my skin. I knew this moment would eventually come. I can only stare at her as the years of silence and thousands of questions and useless apologies hang heavily in the air between us. I have so much to explain. I don't know how or where to start. The words clog up in the back of my throat like fallen leaves trapped in a storm drain. "I wrote you back," is all I manage to get out.

Surprised, she looks at me. "You did?"

I nod. "I just couldn't send them," I admit quietly. The shame is scalding, but I know I deserve it. "I didn't know how to deal with it all." It's such a pitiful excuse. There are tears on her cheeks, and each one is my fault. I know I've hurt her, and wish more than anything I could take it all back. But I can't. There's too much damage. The wreckage is scattered everywhere between us. I'm lying in it. This is all so hard, and I have no way to escape. I fiercely crave a drink. I can actually taste the burn of it.

"I'd like to read them sometime. If you still have them."

"I do." I saved each one in a box in the back of my closet.

I can't help thinking how much she looks like our mother. Everyone told her that. Mama even named her after the character Rebecca Thatcher from *Tom Sawyer* because it was her favorite book. Things were always going to be easier for her, simpler. She is so pretty and kind and sweet, the first to give and help. Everyone loves her. Not a bad word could be spoken of her. She would never have turned out like I did. I wonder if mama had always known life would be harder for me.

I know all too well who I take after. And plenty has been said. I'm the black sheep of the family. It's too painful to remember. But I can't get away from the fact that the one person I swore I'd never become is the one person I'm most like. I don't know how to forgive myself for that. Do I even stand a chance at being someone else? Or is it too late?

"Was Lexy happy there?"

"I think she was trying to be," she answers, wiping the tears from her cheeks with the tips of her fingers. I already know they are not really gone. I'll make her cry again. I can't seem to help it. "She missed you. Talked about you all the time. She was waiting for you."

So am I. We're all waiting for the same thing. For me to change, get clean, start over. For me to want to. As if I know how. Lexy never once gave up on me. I wonder how I managed to have a daughter like her. How did she turn out good when she came from someone like me? I envy how open she allows her heart to be. She's beautiful, inside and out. I'm amazed she hasn't been ruined or spoiled or corrupted by me. I don't want to disappoint her anymore.

"Will I ever stop being afraid of him?"

"I don't know," Becca murmurs helplessly, and we look at each other as the machines beep, the IV drips, and the blood pressure cuff at my arm tightens and loosens. I can't hide how far I've fallen. "I hope so."

The drugs are making me groggy, and I wipe my hand blearily over my face. "I'm so tired." Of all of it. Of being an alcoholic, of running, of hiding, of lying, and fighting. Of hurting everyone I love. Talking is wearing me out. Being alive is exhausting.

"I know you are." Standing, she adjusts my pillows, kissing the top of my head. "Try and sleep."

I don't want her to go and grasp onto her hand. I'm afraid to be alone without her. "Keep watch," I whisper and see her go still as the memory sinks into her. She knows what I'm asking her to do. We always said those words when daddy was drunk, and one of us would stay up to warn the other when he was coming, and it was time to run under the porch. She would fall asleep with her head in my lap, and I would quietly sing to help her not be frightened.

With tears in her eyes, Becca nods, holding my hand tighter. "I will." It's just her and me, tucked into our hiding place away from the rest of the world. It always has been.

I drift into a restless, feverish sleep. The nightmares wait just beyond our little circle and are much too clear and unfiltered now that there is no alcohol numbing my mind and senses.

I only open my eyes once the rest of the night. Becca is still sitting in the chair next to me, standing guard and holding onto me. I'm not sure which one of us won't let go. I dream of the summer nights of our childhood. The air was so hot and muggy that even the sheets wouldn't keep us cool. We'd whisper secrets and stay close and pray for daylight.

And now, more than twenty years later, my little sister is still keeping watch to protect me from me.

Chapter Twenty-Five
RICHARD

I saw a documentary once about a coal mining town out in Pennsylvania that was burning out from underneath itself due to a fire getting out of control in the mines. The town has been burning for over sixty years, and nearly all the residents, with the exception of about five people, had evacuated years before.

The straggling few that have stayed behind live in a toxic wasteland of smoke, ash, and charred trees. Every day they risk falling into a coal pocket or dying from the poisonous fumes.

The town used to be a full, thriving community with festive Christmas parades down Main Street and 4th of July picnics in the park. But now, it is nothing more than rubble and a couple of crumbling homes and an old cemetery. There's barely anything left. The roads in the town are cracked open, swollen, and bulging from the pressure and heat. No cars are allowed through due to the danger of them melting and being swallowed up by the blackened, steaming asphalt. It's not safe to stay or breathe the air.

And yet, the five continue to wait for those that left the town to return after the fire burns out. They still live as if everyone is going to come back any moment, hanging up decorations in the empty, forgotten town square and painting park benches no one will ever sit on. They believe one day, the threat will be contained, that eventually it has to be, and everyone can pick up where they left off.

The town has been condemned by the government, and there is literally nothing left to come back to, yet the few refuse to accept everything is gone and hope that life will return to normal once the smoke finally clears.

I keep thinking about that town and those five people. They haunt and disturb me. They remind me of me, my family, and my life.

I feel like my world has been burning out from underneath itself for years, and we are living in a toxic wasteland, and there is nothing left but ashes and rubble. What if we can't return to each other after the fire burns itself out? What if there is nothing left? What if the land is so damaged and destroyed we can't even rebuild it? What if we are just refusing to accept reality and have spent all this time waiting in vain?

I knew the day would come when one of us would rock the system with a different choice. I'd hoped it would be Victoria choosing to get help for her addiction and coming to terms with her past. But Lexy was the brave one out of all of us. Becca's letters changed the course of all our lives, and I was now in the place I had both feared and hoped for. Feared because I am terrified my wife won't survive this and relieved because the worst has finally happened, and hopefully, we can deal with the pain and move forward. I just pray it's not too late.

I've barely spoken to Lexy since she arrived at the hospital. We haven't had much time alone. I'm in the background, just as

I've always been; quiet, useless, unnecessary, completely inept. It's unnerving to feel invisible when all eyes and expectations and errors seem to be on me.

Doctors, nurses, and machines decide our lives, and we hang suspended, frozen, and paralyzed in this space as we wait and wait and wait to finally see.

I wasn't expecting to be faced with Becca. We've never met and don't know each other. It's been painfully polite and awkward between us; unresolved, misunderstood, stilted conversations. She wasn't at our wedding, and we've never shared the holidays together. I only know of her through the little details Victoria has let slip about her.

They used to be extremely close, but when Victoria left Tennessee, she closed off all contact with her family. But she never threw away Becca's letters, which is telling in its own way. She still needed her sister, secretly hung onto her, and never stopped loving and missing her. Their family history and the trauma they went through binds and seals them together in a way few could understand. In some ways, Becca knows more about her than any of us.

Becca and Lexy have bonded during her time in Tennessee. She's warm and kind, and it's clear how much they care for each other. Lexy has learned to trust her, love her, and lean on her. They huddle together in quiet corners, talking in hushed voices, holding hands to comfort each other. I've watched them over the endless hours and days of sitting and staring at the walls, relieved that at least one thing turned out good in this whole mess.

Becca is in Victoria's room, and the conversation seems intense. They were crying and clinging to each other so tightly that I couldn't even step into the doorway. I had to back up from the sheer force and look away from how intimate, how breathless, and desperate it all was. I wonder if Becca has been the one she's needed to cure her this whole time. It's the first moment they've seen or spoken to each other in over twenty years.

I wanted to give them some time to reconnect. At least that's what I tell myself. Truthfully, I'm avoiding them. I can't bear to face what I know they are all thinking, that this whole thing is my fault. We could blame the drinking, Victoria's past, and her father. And those things are all valid reasons, but I know at the end of the day, where all the fingers are pointed. At me. Because I've done the worst thing out of all of them. Absolutely nothing. I didn't know how to save my family without it completely destroying them. And, so, I stood back and let us burn alive from underneath ourselves.

I'm in one of the private family lounges. I came to get coffee, but then sat down and haven't been able to move for almost an hour. I seem to have used up the last of my energy walking in here.

The television is on. I blankly glance at the late-night infomercial for the latest celebrity skincare product. Eternal youth in a bottle for only $29.95. If only it were that easy. The perky woman's voice grates on me, and I get up and find the remote on a stack of magazines, mute it. The room falls into silence just as Lexy walks in. We both go still. The lounge is empty except for us, making the quiet seem that much louder, echoing, hollow, and achingly obvious that I don't know what to do.

"I thought you were getting something to eat," I finally say and hope it doesn't sound like I don't want her here. I'm very aware of how easily anything I say can be used against me.

"I wasn't hungry. I went back to the room, but Becca and mom were talking, and so I thought I'd come get some herbal tea."

I'm not sure if I should stay or go, so I just stand awkwardly where I am and watch as she walks over to the coffee and tea station. She picks out a packet of Mint Medley. I wonder if her stomach is upset and wouldn't be surprised with the amount of stress she's buried under.

I remember she would often make it for Victoria to help with her nausea from the hangover. Not that it ever did any good. *Old habits,* I think sadly.

Neither of us says anything as she waits for the tea to steep, bobbing the string every couple of minutes. It's a strangely normal thing to do, considering where we are.

Dumping the tea bag in the trash, she turns back around, holding the cup in both hands. It's a recycled one, I notice absently. Hospitals are going green. Another threat and emergency we're up against. It's surreal to think disasters are happening outside the walls of this place. I've been so focused on waiting for Victoria to come back to life.

Lexy leans heavily back against the counter, letting out a weary sigh. *She's too young,* I think, to have to carry the weight of all this. "It's so quiet in here," she murmurs. "It seems so loud and chaotic everywhere else."

She looks exhausted, I notice. She's barely eaten or slept since arriving at the hospital almost two weeks ago. It strikes me as ironic how we are the ones who seem to get worse while we wait for Victoria to get better. Sick with worry should be termed an actual epidemic.

I'm still standing near the doorway. Lexy sits down at one of the tables and sips her tea, the steam drifting up around her face, blurring, distorting, making it harder to read her thoughts and expression. I still haven't moved. The quiet hums and breathes around us, which seems to amplify how much there is to say and how much we don't know how. I wish I still had the distraction of the television noise.

The urge of wanting to try strains in me, to fix something, anything, one thing. I internally push against the years and years of disappointment. I can't think of what to say that will matter or make a difference. No amount of apologies will ever be enough. It's all too inadequate, humiliating, and much too late. How do I get back to her? I have no idea how to close the distance.

She finally looks over at me, and I instinctively brace myself. *It's coming,* I think, she's going to level me with all her anger and accusations, and she'll be completely right. But all she says is, "How are you doing?"

I'm surprised to be asked and just blink for a second, my mouth partly open. I don't deserve to have anyone care, least of all her. "I'm not sure yet. Just coping, I guess. How about you?"

"Same here," she murmurs. She rubs her forehead with the tips of her fingers. "I think my brain actually hurts."

I'm not sure what to say. I've been preparing for this moment for years, but now that we're here, I have no idea what to do. I guess I wasn't as ready for it as I thought. Maybe no one ever is.

"You can sit down if you want."

It's not anger in her eyes, I realize. It's pity. She feels sorry for me. Now that I look back on it, I think she always has. I don't know why it's worse. Even as a child, she was incredibly sensitive, and much too perceptive. Often to her own detriment. Maybe it's textbook behavior or survival instinct, or just simply her. She's taken care of us for years, putting our needs before her own. She still is. I feel the flush of shame rise up, decades of it, churning hot in my belly. The gurgling seems to come from deep within, a dark, sticky tar covering my whole body.

Did she always know how helpless and lost I was? How much I've needed them? Did she come in here to find me and pull me back inside from where I've been stranded in the dark?

"Okay," I answer, making the deliberate choice not to disappear this time. I feel too empty-handed and defenseless and get myself a cup, robotically going through the motions of preparing the coffee. "I've had about six cups of this already," I mutter, sipping it. It's surprisingly good. I'll probably get an ulcer, but it's the least of my problems at this point. Tossing the wooden stir stick in the trash, I make myself go toward my daughter.

I sit down across from Lexy and realize how bone-tired I am. I rub my hands over my face and then look bleakly around the room. Cheery watercolors are on the walls, floral couches and chairs are scattered around, and tables with crayons and books for children. A vending machine with candy, chips, soda, and nuts. Normal things to do while people wait for news that will change their lives for the better or shatter them beyond repair.

"How in the world did we get here?" I meant to only think it, but the words slip out.

"I don't know," her voice is heavy, grief-stricken. She looks across the table at me. It's not large, but it feels as if a hundred miles of lacquered oak are in between us. Her eyes are damp, dark, and tortured, and my heart splits in my chest as I look head-on into her pain. "I'm so sorry. I didn't mean for all this to happen."

I wince as the realization hits. What have we done to her? Why didn't I know she'd be blaming herself? I was certain she held me responsible. I do. How do I make either of them understand how much I love them? Would they even believe me after all this time?

I sit up straight and lean toward her, making myself look directly at her. It's harder than I thought it would be, as I face all my failings in her eyes and the tears on her cheeks. "This isn't your fault, Lexy. You didn't do anything wrong. We should have told you the truth, and I should have gotten her help a long time ago. I'm so sorry I didn't." The words feel weak and much too small for the gravity of pain I've caused. I don't deserve absolution.

"Did you know what had happened to her?"

"Some of it. Most of it she wouldn't talk about." The regret and guilt will haunt me for the rest of my life. "I just thought we had it more under control." I shake my head at how absurdly stupid I am. "I kept telling myself it wasn't as bad as it was. I wanted to believe I could handle it. I didn't know how to face that I couldn't."

Wiping her tears with the back of her hand, Lexy sniffles and stares down into her tea. "How do other people deal with this?"

"I have no idea." We're a statistic, I realize. A sad casualty and part of a percentage. We're just like everyone else. I don't know how I thought we wouldn't be, that somehow it wasn't the same for us, that we weren't as bad off as all of the others. *And now, here we are,* I think, again hit by the harsh reality of our situation. "How was it in Tennessee?"

Almost against her will, she manages to smile for the first time in weeks, as if she can't help it, as if she carries the memory of the ranch around in her pockets. Her entire being changes, lifts, and her fear momentarily falls away.

"It's beautiful there. So quiet and peaceful. Becca showed me pictures of our family. I saw photos of our great-great-grandparents. And mom's parents." Her smile fades, and her eyes turn haunted and serious. "Becca told me what it was like for them growing up, about the abuse and the drinking, how afraid they were all the time. I don't blame mom for not wanting to remember it. I wouldn't want to either. It was so horrible. I don't know how she survived it."

She almost didn't. The thought makes me shudder. I can feel how tense my body is. I'm rigid in the chair, my muscles tight and coiled, ready for a fight. It all makes me so angry. I hate thinking of the fear and pain Victoria had gone through. I hate knowing there is nothing I can do to change it. If she makes it through this, I will do everything I can to make sure she knows she's not alone. I don't know yet if she will let me or if any of them will. Another thing I am waiting to see. "I found a picture of the ranch once that she'd hidden in the bottom of a drawer. It looks like a nice place."

Her smile glimmers back. "It is. They have horses and so much land. It seems like it goes on forever." Her voice has a dreamy, far-away tone to it now. I'm not sure if she notices. "Becca and Ben rescue horses that have been abandoned or are put in shelters. Nick also helps with them. They have this one named Glory. She was a famous racehorse and won a bunch of awards. She's amazing. Nick has brought her a long way. I was helping him take care of her."

"Who is Nick?" Is it my imagination, or did Lexy blush?

"He's friends with Ben," she stammers, looking flustered as if she accidentally let a secret slip. "They grew up together. He lives in the cottage behind the main house and works on the ranch."

He's a lot more than that, noticing how she seems to hold the thought of him close to her. She also won't look directly at me when she mentions him, as if it's too personal to reveal. I'm curious but know I'm not in any position to pry into her personal life. Letting it go for now, I sip my coffee. I don't want to embarrass her. I want to keep her talking to me.

She misses it, I realize. She'd come back different, as if she had found a crucial part of herself she didn't know she needed. I've never seen her look like this before. Excited, content, alive, somehow in her element. Normal. She could be any other girl right now instead of one sitting in a waiting room of a hospital while her mother recovers from an overdose. I smile at the way she lights up when she talks about the ranch, the land, and horses. A life completely different than here. It was all I ever wanted for her. I can't remember the last time I saw my daughter smile. "You were happy there."

She looks guilty, as if she's not sure she was allowed to be. It saddens me to watch her glow disappear as she returns to our stark, sterile, scary reality. It's a far cry from the lush, green pastures I'd seen once in a photograph. "Yeah, I guess I was." She looks at me, and I see Victoria and Becca in her features, mannerisms, hair, and eyes. Beauty and heartbreak passed down through the generations. I wonder if I should worry about what else she's inherited. "Thank you for leaving Becca's letters for me. I'm glad I finally got to know her and Ben. Even with everything that's happened."

This is the first time we've acknowledged what I had done. And now, we're sitting in the consequences and ripple effect of all my choices. I don't know yet if it will be the greatest regret of our lives or the one thing that finally saves us.

Excuses, denials, and explanations spring into my mind, waiting on my tongue, but quickly die and fade. They all feel too meaningless. I have no right to justify anything. "It was the only way I knew to get you out."

She's quiet as she glances around the room. "But we're not out," she murmurs. She looks back at me, holds my gaze, and I'm again forced to stare into all the things I should have done. "It's not ever really over, is it?"

I stare at her as the weight of what she said settles hopelessly over me. She's right, painfully right. It wasn't just about Victoria no longer drinking. Even without the bottle, there was still the battle of her past that we were up against, not to mention all the destruction I'd left her with by allowing this to go on so long. Our marriage is a mess. So are our lives. And she will always want to drink. Even years later, the craving could still rise up. Odd how even destructive habits become normal. There is so much we are going to have to learn how to change. Everything is going to be different. We are completely starting over. Maybe we're all in recovery and in need of rehabilitation.

"No, I guess it isn't."

We sit in silence for a few minutes, both of us lost and trying to find our way through the thick of things. "What do we do now?" she finally asks.

It dawns on me that she's never asked me before. Maybe she already knew I couldn't figure out how to get her mother to make a different choice or that I wasn't brave enough to make it for her. She hadn't trusted me to step in and fight for them, and she'd been right not to. I'm the one who is supposed to protect her, the one who is supposed to have the answers. But I don't know anything more than she does. I never have. The addiction has always been smarter and stronger than us.

"Wait and see, I guess." And then wait some more. "After she's through with detox, she goes into treatment. We'll also be doing family counseling. She'll have a sponsor and go to AA meetings. We just take it one day at a time." I see why they say that now. It literally comes down to making it through one single day, second to second, minute to minute, hour to hour. And then do it all again tomorrow. I'm already overwhelmed, and we haven't even started. How do people do this?

"Will it get better?"

It had to, right? After hitting rock bottom like this, where else could we go? But I'd waited so long, and nothing had changed. I again think of that nuclear waste of a town in Pennsylvania with those few who are still waiting in futility for their lives to get back to normal and come back from the smoldering grave. They believe it will. But what happens when they realize it won't? They can't ever recapture what they used to have. The fire still isn't out. Their hometown, as they've known it, is nothing but rubble and ash. They can no longer stay where they've been. Neither can we.

My daughter is looking at me, young, sad, and scared, waiting for me to promise that everything is going to work out. I want to tell her it will. I want so badly to be able to give her that. But I can't. I just simply didn't know yet. "I hope so."

We fall back into the quiet and do what so many others have done in this same room before us. Drinking our coffee and tea without actually tasting it. Trying to hold normal conversations. Not looking too long into each other's eyes for fear of completely breaking down or seeing that you bear the blame for the tragedy happening to them.

And we wait. And wait and wait and wait in desperate, excruciating hope for the recovery that will either change our lives for the better or the relapse that could bring everything crashing back down around us.

Chapter Twenty-Six
LEXY

The night surrounds me, shadows shifting and seeming to stare, as I lay in bed, yawning and blearily watching the ceiling fan spin around and around above me. The breeze is gentle and light, with little relief.

Los Angeles is in the clammy vice grip of another sweltering heatwave, and our air conditioner is out. California weather isn't humid like Tennessee, and the summer air is so dry and stifling, you could spark a wildfire simply by changing your mind and going in a different direction.

My dad brought me home, and I'm pretty sure he was out cold before his head hit the pillow. We're both worn down and worried. The heat is draining and doesn't help our frayed nerves. The hospital isn't far, and he has driven back and forth over the last two weeks to take showers, change clothes, and pick up things we need.

Becca stayed with my mom. She has a hotel room nearby for when it's our turn to stay up through the night. I hadn't wanted to leave, but they made me go to get some rest. I've barely slept in days, and they were concerned at how disoriented, sluggish, and incoherent I was increasingly becoming.

I was so tired when we walked in the front door, I could barely see straight as I showered and stumbled into bed. I thought I would sink instantly under, but for the last hour, I have restlessly tossed and turned, unable to get comfortable and relax. My thoughts feel jumbled, hectic, and delirious from stress and exhaustion, and I can't shut them off.

I keep seeing my mom in her hospital bed, blankets seeming to swallow her, too still, too small, too unconscious and pale, hooked up to oxygen, with tubes and wires everywhere. The grisly images play over and over in my mind, a stuck movie reel, rewinding, replaying, clicking, and flashing behind my lids, jerking me awake, making sleep impossible.

Everything happened so fast. My dad's panicked phone call, the frantic flight out here, the terrible waiting, wondering, and worrying of the last two weeks. I'm afraid to stand still too long or close my eyes. Every time I do, the nightmares pounce on me, and I wake up gasping, shaking, and sweating when I think of how close we had come to losing her.

I've gotten so used to the constant noise of the machines whooshing and beeping, the drip of the IV, the revolving schedule of nurses and doctors coming in and out, hushed, urgent conversations, the unbearable limbo of the touch and go. It feels surreal to be outside of those white, sanitized walls. I wonder if I'll ever get the antiseptic smell out of my skin, my fingernails, the strands of my hair. Strange what becomes familiar even when it shouldn't.

I haven't been home in over a month. I'm alone, and it's hot, late, and dark. A house on fire. I hear every sound as if it's magnified and much too sharp. Our grandfather clock ticking and chiming on the hour, the neighbor's dog barking, a garage door opening as Mr. Murphy gets home from his night shift at the restaurant. The distant roar of traffic from the freeway. The sprinklers spouting on and coming to life on our front lawn. Everything is the same here, as if nothing has happened. As if my mom hadn't overdosed and our world as we've known it hadn't collapsed.

I wonder how things will change now that my mom is going to be sober. There is so much we don't know yet. I still can't imagine our lives without the addiction stalking and derailing our every move. It's known us better than we have. Will we be happy? Sane? Will she be able to stop? I don't even know what a normal family looks or feels like.

I'm ashamed to admit I don't believe her yet. I've been on the wild, speeding roller coaster ride for far too long; a sweaty, white-knuckled grip on the cold, rickety metal bar, holding on for dear life, blowing through red lights, as she took us up high, too high, dangerously high, frantically, manically, and unreachably high.

And then the crash came, and she sunk lower and lower, further and further down, too far down, underneath the ground down, still unreachable, into the dark, drunken blackouts. I could never get to her either way.

I keep hearing everyone say she's finally out of the woods, but I don't know what that means, or if it will last. Are we ever really safe? She will be transferred to the rehabilitation facility in the next few days and start the long road to getting clean. What if she won't go? What if she refuses at the last minute? I don't think I will stop holding my breath until she's actually inside the doors and they close and lock behind her.

Doctors, sponsors, and therapists will monitor, guide, and help navigate the process and carry some of our burdens. They'll help us figure out how to accept things we cannot change, to have the courage to change things we can, and the wisdom to know the difference. Every day of our lives will now be determined by the twelve steps and mantras of sobriety.

It's a relief to have the control out of our hands and the bottle finally out of hers. I wonder if she will be able to never pick it up again, if she will somehow have the restraint and willpower to refuse. I want to trust her, but I've been disappointed and let down too many times. What if she tries to get clean and then decides being drunk is easier? Will she want to change and get better this time? Can she? The idea seems unreal, like a dream or a miracle, some far-off fairytale I've desperately wished would come true.

Her recovery is a slow, tedious, minute to minute process. We've barely started. But I'm grateful she's alive, and things have calmed down enough for us to begin sorting through the aftermath the alcohol left behind.

My dad and I will start cleaning up the house over the next few weeks after my mom goes into treatment. Find all the vodka bottles and pills where she's stored and stashed them in her odd and obvious places. We will scour every corner, look under every board, behind boxes, and toss over every cushion until we find the very last one. Drain and throw them all out. Detox every room, and our lives. My dad offered to take care of it himself, but I don't want him to have to deal with it alone. He's being sweetly protective, and I let him because we both need it. I know her hiding places better than anyone. It's a sick, deranged way to finally have family time. The thought makes me feel a bit hysterical, and I swallow the urge to laugh, even though there is nothing funny about any of this.

I'm dreading going into her bedroom. The place where she hid out, drank, lost her mind, and tried to take her life. My dad had cleaned up the worst of it. I think he didn't want me seeing it. We will open the windows. Let the light finally shine through. Air the room out. Vacuum and dust, wipe away all the stains and past and pain and evidence. Remove all temptation from her reach. As if the addiction and overdose didn't exist, and there was a way to start over, move forward, and figure out how to live with each other again.

I wonder if this will be the last time we have to clean up after her destruction. I'm afraid we are lying to ourselves. A relapse could easily steal our hope, and her, away from us. Everything still feels very breakable and fragile and uncertain.

It's too much to deal with and think about. The panic is crushing and intense, and I can't breathe, as if a slab of concrete is pushing down on my chest. I press my hand against my heart, feeling the fast, anxious beating through my skin, the cotton fabric of my tank top, into the heat of my palm.

Desperately needing a distraction, I let my thoughts wander, drifting to an easier time, to long summer days and sun-drenched pastures and a color of green I've only seen in Tennessee, and then finally, to Nick.

He's been a quiet hum in the back of my mind, like my favorite song. He's always there, right underneath my skin, just on the edge of my vision, around every corner, love notes tucked into the hollow of a tree. I've thought about our kiss away from prying eyes, behind their backs when the coast was clear, in the quiet when I was alone with my mom late at night as she slept. I take him everywhere with me.

I wonder if he's thought of me, misses me, is worried about me? I haven't heard from him. I keep looking back and forth between the alarm clock and my cell phone on the nightstand, willing it to ring, a text, something, anything. But there's nothing.

For two long weeks, there's only been silence, distance, and white noise. I know he has my number. When I first arrived in Tennessee, Becca made sure we all could get a hold of each other. It was a rule and necessity on the ranch to stay in communication, especially when we were spread out over the five hundred acres. An injury could easily happen. I had gotten used to being able to get to him whenever I needed to, even if it was just a short text to him asking if he could bring over supplies from the storehouse. It's been awful to be so far from him and not having the reassurance of him nearby. I liked him being just one message away.

I doubt he'll call me. I don't think he would let himself, even if he has thought about it. I wish he would, that just once he'd give in, and come find me.

I miss him; his low, lazy drawl when he'd tell me stories about the ranch, how gentle he was with the horses, how intensely he would stare at me as if he had to figure out everything I was thinking. Absence does make the heart grow fonder. All the space and time between us has only made my feelings for him burn stronger.

I don't know the moment I fell for him. I didn't realize how important he was until I had to walk away from him, and the aching took over my entire body. I like having him to think about in the middle of so much being out of control. It's reassuring to know where he is, that he hasn't gone anywhere. That everything on the land stays the same and continues steadily on, even when nothing else in my life has.

I remember the way he'd held me while I had cried, how tender and protective he had been as I fell apart. I couldn't see past him, through him, beyond him. I wish I was still in his arms, wrapped up close, helping me escape, healing me. Kissing me. My eyes drift dreamily shut as I remember that warm, sweet, slow fall into him.

I can still feel the heat beating down on us, sweaty, sticky, damp, his breath hot and shuddering into me as he staggered, and I caught him, held us both up, his hands frantic, grabbing at my waist, his lips wet, searching, stubbled skin scraping, taking me over, away, under, erasing my every thought. I had never been kissed like that before, as if I was the only one who could save him from drowning.

I had completely melted into him, handing over all my fear, shame, and grief, blindly believing he would know exactly how to take care of me inside of them. And for one single, beautiful moment, he had.

But then he'd pulled away, so quickly, so abruptly, the memory makes me flinch. My eyes fly open, and suddenly cold, I roll over, curling onto my side. I had been shocked at how quickly he'd shut down. I hadn't been prepared for it. One minute he was holding me as if I was everything he'd been waiting for, and then the next, I was being blamed for making him believe he could need me. I can't figure out what happened, and I don't know how to get him to tell me. I understand that he feels as if he's betraying Megan. I just wish he would talk to me about it, about anything.

I can't break through to him. He won't let me and has left me stranded here alone. I'm worried he thinks kissing me was a mistake, that he regrets it, that it wasn't as important to him as it was to me. Am I wrong in believing there is something between us?

I couldn't have only imagined that split second when he'd almost kissed me again, the longing in his eyes just before he'd backed up and let me go.

I feel as if I'm constantly banging my head against a wall, calling uselessly out into the dark with no answer. It's enough to drive me insane. I wonder if he deliberately chooses to stay lost, if a part of him likes the idea of being cursed and elusive, off on his own, shut off from the world.

The confusion is making my head hurt. Feeling much too alone and vulnerable, I push myself up, draw my knees to my chest, wrap my arms around them, and look around the darkened room. The loneliness seems to throb off the walls. It's such a long time until morning, and he's so far away. It's a quarter after one in Tennessee, but I know he'll still be awake. I wish I was with him. I wish I was anywhere but here. I don't want to think about what is waiting for me when the sun comes up.

I reach for my phone, checking for the millionth time if I have any missed calls or notifications, even though I know I don't. Radio silence. Trying to distract myself, I mindlessly scroll through Instagram and Facebook but can't handle everyone pretending to have perfect lives and, feeling overwhelmed, quickly close them.

I desperately want to call him, even if he doesn't say much. I just want to hear his voice, his breath, the night around him, only for a second. I can smell the soil, the honeysuckle, the old wood that always felt sad and nostalgic as if it were still waiting too for how things used to be.

My heart pounds faster, thrumming in my ears, as I find his name, and my thumb hesitates, hovering over it, but right before I press it, I chicken out and change my mind. I can't do it. Not after how we'd left things. What if he hung up on me? I couldn't stand to be rejected by him again. My worst fear is that I've completely misread him, and he doesn't care about me at all. I wouldn't be able to handle it. Not now, not when I'm so mentally and emotionally worn out and have no defenses left.

Shakily letting out my breath, I deliberately set my cell back on the nightstand. I'm about to get out of bed and go get some water when my phone rings. Worried it's Becca telling me something happened to my mom, I pick it up and then freeze, my breath catching, as I stare in disbelief at Nick's name lighting up the screen.

I'm in so much shock it takes me four rings to actually answer. "Hello?" I can hear how breathless my voice sounds, how needy, and try to calm down. I don't want him to know I've been waiting for him.

He's quiet on the other end, and I wonder if he's already regretting calling. "Lexy? It's Nick. Were you asleep?"

"No, I'm still up," I finally manage. His voice sounds exactly the way I remember it, exactly the way I need it to. Like it did when he was holding me, rumbling low in his throat, vibrating through me, falling over my hair and skin like warm rain. I would know him anywhere. "I can't sleep." I hold the phone closer to my ear, starving for the connection to him. He has thought about me, I realize, my heart melting.

I hear him let out his breath and clear his throat. Is he nervous? I wonder if he will say anything about the kiss, if he's as aware of it being between us as I am. I feel as if he is trying to figure out how to talk around it. "Yeah…uh…Ben said you were having a rough time out there. Just wanted to see how you were doing."

For the last few weeks, I've had to hold it together and be strong, for my parents, for Becca. I haven't wanted to let myself fall apart. There hasn't been time, even though it feels there's been nothing but, as the hours stretch out in front of me. I finally let myself give in to the fear and exhaustion. "It's been really hard," I answer wearily. "It's just all a lot to deal with."

"How's your mom?"

I prop up the pillows behind me, snuggling back against them. There is nothing else but him in this moment, and I desperately need it to be that way. I feel safe for the first time in weeks.

"She's alive, thank God. She's survived the overdose and detox. It's been horrible to watch her go through that." I wince as I remember the sweating and writhing, muscle spasms, and dry heaves my mom had wrestled against as the withdrawals violently wracked her body. "Ironically though, that was the easy part. The hardest thing for her now is going to be figuring out how to live without drinking. But at least she finally agreed to go into treatment."

"That's good."

"Yeah, it is," I answer, sighing, and shift to get more comfortable. I absently pull at the tattered hem of my pajama shorts I like to sleep in. They are my favorite; soft, gray, and worn. I lost the string that ties the waistband years ago. I need comforting things around me. For some reason, it helps. "I wasn't sure if she would. They are talking about transferring her next week."

"How long is her program?"

"Thirty days, but she can stay longer if she needs to. She'll live at the facility. It's by the beach. The brochure makes it look like a spa."

"Those places always do."

I'm not sure why, but it makes me laugh a little, and the pressure eases, just for an instant. Everything about him feels good. "I've noticed that too. I guess it's supposed to be soothing and relaxing."

"Probably, considering what they're dealing with."

"Yeah." I sigh, my laughter fading into the dark as the heaviness of the situation returns. "It's hard work getting clean. But, she will have a sponsor that monitors her even after she's done. And she will go to AA meetings."

"You must be happy she's finally getting help."

I'm scared to death but don't know how to explain it and I'm not sure I have the strength to try, so I give him an answer that is easier for both of us. "I am. We all are. It's strange to think about her being sober. I realized today I've never known her like that. She's been drunk almost my whole life."

I can feel him listening to me, focusing on my words, leaning in close. I can picture how dark his eyes are, the flecks of gold when the light hits just right in them. I wish I could push through all the distance to touch him. I think of the late nights talking on the porch, in the stable, after everyone else had gone to sleep, and fiercely yearn to go back.

"How's it being back home?" he asks after a few moments.

"Honestly, it doesn't feel like I thought it would." I glance around my bedroom, shadowed by the hazy golden glow from the streetlights outside. These four walls were the only place I'd had growing up where I could come and hide from the chaos and dysfunction. But nothing about them had ever been safe. They are a time capsule that holds our fear frozen in time. "I was actually just thinking that it seems like someone else's house, which doesn't make any sense because I grew up here."

"You haven't been there in a while."

"Yeah, I guess," I murmur, but I'm thinking of the old farmhouse, the horses grazing under the afternoon sun, the peaceful stillness and quiet. "Everything was so much easier on the ranch." I am painfully homesick in a way I don't understand yet and feel too guilty to dare say out loud. I hear the sound of a train going by and smile. "Where are you right now?"

"Out on the porch at my place. Why?"

"I just want to picture it." I hear a creaking and picture him sitting down on the cottage steps. "I really miss it." *I miss you*, I think, and the words wait, perched and ready, on the tip of my tongue. I press my lips together to hold them in. I wonder what he would do if I told him. Does he miss me? I'm too afraid to ask. I glance at the window that faces the quiet street and think of the window seat in my room, how it looked out over the thick, old oak trees standing guard over the lane that led to the tall arch of my Great-Great-Grandfather Beau's gate. Even though I'm back home in California, I've never felt more out of place or so far from where I'm supposed to be. "How's Ben?"

"He's fine. We've been busy with the new horses that came in last week. He went to bed about an hour ago."

I don't ask why he's still up. I already know. It's the same reason I am. Neither of us wants to have bad dreams. I listen to him breathing on the other end and think of how he'd held me up when I couldn't stand on my own. I can still smell the spring scent of the detergent on his shirt, the soap on his skin as if he's in front of me.

He's so quiet. I try to think of something else to say. I don't want him to change his mind and hang up. "How's Glory?" I ask, offering him something he'll know how to talk about.

"She's good," he answers, and I think I hear the relief in his voice. "Getting better every day. I'm hoping to try riding her soon. See how she does. Just waiting for her to get a little stronger first."

"I wish I could be there to see it," I say wistfully. "I really miss her. Maybe I'll get to ride her when we come back after my mom is done with rehab."

"You're coming back?" he suddenly asks, his voice harsh and a bit panicked.

I flinch as his question shoots out quick like a bullet and hits me dead center in my heart. The silky feeling instantly vanishes. I don't understand his reaction. My skin is clammy and cold. "Yeah," I say carefully. I don't feel as safe anymore. "It's going to be part of her twelve-step program. It will hopefully help her face what happened to her out there and get some closure. Why?"

There is nothing but silence on his end for almost a full minute. I bite my lip, holding my breath as I wonder what he's thinking. "I just didn't think you were going to," he answers after a long time, too long, too late. I'm already hurting, starting to shut down.

Does he wish I wasn't? "Oh," is all I manage to say. Disappointment makes my body heavy and weak. My heart seems to fold in on itself, as my hope deflates. Why can't I ever find solid ground with him? I start to think I have, and then he backs up and takes it away. My courage falters, and I give up. He doesn't want to let me in. I'm not Megan. He's not going to allow himself to care about me. The kiss meant nothing to him, changed nothing for him. I mean nothing. How had he broken me so quickly? I'm grateful he can't see my face to know how I'm really feeling.

Tears fill my eyes as I stare at the four walls that are still marred by her addictions, smothering, isolating, and much too sad. I am on my own. "I guess I should let you go," I murmur, feeling defeated and rejected. I'm suddenly so tired. Tired of trying, of fighting, of believing. What was the use? I just keep losing and never can hold on to what he gives me. "I know you've got to get up early."

"Wait. Don't go yet."

Why did he even call me? I wonder, staring hopelessly up at the ceiling fan still spinning and spinning and spinning in circles. Just like me. My emotions are stretched and shredded thin.

I think of the moment he looked at me as if he wanted to kiss me again before I left. I need to know if I imagined it. I just want him to tell me the truth. That look has haunted my every step.

"Are you sorry you kissed me?" I'm too tired to stay strong, and my voice cracks, as more tears fall, but I can't hold myself together anymore. I'm not sure if I actually said it, and for a blurred, whirring second, I wonder if I only thought it. But he's too quiet, stunned quiet, and I realize with a rushing thud that the damage is already here.

I know what I've done, that I've backed him into a corner that is off-limits and restricted. I've bumped up against the forbidden memory of her. It's the scarlet letter sin where he's concerned. I can feel him freeze, his quick gasp as his breath catches. I don't think he thought I'd ask either.

I hear him softly swear, and I sink further away, cringing into the embarrassment of not knowing what to do, futilely wishing I hadn't said anything. "Lexy, I..." he stammers. "I um... I don't... I can't um..." he trails off into a silence that is much too loud and painful between us.

"Never mind," I say dully, still crying, sniffling, on the edge of a total breakdown. All I want to do is hide underneath the covers, close my eyes and disappear, and forget I'd ever met him.

It's the first time since I got home that I've been glad to be back in California. But I'm not far away enough. He can still hurt me all the way out here. "I get it. I shouldn't have asked. You don't have to tell me. I'll let you go."

"I'm not sorry," he blurts out, the words fast and urgent, surprising both of us. He sounds panicked, desperate. "I'd kiss you now if I could."

I'd been ready to hang up and almost drop the phone as his words register. "What?" I'm so shocked I can only whisper the question and instantly sit up in bed. Did I hear him right? "You would?"

I wait, counting eight heartbeats, as I feel him weighing the risk and loss. Megan is between us, a misty reminder, always watching and waiting, wherever he is. I wonder if this is how it all ends with us, if it's over before it even started, and if I'm the one who ruined it, but then he softly says, "Yeah." I hear him blow out his breath as if he's been climbing or running a long, hard distance. Maybe he has. His voice sounds shaky and unsteady. "It's not the same here with you gone."

Tears still on my cheeks, I smile into the dark, my heart full and light. The tension in the air eases, distance disappearing as the fear evaporates between us. Life is instantly beautiful again. He's finally letting me in. "I'm not sorry either." I want to stay in this moment and never leave. I gently trace my fingertips over my mouth, remembering him there. "I wish you were kissing me right now."

"Me too," he drawls, his voice deep and low, as if he knows how much I like it, and my breath shivers out, my skin flushing much too hot, remembering the taste of him, his tongue tangling with mine, the insatiable craving, need, rays of sunlight, desperately clinging and grabbing onto warm denim and cotton, pushing closer, trying to find relief and release for an ache only he understood. "Don't hang up yet, okay?"

"I won't," I promise. He doesn't want to go back to the loneliness either, I suddenly realize, my heart opening even more. Neither one of us do. "Can you do something for me?" I don't wait for him to answer. I already know he needs me as much as I need him. The trust feels different, new, tender, intimate, as if he's next to me. "Please tell me something that has absolutely nothing to do with where I am right now." He must hear my desperation and loneliness; he must understand it, because he does exactly what I ask him to and tells me about a typical day on a ranch in Tennessee.

Tomorrow no longer feels as threatening. There's only the two of us, tied together over the distance. I wrap myself in the sound of him, imagining I'm back on the land, surrounded by nothing but wide open space and acres of green and sultry southern nights. We stay up the rest of the night talking. I finally drift off around sunrise with his voice still in my ear.

Chapter Twenty-Seven
NICK

It's Thursday. Thirteen days have passed since she left. I hate that I know, that I'm counting, watching every minute of the clock ticking slowly by. I've stayed busy. I've had to. It's keeping me distracted from feeling the hole she left behind.

Ben is on the phone with Becca. I stare at the television screen, trying to pretend I'm not listening to every word he's saying. She calls every night to check in. It's frustrating only hearing one side. Impatiently, I wait for him to hang up.

"Sure is quiet without the two of you here," Ben says. "Let Lexy know we're thinking of her." He smiles and glances over at me. I raise my brows in suspicion, wondering if I should worry about what's being said. "Yeah, I'm keeping an eye on him. Don't worry; he's behaving himself. Been a little cranky lately, but that's nothing new." He laughs when I scowl at him. He falls quiet again as he listens. His voice goes low, tender, as it always does around her. "I miss you too. Can't wait for you to come home. Yeah, I'll talk to you tomorrow. Hug Lexy for me. Love you more. Goodnight." He hangs up, setting his cell on the table next to him.

"How's it going out there?" I ask, trying to sound casual and indifferent. I'm not sure if I'm pulling it off.

"As well as can be expected. She's tired. They all are." Even with Becca gone, I notice he still sits on the left side of the couch, leaving the spot where she always likes to sit empty, waiting. "Becca's going to stay out there a while longer. Victoria is finally through with the detox. She's awake and is talking, but isn't strong enough for much else yet. They are transferring her to the treatment center in the next few days. Becca's pretty worried about Lexy. She said she's barely eating or sleeping. Hasn't left the hospital once." He glances over at me. "You talk with Lexy at all?"

My stomach clenches up at her name. I carefully shake my head. I can't make myself look at him and stare intently at the television screen. I feel too guilty. I haven't told Ben about kissing her. He's fiercely protective of his niece. I'm not sure how he'll take it. I'm not even sure what to do with it yet. If I talk about it, it's too real. But it's all I think about.

"You were spending a lot of time together before she left. She's going through a real rough time right now. Might be nice if you called her. I bet she'd like to hear from you."

"I seriously doubt it," I mutter under my breath, remembering how I'd pushed her away, how cold I'd been towards her. I'm probably the last person she wants to talk to right now.

"What?"

I go still, realizing I said it out loud. I can't explain it without telling him about the kiss, which would open up a whole bunch of other questions I have no idea how to answer. "Nothing," I mumble. I lift the mason jar of sweet tea to my lips and swallow, trying to avoid his gaze.

"What's with you?" Ben asks, his eyes narrowing as he studies me. "You've been in a bad mood for the last two weeks. Even more than usual."

Scowling, I swallow back what I want to say and instead tell him, "Nothing is with me." I try to keep my voice calm and even. "I'm just tired. It's only the two of us here, and there's a lot of work to do." When he continues to frown at me and speculate, I shift and rest my elbow on the armrest, leaning my head against my hand, so it shields part of my face. I stare back at the television, but all I can see is her. "Anyway, I'm sure Lexy has plenty of people to talk to out there. I don't even know what I'd say to her."

"You could just ask how she's doing. She'd probably like to hear a familiar voice right now. Poor girl," he murmurs, shaking his head. "She's been through so much already. I can't imagine having to deal with all of this. Richard is taking her back to the house to get some rest. Becca said she was about ready to pass out on her feet."

Even though I know he's not trying to make me feel guilty, his words are like hot coals, branding and searing through my skin, burning me up from the inside out. I already feel horrible for how I'd treated her. Ben wasn't wrong. I have been in a bad mood. I've been distracted, irritable, and restless ever since she'd left.

I'm relieved when Ben yawns, rubbing his hands over his eyes. I can't handle any more questions. "I'm going to bed. I'm beat." He gets up, goes into the kitchen, and puts his empty jar and plate in the sink. It's my turn to do the dishes. He walks toward the stairs, and stops halfway there, glancing back over his shoulder at me. "You know, it's okay if you miss her." Startled, I look over at him and realize he understands exactly what I'm not telling him. I don't bother arguing. We both already know he's right. He doesn't wait for me to say anything and starts heading up. "See you in the morning."

"Yeah," I answer absently, lost in thought. I do miss her. I hadn't realized I would. I thought that her leaving was what I wanted. But every day she's gone, the emptiness seems to get worse. And now I can't stop thinking about her, up in the middle of the night, alone, sad, and scared.

Turning off the television, I make myself get up. Trying to force her out of my thoughts, I distract myself by washing the dishes. I've already made my decision. I'm not going to call her. Ben hadn't changed my mind. He doesn't know the whole situation, what had happened between us, what I'd done to her. By the time the dishes were in the rack to dry, and the counters wiped down, I was still having the same argument with myself.

I turn off the lights and walk out the back door, not bothering to lock it behind me. Abraham will stand guard where he's dozing on the porch. "Goodnight, boy." I ruffle his head as I go down the steps towards my place. Ever since Becca has been gone, Abraham stays near the house to keep an eye on Ben, as if he knows he's missing her. Or maybe they both are.

Lexy didn't need to hear from me. Considering how we'd left things, she'd probably just hang up on me. I know I hurt her, and I hadn't even tried to apologize or explain. There's no way I could have. I had no idea where to even start. So I'd shoved her back, letting her take the fall for everything I didn't know how to deal with.

I walk around the back of the house towards the cottage, still trying to convince myself that calling her was a stupid idea. I should just go to bed, but I already know I won't sleep. I usually can't, but now it's because of her.

I shouldn't have kissed her.

The thought has gone through my head at least a hundred times since she left. What makes all this guilt and frustration even worse is that it's completely my fault. I'm the one who shifted and turned towards her.

If she hadn't been crying and holding onto me, if her life hadn't just fallen apart, if she hadn't been looking up at me, her eyes beautifully broken and begging me to save her, I might have had the strength to stop myself. I could say I hadn't meant to, that it was an accident or a mistake, but now, alone in the dark, I have to admit that it hadn't been.

The minute I kissed her, I collided head-on with my own past, guilt, and despair. I had years and years of hurt pent up inside of me, a thousand things I'd long buried that I wanted to tell her, to lay bare, to shout out at the top of my lungs. Things no one else knew, things I never dared say out loud because I knew they would crush me.

But with Lexy, I didn't need to say anything. I could taste all my loss on her and hungrily fed off of it and found complete release. The rush of relief had been so overwhelming, so euphoric, and exhilarating; I'd staggered backward from the force. If she hadn't already been clinging to me, I would have fallen.

That kiss is the first real thing I've felt in years.

I hadn't wanted to stop, which is why I'd had to. I'd pulled back out of sheer self-preservation. She somehow broke past my walls and made it through straight to the heart of me. She took every ounce of anguish I'd poured into her and kept taking and taking until my every defense was broken down.

She was lost and sweet and starving and even softer than I'd imagined she'd be. It was a dangerously addictive combination. It had been too much. It had been terrifying. It had been everything I'd needed. I'd been completely stripped bare to the point I had to push her away to keep my sanity.

I had almost kissed her again. There had been that one split-second before she'd left that I almost lost my mind. I'd still been aware enough to realize Becca was only a few feet away and barely managed to control myself.

I didn't want her to go. Not yet, not when she'd walked away with so many pieces of me. But now she was gone, and I hadn't had a chance to get them back. And there was nothing I could do about it.

I had watched her leave, not looking away until she was nothing but a speck and silhouette against the shimmering green, seeming to disappear. I'd wondered if she would turn around, and waited for her to look back at me, but she hadn't.

The need is so much worse now that I know what I found with her. I wish I didn't know what I was missing. I'd lost something the day she left. I knew the second she walked away that I was letting go of the one person who could revive me. But now, I'm left here all alone, with a gaping hole in my gut.

The realization stirs up the frustration all over again, and I shove the screen open and step out onto the porch. The cottage feels too small and suffocating. I rub the back of my neck to ease the tension. It doesn't help, and I try taking a deep breath of the fragrant night air, hoping it will clear my head. The muggy heat is inescapable. So is Lexy. I don't want to think anymore. It's hurting me.

I guess when it all comes down to it, none of this changes anything. Now that she is back with her family, she'll probably never leave her mom's side again. Her guilt won't let her. She might come to visit Becca and Ben from time to time, but she wouldn't stay. I'm not sure what would happen with her singing, but that wasn't my business or my problem. By the time she ever made it over this way again, everything that had happened with us would be a distant memory. Her family may own this land, but she didn't belong out here. She'd grown up in the suburbs of California, not a horse ranch in Tennessee.

Funny how I can't picture her out there though. It seems everywhere I look, I can see her. I can see her. In the stables with Glory, singing on the porch, sitting next to me at the kitchen table, working on the land side by side.

Kissing her in the pasture.

The memory sneaks up on me again, and I grit my teeth before the aching takes me over. I can't even walk past the spot where it happened without remembering.

It's the image of the fear in her eyes that finally makes my decision. Her life had shattered and exploded, and I had still hurt her. I had wanted to punish her for making me care about her, for making me feel, for making me believe in something more. Is this really who I've turned into? I hate myself for it.

Not one minute passes that I don't remember how she looked the day she got the phone call, how dazed and dark her eyes had been, how hard she'd cried, how tightly she'd held onto me as if I were her only lifeline. I can't sit back and do nothing.

I'm worried about her. I can't seem to get around it. I want to make sure she's all right. One more time, just to hear her voice, and then maybe this vicious guilt will leave me alone.

I pull my phone out of my pocket and stare down at it, weighing the risk. I know what will happen if I talk to her. She'll pull me back into her. I don't know how to think about both her and Megan. I don't know how to need them both. I can't explain the confusion I feel as I try to hold onto my past while being forced to deal with the present. I don't like that the gap feels as if it's widening, as if I'm becoming two different people. Lexy is the only one who seems to know who I am anymore.

Scrolling down, I find her name in my contacts and quickly press it before I can change my mind. My heart thuds heavily, and my mouth is dry as I count one ring...two...

It's on the fourth ring. One more, and it will go to voicemail. Maybe she finally fell asleep. Or maybe she knows it's me and is choosing to ignore the call. I almost hang up. But, then she answers.

"Hello?"

All the distance I've tried to put between us instantly disappears at the sound of her voice. I close my eyes as my defenses crumble. Maybe I'm not what she needs, but she's exactly what I do. When I open my eyes, I realize I am looking at the exact spot where we kissed a few weeks before. Frustrated, I turn away, and wipe my hand over my face, trying to find some sort of solid ground. She's still waiting. I make myself say something.

"Lexy? It's Nick." *As if she doesn't know,* I think, rolling my eyes. I realize I'm tense, anticipating what her response will be. She has every right to be angry at me. I know I messed up and owe her an apology. But how do I say sorry without talking about the rest of what happened? I wait for her to call me out, to accuse me, to ask, but she doesn't, and I let it sit on the back burner for a bit. "Were you asleep?"

"No, I'm still up. I can't sleep."

I wish I didn't understand what she meant. The loneliness felt like it was waiting for me around every corner. She sounds weary and exhausted. Surrounded, like someone being hunted. I wince, feeling a fresh wave of regret for waiting this long to call her.

Relieved she hasn't hung up on me yet, I slowly let out my breath and nervously clear my throat. I can't seem to get my voice to work. I'm not sure what to do now that she's answered. I hadn't thought that far out.

The kiss is between us and has changed things. The lines that had been there before were totally wiped out the instant my lips touched hers. I have no idea how to stand where we are now. I wonder if she will ask me about it and hope she doesn't. I don't know what to say or how to explain what it has done to me. How much it has changed.

"Yeah...uh...Ben said you were having a rough time out there. Just wanted to see how you were doing."

"It's been really hard," she answers, her voice thick and heavy. "It's just a lot to deal with."

"How's your mom?"

"She's alive, thank God. She survived the overdose and detox. It's been horrible to watch her go through that." She goes quiet for a second, as if gathering herself, and I hear her let out a shaky breath before she speaks again. "Ironically though, that was the easy part. The hardest thing for her now is going to be figuring out how to live without drinking. But at least she finally agreed to go into treatment."

"That's good."

"Yeah, it is." I hear rustling and imagine she's in bed, in that house, alone in her room, too far from here, from me. "I wasn't sure if she would. They are talking about transferring her next week."

"How long is her program?"

"Thirty days, but she can stay longer if she needs to. She'll live at the facility. It's by the beach. The brochure makes it look like a spa."

"Those places always do," I say and am relieved to hear her laugh. I bet she needs it. I haven't heard the sound in a while and realize it's another part of her I've missed.

"I've noticed that too. I guess it's supposed to be soothing and relaxing."

"Probably, considering what they're dealing with."

"Yeah." I notice her voice has flatlined out again. I don't like how empty it is. "It's hard work getting clean. But, she will have a sponsor that monitors her even after she's done. And she will go to AA meetings."

"You must be happy she's finally getting help."

"I am. We all are. It's strange to think about her being sober. I realized today I've never known her like that. She's been drunk almost my whole life."

It was one of the saddest things I'd ever heard anyone say. I can feel the jaggedness of her grief through the line. I don't have any answers or remedies for her, but it's not what she's asking for. I'm as lost as she is, and so I give her what I'd need and stay quiet and simply listen to her, letting the weight of her pain hang in the air between us.

"How's it being back home?" I ask after a few moments.

"I was actually just thinking how different everything feels, like it's someone else's house which doesn't make a lot of sense because I grew up here."

There's something in her voice that makes the hair stand up on the back of my neck, a warning of things to come. I'm not sure what she's getting at. "You haven't been there in a while." A train is going by, its whistle blowing.

"Yeah, I guess. Everything was so much easier on the ranch. Where are you right now?"

I wait until the rattle and rumble of the wheels on the tracks fade into the night before answering her. "Out on the porch at my place. Why?"

"I just want to picture it," she murmurs, and I hear the longing in her voice. "I really miss it."

Do you miss me? I wonder, but don't dare ask. I have no idea what I would do with either answer. Because I'm finally comfortable she's not going anywhere, I allow myself to sit down on the porch steps, the warped wood creaking and aching beneath me. I lean back against the rail, looking out into the dark. It doesn't feel as lonely now.

"How's Ben?" she asks.

"He's fine. We've been busy with the new horses that came in last week. He went to bed about an hour ago." Neither one of us talks about why we're still up. We both already know. I think of the nights I had found her, how late it had been, as if she'd sent out a secret signal just for me, and how it seemed we were the only two in the world who were still awake.

We fall quiet again. I can't remember ever feeling more awkward and foolish and tongue-tied. I don't know how to do this. I'm not good at it.

I keep getting distracted. All I can think about is her lips on mine, her hands clinging to me, the scent and taste of her everywhere. I notice it's uncomfortably hot, even so late when the air has cooled a little.

I try to make myself focus, open my mouth to say something, come up with nothing, and close it again on a helpless breath. I wonder if she'll get bored and want to hang up.

"How's Glory?"

I can't help but smile. I was wondering when she'd ask. I've never met anyone who was able to get a horse to easily come to her simply with a crook of her finger. *Just like me,* I think wryly. Apparently, I'll follow her all the way to California. "She's good," I respond, glad she hadn't said she wanted to go. "Getting stronger every day. I'm going to ride her in the next few weeks, see how she does."

"I wish I could be there to see it. I really miss her. Maybe I'll get to ride her when we come back after my mom is done with rehab."

Fear and need slam into me at exactly the same time. My reaction is so abrupt and unexpected that before I can get a grip on it, I hear myself blurt out, "You're coming back?" and even to my own ears, it sounds like I'm accusing her. Maybe I am. It was too soon. I'm not ready. I thought I'd have more time to figure this out.

"Yeah." Her voice is cautious, wounded, and it's all my fault. Again. "It's going to be part of her twelve-step program. It will hopefully help her face what happened to her out there and get some closure. Why?"

My mind is racing. I don't know what to say. I don't know how to fix this. I'm not even sure I can. I can't pretend she's wrong in what she heard, and I can't take the words back. Floundering, I try to pull myself together. "I just didn't think you were going to," I answer lamely and mentally kick myself for how stupid I am.

"Oh," is all she says. I hear the hurt in her voice, the confusion and disappointment, but don't have my footing back enough to undo what just happened.

Misunderstanding is like static in the air between us. I stare without seeing out in the night, hoping for answers. We'd only been on the phone for about ten minutes, and I've already managed to hurt her. I can't figure out how not to.

"I guess I should let you go," she murmurs dully, and I hear something else in her voice. Is she pushing me away? She's never been the one who does. Even from here, I can feel her shutting down and withdrawing. The panic is intense. "I know you've got to get up early."

"Wait." I don't want to go back to the emptiness, the nothingness, the void she would leave behind. "Don't go yet."

"Are you sorry you kissed me?" Her voice cracks, throwing me off. Is she crying? Her question pierces through the line to me, penetrating through the barriers and walls I tried to put up between us.

I jolt as if lightning struck beneath my feet, surging hot and electric through my arches, tingling up through my body, stealing my breath. *No, yes, maybe. Never.* I can't think straight. I'm grateful I'm already sitting down.

I quietly swear. "Lexy, I..." There are too many thoughts, needs, and feelings jumbled up, a tangled mess, and they slam into me all at once. I can't sift through them fast enough, and don't want her to hang up before I do. "I don't...I can't um..." Feeling lost and overwhelmed, I trail off into the horrible, echoing silence.

"Never mind," she says, and I hear the heartbreak in her voice, making my stomach drop. I'd made her sound the same way the day she left. Devastated. Unwanted. "I get it. I shouldn't have asked. You don't have to tell me. I'll let you go."

She's going to leave again. I can't let her. It's too cold and dark without her. "I'm not sorry," I burst out, blindly grabbing through the distance for her, surprising both of us. "I'd kiss you now if I could."

She's so quiet I wonder if she hung up, but then I hear her breathlessly whisper, "What?" She sounds shocked, stunned. I don't blame her. I am, too. "You would?"

I'm almost afraid to say it, knowing all that will change. Megan gets hazy and blurry as I make the deliberate and terrifying choice to move towards Lexy. I'm intensely aware of the shift happening.

"Yeah. It's not the same here with you gone." I feel lightheaded as if I'm climbing at a high altitude, looking dizzyingly down at the ground so far below me. My voice is jittery and shaky, my limbs weak from the trembling focus and intense exertion. But it's too late to take it back now, and I continue tentatively forward into this new place. It doesn't hurt as much as I thought it would. Maybe the miles between us make me feel safer, brave, invincible.

"I'm not sorry either." Her voice is honey warm and sweet and reminds me of when she asked me not to let her go before we kissed. I'd have done anything for her at that moment. I still would. "I wish you were kissing me right now."

My gaze wanders back towards the spot where we had fallen and collapsed into each other. I can still taste the salt of her tears on my tongue, my own grief, our breath panting, gasping, drowning in the hunger for something we'd waited years and years to find. Her body, her every curve, pressed tight, fitting much too perfectly into my hands, clutching, shaking, melting against me and for me and around me. My gut clenches, and every nerve in my body is on edge and tight. It's seriously too hot out here. The desire is a raw and thrilling punch radiating through my system. I haven't felt it for someone in years.

"Me too," I murmur huskily, remembering the intensity and heat of that kiss, how I'd almost been knocked to the ground by the force of it all. "Don't hang up yet, okay?"

"I won't." When she finally speaks again, I notice the sadness is gone from her voice and feel the pressure in my chest ease up. "Can you do something for me?" she asks, and I realize she understands exactly what I just gave her. She doesn't wait for me to answer. She already knows I'm helpless when it comes to her. "Please tell me something that has absolutely nothing to do with where I am right now."

It's then I have to admit I'd lied. Whatever is happening with us is far from over. Especially since it's in the middle of the night and I'm on the phone with a girl I'd spent the last two weeks telling myself to stay away from. But I can't let go of her. I need her too much. It's that simple and that complicated.

And so I do what she asks me to and tell her about ordinary life out here. I talk about the horses that came in, the new mower Ben bought for the grass, and a bunch of other little things I didn't realize I'd been waiting to share with her. We talk until sunrise. She finally falls asleep just as it's time for me to get up and head out to the barn. I don't hang up even when there is nothing but silence on the other end.

I sit on the porch, watching the sky lighten over the land, letting the sound of her breathing connect us. And for the first time in a long time, I think it's going to be a good day.

Chapter Twenty-Eight
VICTORIA

I'm not sure what makes me open my eyes, but I am suddenly wide awake. I can't figure out what is different. I lay very still, listening and waiting for something to happen.

I slowly begin to realize that nothing is wrong. I'm not feeling anything—no pain, nausea, hallucinations. My skin is not burning or itching. The purple bugs have vanished. I can move without cramping or muscle spasms attacking and seizing up my body.

White surrounds me; bright, pristine, and pure. I feel weightless as a feather, as if I'm levitating. I notice there is a fuzzy lavender halo around the light fixtures as if I've been swimming underwater too long with my eyes open. The whole room seems to have an angelic sheen. I have the surreal sensation of wondering if I'm dead. But I can hear the drip of the IV, the machines beeping, my own heart beating. I can actually feel my pulse throbbing through my wrists, circulating and flowing in my veins.

Sunlight flits through the slats of the blinds, patterns shifting and dancing over my face and arms. I lift my hand, watching the beam glow through my fingertips, lighting me up from within as if I am made of magic or have gained superpowers. Even the hairs on my head are sensitive and tender. My entire system feels changed, reworked, and rewired somehow. As if I've found a way to go back through all the years and start over, and am now renewed and reborn. I feel ironically heroic and victorious, even though tubes still tie me to the bed, and my breath is not my own yet.

I hear the birds chirping and singing outside; their sound is pretty, sweet, and joyful. I read once that they call out at the break of dawn to let the others know they survived the night and are still here. It's the first time I understand their instinct. I have the strongest urge to stand on the rooftop and call out to anyone who will listen that I'm still alive and have made it through the darkest night of the soul I have ever known.

I've been wrestling against the devil, and I won.

I feel like me again—the me who sang and believed and hoped. The me I was before I ever took my first drink, before the vodka swallowed me, before my father got his grip on me. Before I believed him. Before I was ever hit. Before I learned to be afraid. Before I was an abused little girl and hid under the porch and beneath the bed. Before I gave up and decided life wasn't worth living. Before I forgot who I could be, was supposed to be, was born to be.

Before.

Richard is in the chair next to my bed, staring at the television, the sound muted, so he doesn't wake me. He's watching Jeopardy. It's always been his favorite show. I can almost hear him thinking of all the answers, and he's usually right. He's brilliant. So much smarter than me.

He looks worn out. He doesn't know I'm awake yet, and I take a minute to stare at him, absorbing every feature of his face. We're alone, and I like the quiet between us. It feels intimate somehow and reminds me of our early days together when he would study, and I would write songs, and it was just us, in our own private world.

We haven't had much time to ourselves over the last few weeks. There's always been someone else here, in the way, around us, between us, interrupting. His hair is longer, gray at the temples, lines creasing his face from exhaustion and stress. He seems older, aging in minutes and hours rather than years, and much wearier than he should. Deteriorating under the weight of despair. Because of me.

My chest feels as if a heavy, cold stone is pressing down on it. I dreamt he was gone, that he'd had enough and given up on me for good. But he's still here. He's stayed with me and has never left. I feel so tender towards him, hopelessly in love. I have to get to him. He's the only thing that matters at this moment. There is so much I want to tell him. I need him to listen, to hear me out, to know how sorry I am, and give me one more chance before he decides to walk away.

I want real air. Real life. Real anything. I want my husband back. I pull out the oxygen tubes and take my first full breath on my own. It feels exhilarating in my lungs, crisp, clean, clear. Pushing myself up, I try to reach out for him, but my movements set the alarms off on the machine, startling him.

He instantly is at my side, his expression anxious. I hate that I've made him look at me like that; that fear is what I see in his eyes more than desire or passion or love. Can things ever go back to the way they were with us? "Victoria? What is it? What's wrong?"

I open my mouth to tell him I miss him, I love him, I want him to come back to me. But the alarms are beeping too loudly, and he looks too worried, and Nurse Sarah is running in and pressing me back onto the bed, again getting between us, pulling me away. I look past her shoulder at Richard, my eyes panicky, hoping he doesn't leave. He looks confused but can't ask me yet, and to my relief, he stays close.

"Well, I guess you've decided it's time to get up," she chides, but I don't feel scolded. I must look better because she seems relieved.

She turns off the beeping machines, and the room falls back into the quiet. She has a clipboard in her hand. She's my favorite face here. Kind and always gentle as she's cared and cleaned me up and carried me through the long, screaming, sweaty days and nights of detox. "You're alright. Just a false alarm." She fusses around me and checks my vitals. I flinch when the cool metal of the stethoscope presses against my skin. They never seem to warm it up enough. I'm curious if my heartbeat sounds as loud to her as it does to me. It feels as if it's pounding clear through my hospital gown into her hands. "How are you feeling?"

"Really good," I answer, and I can hear my own amazement. "Like every cell in my body is singing."

"That's great news," she says, smiling. She wears the prettiest earrings, I notice. She seems to have a million of them. Today they are pink butterflies that sparkle and flutter whenever she moves. For some reason, I can't stop staring at them, fascinated at how the wings shimmer and change colors depending on how the light hits. They seem appropriate somehow, as if they are trying to tell me something or recognize me. Ever since I was a child, I've loved butterflies; how they are born from a colorless, ugly cocoon and transform into something beautiful and triumphant, just as I've longed to.

She drapes her stethoscope around her neck. "Everything is going to feel very sensitive and raw. You might experience highs and lows and be extremely overwhelmed for no reason. You also might feel some adrenaline rushes and euphoria. It's completely normal." She gives me a tender look. Her eyes are the most compassionate I have ever seen, and I feel the urge to cry and make myself swallow the hot lump in my throat. I wonder if this is the rush of emotion she was talking about. "Congratulations. You're finally clean."

Clean. I'm clean and shiny and new. I thought I wouldn't like it, that I would be too frightened of what was waiting on the other side once the last drop of vodka was gone. But it is so much different than what I imagined. Is this humming under my skin what it feels like to have my blood purified from the inside out? Is this what it feels like to be a human being again? I haven't felt like one in years. Daddy was wrong about me. I'm not like him. I can be different. It's the first time in my life I believe it.

I manage to smile back. "Thank you," I say, knowing she doesn't understand that she's helped rescue me from so much more than just a bottle. She's restored my hope.

"It's a big deal. The withdrawals are one of the hardest parts. They can be brutal. A lot of people don't make it through them." She winks at me, the butterfly wings glittering as if cheering me on. "You must be strong." All business and efficiency, she pulls a pen out of her scrubs pocket. "Now that you're stable, a spot has opened up tomorrow morning at the rehabilitation center. We need your signed consent for the transfer."

"Tomorrow?" My stomach drops, my smile fading. Both Richard and I go still. "That soon?" I wonder if it's quick so I don't have a chance to change my mind and escape.

"Yes. The spots fill up fast, unfortunately." She clicks the pen, getting it ready as if she knows I'm out of options. "Do you consent to go?"

It's reassuring that addiction is such a common problem. It makes me feel less alone. I look at Richard. No one is between us now. We stare at each other, and I see our lives flash before my eyes, wincing as the years of darkness and blackouts and locked doors spin past my vision and then bring me harshly back to this moment of sitting in a hospital bed after an overdose. He says nothing, knowing I am the only one who can choose to get sober. He doesn't move, doesn't blink, but I can actually hear him silently pleading, praying, begging me to say yes. Lexy and Becca aren't here, but I know if they were, they would have the same expression on their faces.

I think of my father and all the pain I've caused because of him. I know I have to do it. I am not letting him win and drag me back into hell. I can't put my family through this anymore.

"I consent," I finally say, my voice unsteady, a little breathy. The two words seem to echo around me off the white, sterile walls. I wonder how many people have spoken them in this exact room. I doubt I'm the first or the last. I don't know why it helps. I watch Richard's shoulders gradually relax, loosen, and lower as he lets out his breath. His relief is so palpable that I smell the tang and sweat of it.

Nurse Sarah nods, holding out the clipboard and the pen. My hand is trembling, the letters spiking, clumsy swirls, and looking nothing like my real name, as I sign on the dotted line. "The doctor will come in and talk to you about the process of what's next."

"Okay." I'm shivering, as I hand the pen back to her.

Nurse Sarah smiles at me, and I feel a rush of warmth towards her. She's helped save my life. "Good job, Victoria. This part wasn't easy, but you did it. It's now time for a new start." That's literally the name of the treatment center, I realize, and wonder if she gets paid to promote it. She removes my oxygen tubes, turning off the air supply. "You don't need these anymore." She gently touches my shoulder before turning to leave. I watch the butterfly wings flit and twirl between the strands of her blonde hair as she wheels the cart out.

Strange how I feel a bit naked without all the crutches I've relied on to stay alive. I can't seem to stop trembling. My teeth are chattering.

Richard looks concerned and sits closer. "Are you cold?" He tucks the covers around me.

I shake my head. My hands clench the white blankets, needing a shield, some protection from the reality of what is to come. "Just realizing it's actually happening."

"I'm proud of you."

Surprised, I look at him. I can't remember the last time he said those words to me. Of course, there isn't much to be proud of over the last few years. "You are?"

"It's a brave thing to do, Victoria. Not everyone can admit they need help."

I nervously bite my lip. I don't feel brave or strong, and I'm not a butterfly. "What if I can't do it?"

"Let's just get you in there. They will help us figure it out."

Us. He said us. As if he will be there, as if he wants to be, to stay. A possibility, long dead, flickers and stirs. "One day at a time?" I ask softly.

"Exactly." He shrugs helplessly, and I understand he doesn't know what to do any more than I do. "Please try."

Feeling overwhelmed, I look away. His eyes are hurting me. They are too blue, beautiful, and heartbreaking. I am very aware of how alone we are, how far apart we've become. Is there still a way to meet each other halfway? "Where's Lexy?"

"I let her sleep in. Becca went to her hotel to shower and change and said she would bring her back here later. Lexy was up pretty late on the phone last night."

"Really?" I ask, curious. "With who?"

"Someone named Nick, I think."

My brow creases as I try to recall the name. "Isn't he the one who works out on the ranch? I've heard Becca talking about him."

"Yeah."

The distraction helps, and my grip loosens on the blankets. I wonder how we are having such a normal conversation as if we are normal people, normal parents, a normal husband and wife. There's no way we could be. I've failed him too many times. "It's good she has a friend she can talk to."

"He sounds like he might be more than that. When I was up going to the bathroom, I heard a little of their conversation from the hallway. It seemed a bit intense."

I meet his gaze, and he gives me a knowing look. *Oh. Interesting.* I guess life does keep going on, whether I'm ready for it or not. "He must be important to her if she was up all night with him. We used to do that." I sneak it in carefully, a message slipped secretly underneath a door, trying to read him, gauging, checking to see if there's an opening, a glimmer of a chance left for me, a way back inside where he is.

"Yes, we did," he answers, his voice low and sad, and I wonder if he still remembers the late nights, the passion, the feverish exhilaration of blissfully unraveling in kisses and skin and hair and sheets. We'd go days on nothing more than two hours of sleep just so we could be together. We couldn't get enough of each other.

The awareness of how things used to be is thick between us. I can feel the heat radiating through his clothes. But he is still too quiet, too far away. I misread his guilt for indifference and resentment towards me and don't know what to do.

I look down at his hand. It's so close to mine, our fingers could brush, but he won't touch me. His wedding ring glints in the morning light. He's never taken it off. He's had every reason to over the years. I stare at the silver band. He hadn't wanted a gold one. Too traditional for us, he'd said. I want to laugh. Nothing about us has ever been traditional. Our initials are engraved on it. Back then, we believed in permanence. In sickness and in health. Til death do us part. All of it, and we were so convinced our love was strong enough to survive anything. I don't think this was ever what he signed up for. I fiercely hope we can find our way back.

I spread out the fingers of my left hand and noticed I had broken one of my fingernails. The tip is ridged and rough and uneven, clean down to the skin, and a little sensitive and sore. I don't remember breaking it, and wonder if it happened in the thrashing of detox. I look down at where my ring should be. My finger is too naked without the familiar weight and rub. I don't like it. "Do you know where my ring is?"

"I have it."

I touch my neck that is still bare. "My locket, too?"

He nods. "They took them off when you...um..." he falters, grief flashing in his eyes, and he clears his throat, taking a deep breath. "When you were brought in," he finishes, his voice gritty and strained. I notice his neck is flushed and remember that always happens to him when he is upset or stressed.

When I almost died. That's what he was going to say, and I involuntarily gasp and feel my body jerk at the shocking reality of how close I came. I would be gone right now, and he would be planning my funeral. The guilt is unbearable and tastes poisonous and bitter on my tongue. I want to break down and sob. He's very still, and I know he's thinking about it, too.

This conversation is what has been waiting for us in between everyone else. We haven't talked about it yet. We haven't dared. I desperately want to fix it and explain and plead for mercy. I open my mouth to say something, anything, but I don't know how, and it's too big and would shatter us completely, and my words fade out on a helpless, shuddering breath. The space between us is tense, stilted, and stalled as if the air itself has been told not to move. I lose my nerve and awkwardly change the subject.

"Do you think they will let me wear them in rehab?"

"We can find out."

"If they don't, will you save them for me?" I hope he understands what I'm asking him and that my question has to do with much more than a ring and a necklace. I want to know if he will wait for me, if he will still be there when, and if, we come out on the other side. I'm terrified of the finality that I'm down to my last few moments and days with him. What if he does leave? I'm relieved to see that at least his eyes look a little less dark.

"I will," he answers, and I think of our wedding vows. Do you take this woman? *I will.* We were so young, so certain, so hopelessly in love. A lifetime ago. *I do.* Two small little words that don't even begin to explain the gravity and complexity of what a marriage and a life together brings. There was so much we were unprepared for.

He's being so polite, so careful, so distant, tiptoeing around me. As if I'm a dangerous land mine or a grenade about to explode. My heart sinks. This is what I've done to us, driven us apart, pushed him to his limit. Is this how it's going to be with us from now on? Painful small talk, sidestepping and skirting around each other, avoiding direct eye contact? Everything I long to say hovers and hangs in the air above us. I don't know how to reach it or where to start. What if he can't forgive me? Or won't?

I look down at his ring again and tentatively reach out and touch the R and V that are engraved in scrolled, cursive letters. Everything in me aches. I feel him staring at the top of my head, trying to figure out what I'm doing, what I'm thinking, and where I'm going to take us next. I remember the look well. As if I'm made of fire or am a siren singing him to his death. I'm a dangerous, forbidden mystery he's always been fascinated by.

I'm so lost in my thoughts and pain I don't notice when he moves his hand, turning it over to where our fingers link, fitting perfectly, a missing puzzle piece. He wraps his tight around mine, and our palms touch. He used to say the creases of my lifelines led to his, and I wonder if he still thinks they do. Startled, my breath catches as I look up to see his face, unsure of what I will find. He's staring back at me, and I see the same questions, uncertainty, guilt, loneliness, and need.

Tears fill my eyes, my body flushing all over, the heat rising clear up into my scalp. I feel embarrassed, too exposed, and vulnerable.

I feel like an alcoholic. "I miss you," I whisper hoarsely and shake my head at how useless the words are. "I know I have no right to, and I understand if you don't love me anymore, but I—"

I don't finish the rest of my sentence because he's kissing me, his mouth hard, hot, and desperate. He hasn't touched me in years, and for a second, I'm stunned still at the surge of sensations. He's not careful now, and his hands are firm and a bit reckless, gripping at the back of my neck, pulling me close, holding me in place so I can't move. His fingers tangle into my hair, the roots pulling, tingling, and I don't care that it hurts. I crave it. I am starving for him, as we make up for lost time and broken promises, trying to reverse and repair the damage we left each other with. His mouth is greedy, his tongue hungrily parting my lips and diving into me as he breaks through all the years and barriers and doors I had slammed in his face, determined to get back inside, refusing to be shut out ever again.

I'm flung back twenty-five years to our first kiss in the parking lot behind the diner. The traffic had roared and rushed from the strip; car horns blared, music and voices echoed in the distance. Steam radiated off the grate, drifting hazily around us; the greasy scent of fries and burgers had mixed with our breath. And he had found me in a way no one else ever had. I knew then I never wanted to live without him.

Caught up in the frenzy, I grasp onto him, frantically touching anywhere I can find, holding on for dear life. He tastes the same, feels the same, is exactly the same. He's still in there, under all years of drunkenness, devastation, and disappointment. He still wants me, loves me. I haven't lost him. This is what I wanted. This is the part of his heart I needed to know still belongs to me.

He kisses me as if searching for reconciliation, as if trying to offer it to us both. As if he's remembering me, rediscovering me, reminding himself of the curve of my mouth, the taste and feel of my tongue, how it fits, melts, mixes with his. I thought we wouldn't know how to do this anymore or would have forgotten each other after all this time, that it would be awkward or uncomfortable or clumsy or too different. But it all comes rushing back so easily, so effortlessly, and I let him take me away into our past, our memories, our history, our habits, the intimate parts of each other only we know, reminiscing over how we were. As if he's recovering me, and it's still possible and worth it to find me.

After a few moments, he breaks the kiss, leaning his head weakly against mine. Our faces are close, our breath ragged and warm as they mingle, moist on our skin. His eyes are intense and beautifully blue, just like I remember. They are all I can see. I used to drown in them, and it was the most exquisite form of suffering I've ever known. He's crying, I realize, jolting. I didn't know he was and gently touch his damp face as my heart breaks. Why didn't I understand he needed this as much as me? Why didn't I see the guilt he was carrying? All I could feel was the crushing weight of my own and the shame over what I was doing to us.

"Don't leave me again," he says, his eyes burning intensely into mine, his words thick, each syllable pronounced, fierce, and forceful, making me listen and understand and go breathless. It's a thrilling relief.

"I won't." I'm sobbing, apologizing, begging his forgiveness, hoping there's still a chance at redemption. "I'm so sorry."

"Shhh. I know." He's kissing my face, my eyes, my tears. He whispers how sorry he is, how much he loves me, over and over, the words healing me, a balm on my bleeding soul. I don't want to let go of him, and he climbs into the hospital bed with me, being careful of the IV and tubes and tangled blankets. Still crying, we cling to each other.

"I kept dreaming you were gone," I muffle tearfully into his shoulder. "I was so afraid I had lost you."

"I'm not going anywhere," he soothes, his lips staying on the surface of my skin, as if needing constant contact. I think we both do. "I'm here."

I burrow into him, I can't get close enough, and he holds me tight. We lay together, arms, limbs, legs, hands wrapped and intertwined. Two bodies melded into one. It's been so long. My head is on his chest, and I imagine I'm eighteen again, in the back of his beat-up black corvette, two young dreamers in love, steaming up windows, listening to the radio, our hearts pounding just for each other.

"Do you remember our first date?" I ask, after a long while, when the quiet has lulled us and our tears have dried. He's holding me as if I am fragile and precious and important, and I desperately need him to.

"Yeah," he answers, and I hear him laugh softly. "We couldn't get a table at that Italian restaurant."

"You took me to the Santa Monica Pier, and we ate three dollar tacos and watched the sunset." That night seems like a hundred years ago, but the feelings are still so close and raw as if we were on the pier yesterday.

"Best first date I ever had."

My body is warm, content, against his. "Me too. That was the night I knew I loved you."

Chapter Twenty-Eight

"I knew way before then," he says.

"You did?" I ask, drifting in the afterglow of our conversation, a lovers haze glossing over us, lazy and hushed and intimate.

"Yeah. I knew the second you walked towards me in the diner."

"You just liked my southern accent and my waitress uniform," I tease, remembering how I used to leave the two top buttons undone just for him.

"Yes, I did," he says huskily, and I actually blush. I feel gloriously young and beautiful again.

I smile into the crook of his throat, where my lips always fit just right. I breathe him in. He even smells the same. Shampoo, Ivory soap, and the polo cologne that is his favorite. He's worn it ever since I've known him. He's so familiar, exactly where and how I left him. I feel safe for the first time in years, as if I've finally found my way home. Tilting my head, I study his jawline, the faint stubble on his skin, the dark fan of his lashes. I would know each feature with my eyes closed. I have him memorized. "When I'm out of rehab, can we go get another taco?"

I feel his smile. I somehow always could. I watch as it erases the lines of grief I had put on his face. "It's a date," he answers, as his fingertips trace lightly over the back of my neck, just under my hair, and I know he remembers it is my weak spot.

I ease back into him, into the groove and niche of his body, as if molded there, intricately carved into the shape of me. The doctor will be in soon to inform us of what our next steps will be. But, for right now, I'm not an alcoholic who is going into rehab in the morning.

For a few more minutes, it's just us, and we get to be two normal people who fell in love over twenty-five years ago at a hamburger joint in West Hollywood.

Chapter Twenty-Nine
BECCA

I never thought the first time I saw the ocean would be the day I dropped my sister off at rehab.

We say our goodbyes in the lobby as the staff checks her suitcases for stashed alcohol and weapons she can hurt herself with, inspecting each and every bottle of her deodorant, tubes of makeup, and tampons. They confiscate her mouthwash when they discover it's a brand with alcohol in it. I've already been patted down, my purse searched. Security is tight.

Victoria is visibly shaking as we hug. I feel her trembling against me. "I'll see you soon," I promise, trying to reassure and comfort her. Her eyes are wide and glassy, her breathing shallow. I don't think you're ever ready for something like this, and keep my arms tight around her, giving her something secure to hold onto. "I love you."

"I love you, too," she whispers, cringing as they rifle through her underwear and delicates. For a place that is anonymous, there is no privacy for the people who are admitted here. I notice her blushing and empathize with how violating and invasive this feels for her. Her rights were left behind at the front doors.

She releases me and turns to Richard and Lexy, desperately latching on as if seeking protection. They huddle together, holding hands, and clinging to one another. It's a sweet relief to see how close and connected they are. They will need each other to get through this. I will stay a few more days, just in case, until I know she's settled and staying and still willing to be sober. I don't want her to hurt herself again. I'm grateful her every move will be monitored.

The facility grants permission to wear her locket and wedding ring, explaining it helps to have personal reminders of the people you are trying to get clean for. Richard puts both on her himself, kissing her as if proposing as he slides the ring on her finger. The exchange is so tender, so intense, and intimate, tears fill my eyes, and I quietly step outside to give them a moment to themselves.

Fresh air fills my lungs as I take a deep breath and walk out into the bright California sunshine. Wiping my tears, I lift my face and let the golden rays warm my skin. The glare off the water is dazzling and blinding, and I put my sunglasses on to shield my eyes. All the stories I heard growing up were true about the breathtaking beauty of the Pacific Ocean.

The treatment center is tucked up in the Malibu hills, high above the loud, hectic bustle of the city. Palm trees stand in a tall, crooked line, their leaves spiking up against the wide, blue cloudless sky. I scan the horizon looking out across miles of sparkling waves. The scenery is so different from the flat green acres of our ranch. The breeze is light and a bit cool and smells of sand and seaweed, and I can taste a hint of salt on my lips.

It feels good to be out of the hospital. The last few weeks have been a whirlwind of worrying and waiting. I've barely had a second to think. And now, here we are. I still can't believe Victoria is agreeing to do it, but I think, after her overdose, she realizes she has no other choice. I turn away from the view and look up at the blue logo, *A New Start*, displayed above the doors of the facility. Waves jut off the side of the letters as if rising. It's a nice, hopeful touch.

The staff is kind and understanding, but strict, and you are only allowed so far past the front desk. Rules and routines will be enforced and followed. It is rehab, after all. I'm very aware of the fact of how easily I could have been the one admitted to a place like this if I had made different choices. The thought haunts me.

Even outside, I still have the sense of being watched. Security guards stand near the front door and around the grounds in case of conflicts or confrontations between staff and patients. They also make sure no one from the outside tries to sneak in any drugs or alcohol and keep a close eye on everything and everyone who enters and exits the property. I'm at the edge of how far the residents are allowed to go. There's another gate we pass through to be granted permission to leave. Cameras are on the roof, and I wonder if they recognize the same darkness in me that my sister wrestles against. We come from the same bad seed. Feeling exposed, I turn back towards the stunning, serene view of the water.

The beauty makes me homesick for the land and horses, the heat and humidity. My own bed. Ben. I wish he were here to share this with me. I miss him terribly. He's too far, hundreds of miles from my reach. I've never been away from him this long.

Hearing the doors open behind me, I turn, thinking it might be Lexy. Richard steps out. He's alone. Seeing me, he walks over, seeming glad to have someone he recognizes, even if we barely know each other. I think he's a bit shaken up.

"She's all checked in?" I ask when he's in earshot.

He nods, looking dazed and overwhelmed. He has a dark blue folder in his hand with the facility information and a schedule for their family sessions and visitor rules. "They just took her back to her room."

I notice how pale he is. "You okay?"

He seems surprised that I would ask. We're family, but not friends. He sighs, shaking his head. "Don't exactly do something like this every day."

Who does? I wonder. Probably more people than we realize, and I bet all of them thought it would never happen to them. "No, I guess not." I turn and look back towards the double doors. They are tinted dark for privacy and anonymity. "Where's Lexy?"

"They needed her signature on one of the forms, and then she was going to the restroom. It's almost an hour back down into the valley. She'll be out in a minute." He falls quiet again, gazing out over the water, and I wonder if he feels as awkward as I do. "At least Victoria will have this view to look at for the next month."

We're standing side by side, but we couldn't be further apart. "It's definitely beautiful here." I watch a seagull soar and skim over the waves, dive under, the foam splashing as it penetrates and disappears beneath the surface. It re-emerges less than a minute later, drifting and bobbing along with the tides, seemingly happy and content with its catch. The simplicity soothes. "First time I've ever seen the ocean, so it's worth the trip."

"You've never been?" He's asking as someone who is used to being around water instead of pastures and horses.

"The nearest beach to our ranch is about a six-hour drive. We're inland, " I explain, even though I already know he doesn't relate to the geography of East and Middle and West Tennessee. Country life is a foreign concept to him. He doesn't seem like the farm type. "It's nothing compared to this."

I'm not sure what to say next. We've run out of small talk, and the only thing we have in common is Lexy and Victoria, which is a whole other can of worms. I haven't been alone with him since arriving in California. With all the chaos and confusion, I haven't had a moment to give much thought to more than just praying Victoria stays alive. But now, it's only the two of us, outside a rehab center, waiting to find out where our lives have finally landed after the tornado has passed. Debris from unresolved family history is everywhere.

One of us has to offer the olive branch, I realize. We're both here with no way out. And I have years of things to say. Sunlight streams from behind him, around him, bringing out the gray in his hair, shadowing and accentuating the lines of grief and stress on his face. His eyes are rimmed red from crying, causing the blue to shine more brilliantly. He's handsome in one of those effortless ways men like him don't have to think about. He still looks like a lawyer, even dressed down in casual tan slacks and a black polo shirt.

I can feel him wanting to explain himself to me, to defend himself, but he doesn't. It's almost as if he's accepted the judgment and condemnation he's so certain I've placed on him. He isn't wrong. I have thought exactly what he thinks I have. But now, face to face with him, all I feel is pity. Watching him with Lexy and Victoria over the last few weeks has changed my mind about him, and helped me see him in a new light. He never once left their side.

"Lexy told me you are taking a little more time off work."

He glances at me and nods, the tension in the air easing a bit now that one of us finally said something. "Just until we see how all this goes. I'm still checking in every day and am consulting on some cases, but I have handed most of the load over to one of my associates. We're going to be back and forth here for the family therapy sessions, so I wanted to make sure I was available."

"That's probably a good idea. When do you come back?"

He opens the folder and looks at the schedule, the breeze rustling the papers. "Wednesday is our first meeting. And we will be here on Saturdays for visitor days."

"I didn't think they would let you visit so soon."

"Me neither, but they said it's good for her. It will help her feel more supported and know she's not alone. We just have to make sure we follow the rules." He closes the folder, tucking it under his arm.

I hear what he's not saying. Them being here will give her something to live for and a reason to stay sober. "Seems like there's a lot of them in there." I glance behind me at the security guards again. They stare straight ahead, but I know they miss nothing. Uneasy, I deliberately look back towards Richard. "I imagine it will be reassuring for you and Lexy to be able to see her."

He nods. "When do you have to fly home?"

"Tuesday morning, but I told them I'd call in if they need me for any of the sessions. The front desk has my numbers." The breeze has picked up, strands of my hair are blowing across my face, and I push my sunglasses up on top of my head to hold them back. I feel like he needs to see my eyes. Or maybe I want to see his. He watches me closely, carefully, reading me, his gaze penetrating, riveting, and I wonder if he looks at people in court the same way. He knows how to put people at ease and disarm them, and I can see why he's a good lawyer. I read he was the youngest to make partner in his firm. Ironic how you can be so successful when the rest of your life is falling apart, but I guess if you're failing at one thing, you desperately seek control somewhere else. "What about school for Lexy? Isn't she supposed to start soon?"

"Yeah, next week. She's going to do this semester online. It's easier for now. There's just a lot we don't know yet."

"Taking it one day at a time?" I ask.

He shrugs helplessly. "What else do we do?"

He's so lost, I realize, my heart softening a little more. I feel strangely protective of him. Addiction is an odd way to level the ground between people. I realize I haven't wanted to like him and have held a barrier up between us all this time. I have blamed him for the years of silence, believing he agreed with my sister's reasons, not understanding the fear and consequences he was up against. The walls between us begin to shift, erode, and crumble. "I don't know," I murmur.

"Thank you for being here. It's really helped. I know it's meant a lot to Victoria. And of course, Lexy."

"It's meant a lot to me, too." I look at him and decide it's time to lay it all out, break through the ice, the past, all the years of silence and misunderstanding. And all the things I understood much too perfectly and painfully. "Lexy told me you gave her my letters. Thank you for doing that."

He faces me then, fully, completely, hiding nothing, and I almost back up from his intensity. I'm surprised at how easily he lets his guard down as if he's been waiting for me to ask him to. His eyes are heartbreakingly earnest as they meet mine. "I wanted Lexy to find you. It was the only way I knew how to save her. To save both of them. I knew how important your letters were. Victoria needed them even if she didn't know how to tell you or reach out. Maybe I was doing it for all of you. Thank you for taking care of her."

I smile tenderly, thinking of my niece. "It was kind of the other way around. She's a great girl."

He glances behind him at the doors, as if wanting to make sure Lexy is never far off and still safe. "Yes, she is."

"I appreciate you bringing the letters Victoria wrote back to me." I had stayed up all night, reading every single one. I sobbed as she confessed her fears and told me about the nightmares and her drinking. She knew it was getting out of control and didn't know how to stop it. It was as if I had been her secret diary all these years, just like when we were young. She's always been the one person I've trusted most.

"I had no idea she was writing to you. But I think it helped her. Even if she never sent them."

"I'm guessing she didn't really talk about what happened to us."

"Some of it. But there was so much she wouldn't tell me. And then the drinking took over. Sometimes I think it made things better," he murmurs absently, and I don't think he meant to say it out loud. I see the flicker of disgust when his words register, and he shakes his head, appalled at himself. They are absurd, but they somehow make sense to me, too. I lived it and know all too well how chaos can somehow become normal. You get used to it. He rubs his hand over his face. "That's such a sick thing to say. I know that. But it took away her pain, and just for a moment, she didn't have to feel or remember any of it. I didn't know how to help her. But somehow, the drinking did." His eyes are dark, dulling as he stares at the front doors of the rehab center. "Until it didn't." He looks back at me, his expression anguished. "I'm sorry I couldn't get her to come back to you. I swear I tried."

He is asking for more than me just to believe him. He wants my forgiveness, for someone to finally let him off the hook where he's been dangling for over twenty years. I wonder when the last time he was asked how he felt, what he wanted, how close he was to losing his mind. He's no different than me. He's just hiding under a different porch. He looks so young and stranded as he says it, so vulnerable. My heart aches for him. I know exactly what it's like to love someone even as they are destroying you. I want to hug him but make myself stand still. Maybe we have more in common than I thought. "I understand."

He lets out an unsteady breath as if I handed him permission to finally release the past. "Can I ask you something?"

I nod. He's surprisingly easy to talk to. I hadn't thought he would be. I was wrong in a lot of ways about him. "Sure."

"How didn't you end up like her? You grew up in that house, too. Why didn't you drink?" He hesitates, his eyes apologetic. "You can tell me it's none of my business."

"No, it's fine. I ask myself that all the time." I sigh, thinking back over my life, every decision and chance. All I can see is my father at each crossroad. His face and fists made me who I am today, for better or worse. "I saw what the drinking did to all of us, and I never wanted to turn out like him. I always knew there was a good possibility I could and that I wouldn't want to stop. So I just never drank."

"Never?" He asks, his voice incredulous. "Not once?"

I shake my head. "No. Not one sip. There's not even any alcohol in our house. After daddy died, Ben helped me dump out every last bottle. It took us a while, but we finally found them all."

"We're doing that now. I've already thrown out most of it." He looks past me, towards the direction of where his house is, as if he can see it from up here, thinking of all the corners, cushions, cabinets where she stashed her supply. "I hope anyway. She has a lot of hiding places."

"They usually do," I murmur, thinking of daddy tucking bottles of Wild Turkey under floorboards in the storehouse. He was a mean, sad, desperate drunk. "It's strangely cleansing."

He seems to think about it. "Yeah, it is." He studies me as if realizing he's found an ally and fellow survivor. I can't help thinking how different he is from Ben. He's intense, charismatic, a lot like Victoria. People always stop and stare whenever she walks into a room. I've never possessed the same presence as her. Mama always said she'd have her name in lights one day. Ben is calm and steady, a solid rock, ruggedly handsome, salt of the earth type. I can't wait to get back home to him. "I guess we'll be seeing you in Tennessee whenever she's released. I saw the pictures you sent. It looks like a beautiful place."

I nod. "It is. I think it's going to be a really important part of her healing and recovery. That land is why she's here." I motion over my shoulder at the treatment center. "Hopefully, she will be able to handle it."

"We'll see," he murmurs, and I think he will be saying that a lot in the uncertainty of the days ahead. "I hear it's pretty hot and humid there."

"Yeah, but you get used to it." I shrug, smiling. "Sort of."

"I'm looking forward to finally meeting Ben."

Even his name makes my heart beat faster. "You'll like him. Everyone does."

He sends me a sly glance. "And Nick?"

I can't help laughing a little. Lexy told me how Nick called her, and they stayed up all night talking. He's still texting her, sending pictures of Glory, and saying a few other things that make Lexy blush and tilt her phone away so none of us can see. I'm happy to see the nudge I told Ben to give him worked. Or, in Nick's case, a swift kick in his stubborn pants. Watching Lexy's face light up is a precious distraction. For a few moments, she gets to simply be a young, normal girl who likes a boy. And they will be good for each other. Wounded finding wounded. Funny how you always seem to recognize your own.

"Yeah, something tells me you'll be hearing a lot more about him." My smile widens a little more at his concerned expression. "Don't worry; he's a good guy."

I know he wants to ask me more, but doesn't, and I wonder when he will finally feel like he's her father again, or if he's ever felt like one. "So, now what do we do?" he asks, but I think he's talking more to himself.

"I have no idea. But I do know one thing." I reach out my hand to shake his. "It was nice to finally meet you."

He looks startled and studies me as if trying to figure out if I'm serious. After a moment, he smiles for the first time in weeks and takes my hand in his. "It's nice to meet you, too."

Lexy comes out of the doors, and we both look as she walks over to us. I see her take a deep breath and let it out as the view of the ocean greets her. I have the thought she's been waiting to breathe freely for the last eighteen years. I feel the burden lift off her and imagine she's relieved to finally have someone else carry it for her. Her cheeks are pink and flushed from crying. I know how worried she is for Victoria. She notices the guards, and her steps quicken to put distance between her and them. I think they make her nervous, too, and reach out my hand. She takes it as soon as she's close enough.

"They are going to let mom keep her phone," she says.

"Really?" Richard asks. "I didn't think they would."

"Yeah, the lady at the front desk just told me. They will monitor her though. But she can still call and text us."

"That's good." Richard smiles, relieved to still have contact with his wife.

"Here's her room number." She pulls a card with writing on it out of the back pocket of her jeans, hands it to Richard, and he puts it in the folder. "They said she's going to meet her sponsor today."

"Her sponsor," Richard repeats numbly, and I feel him trying to process and keep up with the heavy reality of where we are. "It's all really happening." He stands a little closer to Lexy as if trying to shield her, and maybe himself. "Are you okay? I know this is a lot to deal with."

Lexy nods. "I'm alright," she reassures him. "I'm just glad she's finally here."

"Me too," he says, still watching her, checking and rechecking. I can tell he's trying to make up for lost time and is afraid of losing her again. We're all balancing on breaking branches, struggling to find solid ground. "Are you hungry? You haven't eaten anything since last night."

"Yeah, a little."

He looks at me. "Would you like to come over and have lunch with us? We don't have a lot in the house right now, but maybe we can order pizza or something."

I realize he needs it, the connection, normalcy, and stability in a situation where there is still so much unknown. Something to do to keep from going crazy during the time in between the days they can come see Victoria. I'm not ready to be alone yet, either. The hotel room is too quiet and lonely. Pizza is familiar and comforting. Pizza is what a family eats together. "That sounds perfect," I say. Lexy smiles at me and squeezes my hand.

Richard nods, and we head down the hill towards the parking lot. We have the luxury of being able to leave. We all try not to notice the camera angling and zooming in on us as we exit the grounds. The guards check our ID at the gate but let us go. As we drive away, I take one last glance at the ocean, hoping the next time I see it won't be at a rehab facility. We make small talk about the weather and how pretty the view is—ordinary, almost boring, mindless things. I think we need a break from the stress. None of us acknowledges how we're all waiting for Victoria to decide where this one day at a time will take us.

Chapter Thirty
VICTORIA

Sunlight warms my face as I look out the window, watching my family walk down the hill, talking and laughing together, as if it's a normal day, as if there's such a thing for us, and we are a typical family and have been this way all our lives.

Becca and Richard seem to have cleared the air and come to a truce. Curiosity has me wishing I could have gotten closer, followed them, eavesdropped. Their conversation is one that's been waiting to be hashed out for years. And I'm the reason they've never spoken before now, leaving them all to clean up my mess and repair the damage my drinking caused.

Steam from my breath mists the glass, blurring the three of them into ghostly silhouettes. They're out of sight now, leaving, disappearing, achingly too far away.

Feeling abandoned and much too vulnerable, I wrap my arms around my body and look around. My room is pretty; the colors deliberately designed to soothe, decorated in pale shades of green and mauve and cream. The double bed is plush, the blankets thick and fluffy and comforting. Lexy was right. It looks like a spa here.

I'll have to remember to tell her, and I am relieved they let me keep my phone so I can.

My gaze lands on the serenity prayer hanging in a wooden frame on the wall. Walking over, I stand in front of it. I'm pretty sure they have it posted in every room. There is even a plaque in the lobby.

God, grant me the serenity to accept the things I cannot change, the courage to change the things I can, and the wisdom to know the difference.

I read the words over and over, mouthing them to myself, hoping they will magically sink, soak, seep through my clothes into my skin. Cure me. Heal me. Change me. I'm desperate for something more, something else, somewhere other than the darkness of where I've been.

Serenity. Such a small, simple phrase with a big impact. I don't even know what it means, much less feels like. I don't think I've experienced it in my life. The drinking fooled me into thinking I had found it, but the glossy high haze eventually wore off, forcing me to come thudding painfully back down into the ugly reality and consequences waiting for me.

The hangovers were never peaceful. They were sour, excruciating, throbbing, and violent. That will be one thing I won't miss about being a drunk, and I have a feeling this prayer will become my mantra and battle cry—an alcoholic's survival guide.

To distract myself from the loneliness, I unpack, but I'm done too quickly. The silence makes me edgy, and I am not sure what else to do. It's 1:42 in the afternoon. I'd be blacked out by now. I haven't been sober in years and don't know how to be alone.

I'm too awake, too aware, feeling way too much, and I have nothing to protect me from it. My thoughts sound urgent and loud inside my head, and each one wants a drink. Badly. Sweat breaks out over my skin from the craving. My old habits are definitely dying hard. A familiar screaming madness rises up in me. My palms are hot and itching, and I wipe my damp hands on the thighs of my jeans, tucking them deep in my pockets to keep from reaching out for something I can no longer have. I would normally be holding a bottle and miss the cool, heavy pressure and grip of it, like a phantom limb.

A knock on the door makes me jump as if they heard what I was thinking, and alarms silently sounded, and they came running. Feeling guilty, I turn as it opens, assuming they have their own set of keys and wonder how many people have tried to escape. Quite a few, I'd imagine. The staff probably doesn't want to leave us on our own for too long. I can see why. The interruption was just in time.

"Hey, anyone in here?" A brunette woman with a sleek bobbed haircut and warm hazel eyes steps in. She's a little shorter than me. "You must be Victoria." When I nod, she smiles. "I'm Andie." She holds out her hand. "I'm your sponsor."

No backing out now, I realize. I'd never make it past all the guards surrounding the grounds anyway. And how would I face my family if I left? Anxious and unsure, I shake her hand. "Hi."

"I understand if you think it's not nice to meet me yet. Hopefully, I can change your mind." She glances around the room, and I wonder if she's searching for a secret stash. "Looks like you're getting settled in."

"Yes." The air smells like Caribbean breeze diffuser oils. I think they want rehab to feel like a tropical vacation. "It's a pretty room."

Andie nods. "Not a bad place to get clean. I dried out in a place that looked like a motel in a horror movie, so this is definitely a step up. I want to make sure you have my cell number." She holds her card out to me. "Please put this in your phone. Call me day or night. I mean it. I'm here to walk you through all this."

I take the card from her. She stands there, expectedly waiting, and I realize she means right now. Flustered, I pull my phone out of my jeans pocket and nervously program in her name and number. My hands are still shaking from the shock of being here. She watches, making sure I save her contact information, telling me to send her a text, which I obediently do. She's smaller than me, but somehow, I'm intimidated. She already seems to know too much about me. It's unnerving.

Her phone dings. "Good," she says, as she programs me into hers. "Use it as much as you need to. I'm your life raft in all this, but I can only help you as much as you let me."

I set her card on my nightstand next to the Holy Bible. I bet they have those in every room, too. I haven't read it since Sunday school with Grandma Rose and wonder what Jesus would think of me now. Am I too far gone to be saved? "I'm surprised we are allowed to have phones and computers in here. I didn't think we could."

"Some facilities don't let you, but we do. We have found that people respond better if they feel like they are trusted. You only lose it if you abuse it. You always have a choice. You can even leave if you want to." She studies me, and I feel myself flush, fighting the urge to squirm. Her eyes are too direct, and I have too many sins. "Something tells me you won't. Since you're already unpacked, I wanted to ask if you'd like to join us for support group. It's in about fifteen minutes."

I freeze. "Now?" My voice comes out with a squeak. "I just got here."

"You're already at rock bottom. You have somewhere else to go?"

Who talks to someone like this? I wonder, my mouth falling open. I should be offended, annoyed, and angry even. If I were anywhere else, I might be. But I'm in rehab, and I lost the right to be upset about someone's comments the second I walked through the doors. I don't know why it makes me laugh. It shouldn't. There's something about her I like. Her eyes remind me of my mama, somehow gently tough. She has deep lines creasing her face that seem to be more from pain and suffering rather than age. She has the weathered feel of someone who has seen things no one should ever have to and survived it. War-weary.

I don't realize yet that this woman will become one of the most vital, important, and dearest relationships I will ever have. I don't know that in a matter of two years, I will be a sponsor just like her. I don't know how hard and fiercely she will fight for me and how drastically she will change my life.

All I do know is how desperately I still want a drink.

"No, I guess not." I'm still laughing as the words come out. Adrenaline is surging, making me jittery as I try to cope.

"There you go," Andie says, smiling. "It's good to laugh. People tend to forget how in all this. It's important to enjoy the simple moments."

"I haven't laughed in a long time," I answer, realizing it.

"You'll remember," she assures me. "I'm leading the group. And the coffee here isn't half bad. Come on. I'll show you around. You will need to know anyway. You'll be with us a lot. The women here will become as close as an annoying sister you can't get away from."

Following her out, I try to absorb my surroundings as we walk side by side down the hall. The sage green carpet is patterned with swirling gold leaves and acorns. Dreamy paintings of seascapes are on the walls. I think I hear Enya ethereally singing around us. Everything about this place feels like a cozy, warm cocoon, and I imagine they did that on purpose. Andie is still talking, and I make myself tune back in.

"Just wanted to give you a little background on me since we will be spending so much time together. I was an alcoholic for eight years. Lost my job, my husband, my home. I alienated my kids. I didn't want to get clean. Didn't think I needed to. Everyone else was the one with the problem. But, I have a brother who loved me no matter what, and he rescued me. I was living in my car when he got me into rehab. I fought him. Cussed him out. Even punched him and broke his nose, but he didn't give up on me." She looks at me. "You have people who love you?"

A few weeks ago, I would have been afraid of that question. I wouldn't have known the answer. Out of instinctive habit, I touch the locket around my neck, relieved to have it back. My wedding ring is securely on my finger. I blush, remembering the kiss Richard gave me, and press my lips together, trying to hold onto the taste and feel of his mouth, already missing him.

"Yes." I'm surprised when I choke up. My emotions are so raw, so close to the surface. Even my skin is sore and tender. I'm used to being numb, nothing and no one. It's hard adjusting to feeling human again. "My husband and daughter," I answer hoarsely. "I also have a sister." My face is hot. Embarrassed, I wipe my eyes. "I'm sorry. I don't know why I'm crying."

"Don't apologize. It's a good thing to know you're loved. It's hard to believe it after everything that has happened. Hold onto those people, Victoria. They will help you find your why."

"My why?"

"Your reason to get clean and stay clean. My brother helped me find mine. Some people have God. Others have art or music. Even exercise. Find something you're passionate about. Who did you used to want to be?"

My mind rewinds back to the day I ran from the ranch with Grandmother Rose's guitar, reckless and determined, my entire being on fire with the love of music. "I wanted to be a singer," I admit, shaking my head. It seems like a fairytale now, childish and ridiculous and foolish. I can't remember where my guitar is. I hid it in one of my drunken stupors, unable to bear being reminded of how far I had fallen. "But, I haven't sung in years."

"Well, this is a great place to find your way back to that. You need more to live for than your next drink. We have a strict routine and schedule here. The main rule is that the AA meetings are mandatory. You can't make it through this without them. We have one at ten in the morning and another at seven in the evening. You must go to one every day. Since you missed the morning session, you go tonight. Do you understand?"

I don't dare argue. "I understand."

"Good. I'll be there with you. You won't be alone in any of this. Breakfast is from seven to nine. After that, we have our quiet reflection times where you will journal, take inventory, and do your study work. Then we have meetings and support groups. You'll do weekly therapy sessions. We have yoga classes and meditation. A gym. A pool. We want you to stay active. Keeps the mind clear and your hands from becoming idle. Staying a good kind of busy will help with the cravings. Channel them somewhere else. Lunch is at noon and dinner at six. No visitors are allowed after eight at night and lights out at ten."

"That's a lot to remember." I'm breathless, trying to keep up. Her pace is as fast as her words. The ring of keys she's holding jangle and clink together as we walk. They sound like notes in my head. Maybe the music isn't silenced after all. I used to hear it everywhere, in everything, and wonder if I could ask Richard to find my guitar and bring it here. I'll need something else to hold onto besides a drink.

"You have a schedule in your room, along with the pamphlets of all the activities and classes. I encourage you to get involved with the women here. You'll need them, even if you think you won't. I met my best friend in rehab. We got clean together and still talk every day. For now, let's just start with one meeting and take it from there. I've been sober for sixteen years, forty-two days, and..." she checks her watch, "...nine hours. And still counting."

Astonished, I stare at her, and she smiles. I like how honest she is. I didn't think I would. It's oddly refreshing.

"Recovery is possible, Victoria. I'm living proof of it." She brushes her bangs out of her eyes. "What part of the South are you from?"

My heart sinks, dropping queasily into my stomach. I have a feeling I will be talking a lot about the ranch, my drunk of a father. His fists. The porch. "Tennessee." I hear the flatness, the death, and bitterness of my tone.

"I have a cousin who lives there. Out in Knoxville. It's beautiful."

Flashbacks of the old, warped floorboards pressing into my sweaty cheek as Becca and I cowered under the bed crash into my mind. Wincing, I look away, not answering, focusing on the swirling gold leaves on the carpet disappearing under my feet.

Andie studies me. "Did I hit a nerve?" I don't look at her as I stiffly nod. "Good. Get used to it. That's why you're here."

Wounded and bruised, I warily look over at her. I'm already exhausted.

"You're only as sick as your secrets," she says as if I asked her something. Maybe I did.

"I have a lot of them," I confess, trying to warn her what she's getting herself into.

She stops abruptly and faces me, meets my eyes, and holds them. Startled, I go completely still. I don't look away. I can't seem to move. I feel like I'm being seen for the first time in my life. One addict rescuing another.

"Who doesn't?" she asks gently, and my body flushes warm with a strange release of relief. "You're more than an alcoholic, Victoria. I'm going to help you remember how to believe that. You just have to trust me." She starts walking again, and feeling a bit shaky and stunned, I follow silently beside her, trying to absorb the chance she's offering me. We reach the end of the hall, and she opens a door. "Here we are."

Hesitating, I pause, but then realize Andie is right. I have nowhere else to go. Forcing myself to cross the threshold, I walk into a room that looks more like where a family would hang out rather than a support group.

Comfy, overly large couches and chairs are positioned in a circle, facing each other. A round mahogany table with coasters and Kleenex boxes is in the middle. Against the back wall is a coffee and tea station. Chocolate chip cookies are piled on a plate, and a box of donuts is next to paper cups, napkins, sugar, and creamer. I wonder if sweets can become a new addiction. You have to get a fix somehow. Trade in the high for something else.

There are ten other women in the meeting. They look over when I walk in. Andie introduces me. "Good afternoon, everyone. This is Victoria. She will be joining us today."

The women smile. Some say hello. I nervously nod. I'm not sure if I say anything. Feeling exposed, I don't look anyone in the eye for too long, fearing they all have X-ray vision and can see every mistake I've ever made. Guess I'll have to get used to that, too. Andie moves away from me to talk with an older lady with gray hair, and I realize addiction can get a hold of anyone at any age. Left to my own devices, I stand by the coffee station, fidgeting with my hair, and adjusting my shirt. A stained, tainted wallflower.

A swatch of green catches my eye, and I notice a packet of Mint Medley herbal tea tucked in with the other flavors. My heart wrenches as I think of Lexy. I can still see how worried and frightened her eyes were as she wiped away my vomit, combed my tangled hair, and dressed me. I was a pathetic, pitiful, helpless mess. My hands tremble slightly as I pick it up, the smell of mint wafting through the wrapper. The scent is painfully familiar and reminds me of too many disgusting, nauseating, hungover mornings.

I almost put it back but then decide to use it as a reminder of who I don't want to be ever again and deliberately open it. As I drop the bag into the steaming water, I can't help thinking of the irony of Lexy making it for me, and now I'm drinking it in rehab. It's funny in a sick, twisted way how life works out.

Waiting for the tea to steep, I look up at the sign on the wall where the rules for the group are posted. No cross-talk. Give everyone a turn. No interrupting. No touching. Tell each other the truth. The last line strikes me, and I stare at it. How am I supposed to do that? I haven't told the truth in so long. It's too traumatic and ugly. What if I can't handle it? What if the others can't stand hearing what I've done? Where I've been? I start to panic. I don't know how to do this. What have I gotten myself into?

A bit frantic, I move to back up towards the door, but just as I do, a young woman with long dyed blonde hair comes up next to me, blocking my path. I distractedly notice there are streaks of pink and blue hidden within the light-colored strands. She reminds me of a mermaid. She doesn't look much older than Lexy, and I'm curious how she ended up here. She smiles at me as she prepares a cup of coffee. I don't think I smile back. I can't feel my legs. "I'm Kayla. Your first day?"

"Yeah." Still reeling, I notice she has a nose ring and a tattoo on her wrist that says breathe, and I wonder if she needs the constant reminder. I think maybe we all do and unconsciously let out the breath I'm holding. "I'm Victoria."

"Nice to meet you. I like your accent. It reminds me of that movie Sweet Home Alabama." I don't tell her I'm not from there. I can't seem to say anything at all as she stirs in cream and sugar, but she doesn't notice as she keeps talking. "I know this all is a lot to take in. You have that deer-caught-in-headlights look. I felt the same way when I first got here." She blows on her coffee, waiting for it to cool, watching me over the rim. "I can tell you're trying to figure out how old I am. Everyone asks. I'm twenty. My mom was a drunk. Guess I wanted to be just like her," she jokes, but neither of us laughs. "Had my first drink at thirteen and never stopped. Until now. I'm twenty-six days clean. How many days sober are you?"

I realize not drinking literally comes down to counting the seconds and minutes and hours of sobriety. "Um...I'm not sure. I haven't had a drink in fifteen days, but I've been in the hospital though, so..." I shrug, trail off.

"Overdose?" she asks, and I blink, stunned at how blunt she is. She doesn't even flinch.

For some reason, I nod. "Uh...yeah," I admit. I should feel humiliated, but I don't. There's no judgment from her at all, only raw empathy. She's easy to talk to and doesn't seem to mind uncomfortable silences. I have the sense she also grew up trying to outsmart the fist and dodge the blows. *Just like I did*, I realize, and have the urge to wrap a blanket around the two of us, to somehow keep us both safe from more harm. I feel as if I'm looking at myself twenty years ago. "How did you know that?"

"You still have the puncture marks on your wrist from the IV."

"Oh," is all I can manage, flushing hotly. Feeling ashamed, I try to pull my sleeve down to cover the evidence of my attempted suicide.

Noticing the movement, she touches my arm as if trying to offer me comfort. "You don't have to hide anything with us. A lot of people in here have tried to end their lives. They think there's no other way out, and we've all done things we wish we hadn't," she says, and I think she's trying to remind herself as much as me. "Rock bottom makes people desperate."

"Did you? Overdose, I mean?" I can't believe I'm asking the question. This is a typical conversation in rehab, I guess. Gritty, gross, graphically real.

She shakes her head, still unfazed and so matter of fact, the way someone responds when they've seen too much and haven't lived a sheltered life. Innocence lost. Nothing shocks her anymore, and I wish I could somehow protect her from that, too.

"No. I was found blacked out at a bus stop. I don't even remember how I got there. I ended up spending the night in jail for resisting an officer. Can't remember that, either. My boyfriend wouldn't let me come back home or see my son until I went into rehab. But I get my thirty-day sobriety chip soon. You will get one for your first twenty-four hours of being here."

"Twenty-four hours?" I repeat, confused. "Why?"

She picks up a cookie and bites into it. Her fingernails are painted with glittery purple nail polish. Everything about her seems to sparkle with the resilience of youth. "It's not as easy as it sounds. The first few days are the hardest. A lot of people leave," she says with her mouth full. "They can't handle it. You have to learn how to be you again." She points the cookie at me as if making a point. "Without the bottle."

I've never known how to be me. I haven't wanted to. It was the whole reason I drank in the first place. I think of the few moments alone in my room where I could actually taste the vodka on my tongue and swallow hard. I miss the clink of the glass rim against my teeth. My mouth instinctively fills with saliva, already anticipating the burn and rush. The back of my neck under my hair is clammy. "Yeah, I guess I do."

"Don't worry," she reassures me. Swallowing the last bite of cookie, she licks the chocolate from her fingers. I'm surprised she can eat. Nerves are making my stomach knot up. "It gets easier. I can't wait for my chip. I'm getting clean for my son. He's two. I'm here, so I don't lose him. His name is Adam. Want to see a picture?"

Before I can answer, she's setting her coffee down on the table and pulling her phone out of her pocket. She's one of the people here who didn't abuse the privilege of having it. She's beaming with pride as she shows me photos of a curly-haired little boy grinning from a sandbox, his face smudged with dirt and sticky from whatever it is children find to shove in their mouths. I can't help smiling at his simple joy and sweetness. I don't remember ever seeing Lexy smile like that. "He's beautiful."

"You have any kids?"

I nod. "A daughter. Lexy. She's eighteen." We're both aware of how close in age they are and the choices Kayla has made.

"Hope she doesn't drink."

I don't think Lexy has ever had a drink in her life. I hope to God I haven't passed my addictions onto her. I uselessly wish that I could go back in time and never buy that first bottle of vodka. Or the second or third or hundredth. "She doesn't. I probably scared it out of her."

"Let's hope so," Kayla murmurs. "Don't want her ending up here." The thought terrifies me. I'm not sure what else to say and quietly sip my tea, my hands shaking slightly. She must sense how overwhelmed I feel because she changes the subject. "It's a lot to talk about over cookies and donuts, isn't it? You'll get used to it. And then you'll start to need it. Recovery becomes your new addiction. Don't ask me how that works. I still don't get it. But it's definitely better than where I was."

"Okay, everyone," Andie says. "Let's have a seat. Make sure your cell phones are turned off." She motions for me to sit next to her. The thought flashes through my mind that I could still try to make a break for it. But I realize I no longer feel like running. I have too much to lose and find myself sitting in a circle with ten other women at my first AA support group. Kayla is across from me on the couch. It helps that I can see her, and I'm hoping it's also reassuring for her.

Andie reiterates the rules and then opens up the space for sharing. She goes around the circle, one by one. I'm not sure what to expect and am relieved I'm last and can wait and listen as the women share about how they ended up in a place like this.

For the first few minutes, I sit there, guarded and closed off, wary, mistrusting, reluctant. I don't see how any of this will apply to me, and I can feel my own resistance, and even arrogance, that I'm somehow different from all of them. What could any of these women say to help me? They don't know where I've been, what I've done. I'm nothing like them. I'm not even sure I belong here.

But as we go around the room, their stories, testimony, and tearful confessions shock me and pierce my heart. They are gut-wrenching, depraved, horrific, and devastating. They are exactly like mine.

I don't notice I'm leaning forward, identifying with their struggle, empathizing with their pain, listening intently, paying very close attention, crying with them, for them, in front of them. It's as if someone is shining a spotlight on my darkest, dirtiest, dustiest corners, finally finding me, saying everything I've never known how to speak aloud. I'm in awe at their courage and willingness to be vulnerable and split wide open and bleed so freely. I can feel the relief radiating from them as they purge their demons.

You are only as sick as your secrets.

I understand what Andie means now. Bringing out what is hidden into the light makes it lose its power over you. I can actually hear and feel their chains falling away. And as I sit there, surrounded by their grief and transgressions, I begin to realize that underneath the tragedy, there's a hope they cling to. They believe in redemption, in forgiveness, in the future. They have faith there still is one for them, that they can and will beat the alcoholism and get and be better. I start to accept I'm not alone, that I'm not the only one who fell into that slimy, bottomless pit and couldn't get out. The bottle can find anyone, anywhere, at any time. And we each have our reasons for needing it and trying to hide in it.

It's my turn. I can choose to share or not. It's up to me. All of this is. Everyone is watching and waiting. The heat and weight of their gazes sear into me, and I anxiously look over at Andie. She's the safest face in the room. She smiles, silently encouraging me. I don't know then that she will one day be at Lexy's wedding, how many nights she will stay up and talk me down from the sweaty, vicious temptation and cravings, be the hand and voice I will reach out and hold onto for years to come.

My gaze again fixes on the sign hanging on the wall. Tell each other the truth. I think of Richard and Becca, and the lies and burdens they both carried for me all these years. I look at Kayla, who is here so she doesn't lose her son. The scent of mint drifts up from the tea gripped tightly in my hands, reminding me of my beautiful, young daughter, who I dragged into hell with me. And lastly, I think of my father and how I've been running from the curse of his addiction and abuse my entire life.

And, I find my why. I'm not going to let him hurt me, or the people I love, ever again.

Nervously, I clear my throat, open my mouth, and take the first step that will lead me into the first day of the rest of my life. "My name is Victoria, and I'm an alcoholic."

Chapter Thirty-One
VICTORIA

I swore I'd never come back to Tennessee.

I definitely have not missed the heat. Sweat glistens on my upper lip, and I can taste the dust, grit, and moisture of the irrigated soil and pastures in the back of my throat. Cicadas swarm constantly, their whirring song still so familiar.

Scents of jasmine, gardenia, and honeysuckle drift over to me on the slight breeze and are a sweet syrup on my tongue.

My energy drains as the humidity falls over me and seeps through my clothes, dampening my shirt and jeans; perspiration trickles slowly down my spine.

Even late in September, the air is warm, sticky, and muggy. The weather will turn crisp and cool when October comes, and the seasons predictably change the land, but for now, the last days of summer stubbornly hang on and linger.

Needing the constant reminder, I uncurl my fist and stare down at my thirty-day chip in my hand. The serenity prayer is engraved on the back. I'm gripping onto it so tightly, indentions chafe and redden my skin.

The coin is proof of my sobriety, freedom, breakthrough, and healing. My strength, courage, and ability to overcome and defeat the bottle. One day at a time.

I made it through to the other side and keep the coin with me at all times as a reminder and anchor, weapon and shield for when temptation and the nightmares come.

For the last month, I've wrestled myself to the ground by getting clean and sober, doing my inventory, attending every AA meeting, walking through the twelve steps, digging down deep, confessing my sins, and facing my past.

And now, everything I've worked for has led me to the one place I fear the most and spent my entire life trying to forget. I fiercely hope thirty days is long enough for what I'm now up against.

The house stands before me; paint chipped and peeling, the wood warped, white, and old, resilient against time, tears, tragedy, and history.

As a child, I used to pray for a twister to come ripping through and blow it down, fervently wishing every part of this land would be torn away and destroyed, so there was no trace of him left; no memories, no past, no drinking, no fear. Everything would be gone, completely wiped out until it was unrecognizable. Until I was.

But this home, the land, the porch, the stench of him, is still here, and now, so am I.

Every window, board, nail, and blade of grass is a reminder of the terror and trauma. I can hear his voice bellowing and slurring down the hall, whiskey sloshing and stairs creaking as he staggered closer to our room, his boots thudding, heavy and threatening. I can hear my sister's desperate whispers as we huddled together under the damp, moldy porch, the only light coming through the gaps and slats between the boards, and the crack of his palm slapping across my face when he found me.

He hasn't laid a hand on me in over twenty years, but I still flinch as if I'm being struck.

Nothing has changed, and yet, everything has. It's a strange reality to reconcile myself to who I used to be and who I am now.

I haven't stepped foot on this land since I was eighteen, but I still know all four corners from east to west and back again that belong to the Montgomery family line. Each acre and perimeter post and boundary marker is engraved into my blood, passed down to me through the generations.

I'm tied to this house, no matter how far I go or how long I'm gone. In some ways, it knows me better than I know myself. I left a part of me behind when I ran that day, and it's been waiting all this time for me to come back and pick up the scattered, wounded pieces.

Letting out a shuddering breath, I pull out my phone from my pocket, my hands trembling as I send Andie a text to let her know we arrived safely and are about to go inside.

Her response is immediate, reassuringly so, and I take a small amount of comfort in her reminding me how far I've come, how proud she is of me, and she's only a call away.

My trust in her over the last month has become absolute and unwavering. She has walked with me through the darkness, the screaming close calls and cravings, the gritty, gross depths of recovery, and I willingly followed her out into a new life.

But, as much as I want to think I've grown and learned and become stronger, this place brings me instantly to my knees, as if

I'm a scared little girl again, hiding under porches and under beds and cowering in the corner.

I refuse to believe I'm the same person I was when I left over twenty years ago. I'm still his daughter, but I'm not a drunk anymore. I made it out of the pit. He didn't completely destroy me, no matter how hard he tried.

I've spent years trying to drown out his voice in my head telling me I was never going to amount to anything, that I was exactly like him and would never be able to get away from him. I'm desperate to prove him wrong.

The time has come to face the past, the abuse, and myself. Without the vodka.

"Are you ready to go inside?" Richard asks, standing next to me. I must look as vulnerable as I feel because he seems concerned and takes my hand. His is warm, safe, and solid, and I weave my fingers tightly into his, securing me to the ground where I stand. My legs feel as if they are about to give out, and I'm grateful to have him to hold onto.

Everything in me wants to say no, to run as fast and far as I can. Glancing behind us, I scan down the gnarled line of oaks that always seemed nostalgic and romantic as I passed under the canopy of leaves and branches, the lush green wild grasses where we would run for cover, my Granddaddy Beau's gate that he and Adelaide built themselves, his boot still perched in an invitation, out to the shimmering, long road just beyond.

I could escape, but I know I would never be free. I'm tired of hiding and force myself to stay where I am.

Turning back toward Richard, I hear myself say, "Ready as I'll ever be." My voice is a bit breathless and shaky, and still not as certain as I'd like. Lexy is on my other side, close and watchful of me, and it's comforting to have them both here.

Becca is standing at the front door. Keeping my eyes firmly fixed on her, I hold onto my family as we walk the rest of the way up the dusty lane. We pass the tree where the tire swing still dangles, up the porch steps where we spent hours hiding underneath in the sweltering heat, the post where our names are jaggedly etched and carved as we waited for the coast to be clear, until I finally reach my sister who has always been on this land, waiting for my prodigal return.

Relief and fear are both bitter tastes in my mouth as she embraces me, holding on tight. I don't look at anything else but her eyes, just like always, and before, forever as we promised.

"Hi, honey," she says, her voice warm and soothing, reminding me of all those nights clinging to each other in the dark. "I'm so glad you're here." Still keeping me close, as if she knows how badly I want to flee, she opens the screen for us. It groans exactly how I know it will, and I instinctively want to lay low. Daddy was always waiting just on the edge of my blind spots. "Let's get you all inside. This heat will melt you where you stand."

As I walk through the front door, the sights, scents, memories, swirl, rush up, swallow and surround me, much too vivid and clear.

Time seems to have stood still in this house. Even the stains on the faded floral wallpaper are the same. Old photographs of my family scatter the wall by the narrow staircase, and I recognize each name and face without having to look. The wooden floor is worn and scarred and creaks under my feet in all the places I remember.

I know the layout of each room with my eyes closed, retracing my steps, rewinding time, recalling the nooks and crannies where we crouched and cried. The hand-built cupboard where mama kept her spices and the loose floorboards where daddy hid his bottles. The faint scent of Tabu perfume that Grandma Rose used to wear waits around corners like a lost, forgotten ghost in these haunted halls.

This house built me, molded, and shaped me into who I am today. For better and for worse. I wonder if it has remembered me, missed me, and if I turned out how it thought I would.

Tension burns and swells, building in my belly, my chest, my bones, the anticipation of an inevitable showdown coming. He's waiting for me here, beckoning me, daring me to challenge and face him, and I wonder if he somehow knew I was coming for him.

Becca is still in front of me, gently smiling, waiting to take us upstairs and get settled. From a glazed over place in my mind, I watch her lips move as she tells us Ben and Nick are still out on the south side of the ranch, but are heading back in, and dinner will be ready in an hour.

The chatter soundlessly hovers around me, above my head, not registering or sinking in. My ears are ringing; white noise, muffled, hollow, echoing. I'm grateful Richard and Lexy fill in the humming silence for me.

My shoulders are tight, and I realize I haven't taken a breath in a few moments. Senses overloaded, shocked, and overwhelmed, my feet seem to be stuck and frozen in the same spot. A wild animal cornered. I resent that I don't feel stronger, that he can trigger and trip me up so easily.

Falling back on the calming techniques Andie taught me, I breathe in deep, mentally count to ten, and let it slowly out. And then do it three more times until my muscles loosen, and the buzzing in my head stops.

Feeling a little more steady, I again look down at my sobriety chip clutched in my hand, desperately seeking the reminder that I'm different now and am not going to fall back into old habits.

Feet shuffle, and bodies shift, brushing against mine, bringing me back to the present, and I realize we're moving forward, deeper into the house. Steeling myself, I follow my family up the stairs, past the photos of my family tree, their eyes watching and seeming to whisper and warn me, each step conjuring grainy images of long ago.

Becca makes small talk with us about how our flight was and the drive in from town, as if she knows I need the distraction as we reach the landing on the second floor. The air is heavy, thick, musty, as if the heat, my thoughts, pain, and fear are all trapped in these walls. If they could talk, they would only be able to weep.

I still can't say much, trying not to see what I know is waiting for me, as she leads us past mama and daddy's old bedroom where they fought, and she begged him to stop hitting her.

She has Lexy take our childhood bedroom, with the window seat and the closet where we hid, and I'm grateful not to have to face it yet as Lexy goes to put her suitcase away. I know she's eager to see Glory. And, of course, Nick. I'm more than a little curious to meet him. He's all she talks about.

"I thought you'd like to be in Grandma Rose's old room," Becca says to me as she opens the door to the far-back bedroom. "She always loved the morning light in here."

Stepping inside, the room is warm and smells of lemon dust cleaner, cedar from the hope chest in the corner, and the lilac potpourri satchels hidden within its drawers. A hazy memory of us searching for secret treasure within the velvet pockets flits through my mind.

The white wrought iron bed and handmade quilt are the same, as is the high back antique rocking chair near the window facing the fields. Her silver brush and mirror set are still on the dressing vanity next to her collection of crystal perfume bottles. Lightly tracing my fingers over the ornate handle, I think of when Grandma Rose used to brush and braid our hair before bedtime. She would sing to us to soothe our bad dreams and frightened tears.

This was always my favorite room, too, and I wonder if Becca knew it would comfort me. It's quieter, safer, and lighter than the rest of the house, far enough away from where daddy used to sleep, and the view of the horses and pastures is peaceful.

"It's perfect," I answer, attempting a smile, not really pulling it off, wanting to help Becca feel better. I know how hard she's trying to make this as easy as possible for me.

"Good. I'll let you both get settled. I'm going to finish dinner," she says, understanding I need a minute to take all of it in. "Come down when you're ready." She quietly closes the door, and I hear the sound of her footsteps treading and fading. Hers I recognize and was always so relieved when I used to hear her coming to my rescue.

Alone, Richard turns to me, his blue eyes seeming to glow in the tranquil violet evening. Daylight savings is making the rays of sun leave faster, shadows slinking and lengthening along the wide plank floors, inching closer to where my feet stand. "You okay?"

It's a minute-to-minute question, I realize. I want so badly to believe I am. "I'm trying to be." The window is open, bringing in the fragrant scents of fertile, plowed earth, and I turn to look out at the wide, open acres. The green here is unlike anywhere else and achingly beautiful and bittersweet. As a little girl, I sat at this window for hours, dreaming of my escape. "At least I made it through the front door."

Nodding, he comes up beside me, putting his hand on my back. His touch calms and eases my frazzled nerves. "Yes, you did. It's a big step."

One of many I will have to take and face here. Leaning closer to him, I absorb his body heat, his strength, his protection, and he holds me tighter just as I need him to. "Why is this so much harder than getting clean?"

"Because everything that happened here is the reason you drank in the first place."

He's right. And now I'm facing the fear and abuse without a bottle. But I'm not empty-handed, I suddenly realize. I'm not alone. My family is here; Andie is a text and call away. I'm clean and sober. I tighten my hold on my chip, the shape and pressure of it reassuring as it presses deep into my sweaty palm. I keep it between us as I look up at him. "Thank you for coming with me."

His gaze holds mine as the last glimmer of daylight disappears behind the trees, dimming the room, turning us into silhouettes against the sky. I'm relieved he will be here when darkness falls. The house changes at night as if it's breathing and alive. "Thank you for letting me," he answers softly.

There's so much to say, but I don't have the words yet. They feel too raw and painful, hanging in the air around us, with the ghosts and dust-covered memories. Thoughtful and pensive, I fall quiet again as I look out over the land that is both a birthright and my heaviest burden.

I'm very aware that I'm up against the biggest test and fight of my life. I'm not sure yet which one of us will make it through this still standing.

Daddy, the bottle, or me.

Chapter Thirty-Two
LEXY

While my parents unpack and get settled, I quietly slip out the front door and head over to the stables, my eyes scanning the glowing horizon for Nick's return, as I follow the worn path in the grass.

Twilight creates shimmering streaks of pink and lavender across the sky as the sun sets lower behind the trees, making the warm September air, the insects, and even the pastures, seem to sing and hum and ripple. I remember this time of day here and have deeply missed the serene hush as evening falls.

The land is how I left it, and it's reassuring how constant, green, and fragrant it still is. The scattered outbuildings, old rickety windmill, and barn are uneven, familiar shadows against the darkening sky, and I experience a bittersweet sense of coming home.

A part of me feels guilty for loving a place that causes my mom such deep pain. Our experience on this ranch is drastically different, and I can only empathize with the stress and struggle she is wrestling with.

My heart aches for how trapped she feels in this house. Painful reminders of her childhood wait around every corner and down the hallways. And the violence that happened here isn't something she will ever forget.

I hope our time here will be healing for her and not cause more pain. Or a relapse. She's sober now, but that doesn't mean she won't still want a drink. Triggers are everywhere; on the stairs, out every window, even collected in the dust under my bed where she hid with Becca when they were young.

We've only been back a little over an hour, and it's already difficult for her. She seems a bit shell-shocked and fragile, and I know better than anyone that the nightmares and flashbacks are always worse the later and quieter it gets.

There is a heavy, unspoken understanding between all of us of how necessary and crucial this trip is. I'm grateful her sponsor is only a quick call away, and the AA meetings are still required daily. She can do them online, but Andie will monitor her, and she has to make sure she checks in at each one.

Recovering alcoholics don't get a break, even on a horse ranch out in the middle of nowhere in Tennessee.

Nick knows I'm back. I texted him the second we arrived. My skin, heart, and even my nerve endings are tingling with excitement to finally see him. I think he's looking forward to seeing me too because he sent a message saying he'd head in as soon as he could.

We haven't seen each other in two months, since that terrible morning I found out about my mom's overdose and had to leave him behind with so much misunderstood and unsaid between us.

We've talked every day since that night he called me; texting back and forth, he's sent pictures of Glory, and rustic, simple snapshots of where he is on the land during his workday, sunrises over the pastures, the wide, open view from the porch of his cottage.

He knows how much I've missed this land, how connected I feel to it, and long to be a part of the day-to-day things.

We've shared sleepy late-night conversations while the rest of the world dreamt. Whispering, confiding, confessing feelings, staying up until dawn, just to hear the other one breathe and sigh and say our name.

He's kept the loneliness away and helped get me through the uncertain days of my mom's rehab and recovery. I can't wait to see him, be close to him, hold him, kiss him.

I remember the feel and taste and heat of his mouth, his breath on my skin, his arms wrapped so tightly around me I could feel his heart thundering against mine. My body flushes with anticipation and need.

Sliding open the heavy wooden door of the stable, I step inside. The overhead fans slowly spin, lazily stirring the earthy smell of grains and sweet hay, leather, and saddle oil hanging in the air.

I wonder if Glory has missed me and will let me back into the bond we had before I had to abruptly leave. I didn't even get to say goodbye.

She's in the third stall down. The other horses stick their heads out, curious, and shamelessly hoping for treats, silently watching as I pass.

Reaching her, I stand back, waiting to see if she recognizes me. Even though I want to touch her, I'm careful not to move too fast. I don't want to startle her by invading her space if she's not ready.

She is as beautiful as before, her mahogany coat deep and rich and sleek, her body full and strong. She was still healing and finding her footing when I left, but now she's powerful and majestic and somehow much larger than I remember. She looks like the champion racehorse she's born to be.

Her soulful brown eyes are no longer sad and suspicious as she looks out from her stall at me. She's calm, confident, and at ease; the threat and defense against pain are now gone as she's learned to trust the hands that feed and care for her.

Saying nothing, I stand very still, letting her get used to me again. She sniffs the air and snorts, seeming to recognize my scent. Bobbing her head, she lets out an excited neigh, pushing against the stall door as if trying to force it open, or break it down, to reach me, granting me permission to approach. Smiling, I walk up to her.

"Hi, sweet girl," I murmur, reaching my hand out for her to smell, and she presses her nose eagerly into my palm. "I'm so happy to see you." She bows her head, and I kiss her forehead, wrapping my arms around her, trying to get as close as I can over the barrier of the door.

Her wounds have healed, only the white jagged scars a reminder of past pain. She trusts my touch, and we both lean in, reacquainting ourselves with the feel of each other. She nuzzles my hair, and I laugh as she butts the top of her head into my shoulder as if scolding me for leaving her so long.

"I'm here," I soothe, inhaling her musky scent. "I'm sorry I went away."

"I figured this is where you'd be."

Even his voice is the same. Low, deep, drawling. Jolting, my heart catches as I look over and see Nick standing a few feet down.

I'm surprisingly nervous and unconsciously bite my bottom lip. We've talked every day, but it's different in person, more intimate and exposing, with no walls or distance between us.

His gaze is direct, intense, staring at me, into me, absorbing me. His eyes have changed, I notice. They are lighter somehow, not as sad or tragic or bruised. His hair is a little longer, falling over the scar on his brow, his ears, the nape of his neck, the frayed collar of his shirt.

"Hi," I manage, smiling shyly.

"Hey." He continues to stare, saying so many things with barely saying a word, and I blush in the way I always did around him.

I'm not sure what to do and awkwardly glance back to Glory. "She looks beautiful."

He comes closer, and I can smell the land, sweat, and soil on him. The back of my throat is dry. The air between us feels electric, surging, charged.

"Yeah, she's come a long way," he answers, reaching out to scratch behind her ears, and she tilts her head towards him. It's distracting watching his fingers, the way his mouth moves. I vividly remember them on me. "She kept looking for you."

"Really?" I ask, stroking her neck as if trying to apologize. "I felt so guilty that I had to leave her the way I did."

"Couldn't be helped," he says, resting his arm on the stall door, his body facing mine. "You had to go."

"I know. But I'm happy to be back for a bit. At least for the week anyway. I loved all the pictures you sent me of her."

"Good." He nods his head towards Glory. "I knew you were missing her."

And you, I think, the words suspended like a red string in the space between us, tying us together, but I am hesitant to say them. He still hasn't touched me or reached for me. His body is mere inches from mine. It's the closest we've been in months. Feeling too needy and flustered, I keep my hands to myself and try to focus. "Did you get to ride her yet?"

He shook his head. "I was going to, but then you said you were coming back. I wanted to wait for you. Thought you might like to be the first one to take her out."

Thrilled by the idea, my whole being lights up as I smile brilliantly at him. His eyes flicker with need, desire, fascination, the flecks of gold shining through. His guard is completely down, and he lets himself smile back in that tender, sweet way I remember from the photograph in the paper. But, this time, it's for me. I'm very aware there are only a few people he looks at like this or allows to see him. I don't take the gift lightly.

"Do you think she's ready?"

He nods. "Yeah, I do. She's strong enough now, and she trusts you."

"I hope so," I answer, looking back at Glory, who continues to stay near me as if making sure I don't disappear again. I keep my hand on her, giving us both the reassurance of constant contact. When I turn to Nick, I notice he's still watching me with that focused, searching stare that always made me tongue-tied, and my thoughts spin out and scatter. "Will you help me ride her? I want you to be there."

"I wouldn't miss it," he answers, and I realize he's moved to where there is barely any space between us, close enough that if I shift, I'll brush his arm, his chest, my hair will skim his jawline.

He does the same thing with the horses, I remember; biding his time, inching in, letting them get used to the feel of him in their space until they are within his grasp. I smell the faint scent of his shampoo, his aftershave, and feel the heat coming off him, mixing dizzyingly with mine. I'm completely surrounded by him.

"Thank you for waiting for me," I say, meaning more than just this moment.

He doesn't respond, his gaze lowering to my mouth like he did the morning I left as if searching for something, a sign, an opening, a chance, a yes.

My lips instinctively part in expectation and an invitation. The air crackles, thickening, making it harder to catch my breath.

I had wondered if he might change his mind or decide he didn't want to let me in or be with me. That he might not want to let go of his past and come towards me.

But then he's reaching for me, his arms moving around my waist, pulling me to him, and any insecurity or doubt I am feeling instantly falls away and vanishes.

"Come here," he says, his drawl husky and low, just how I like, as if he's reading my thoughts, closing the last of the distance between us.

My breath shudders out as I look up at him, his face a sweet, hazy blur. All I can see are his eyes, dark and hot, before he leans in to kiss me. I sway toward him, and this time, he's there to catch me and hold me up, his arms tightening around me, his lips covering mine, greedy and starving as if he can't bear for us to be apart anymore.

I lift my hands to finally touch him, over the soft, faded cotton of his shirt, up his shoulders, into the ends of his hair. His jeans rub against my legs, denim pressing against denim, and I shiver as he runs his hands up my spine, the heat of his palms leaving a trail of sparks even through my clothes.

The kiss is like before on that devastating morning when the sun was too bright and harsh, and my tears stained and burned his skin. Wounded finding wounded, a raw, soothing remedy for our scars and bruises and pain, gently running our fingertips over the cracks and cuts left behind by years of loss, grief, and heartache. I can taste his relief that I'm finally here, and he's not alone in all the things still unknown to us.

An understanding passes between us that things are different now; we are letting them change, breaking them open, barriers crumbling, and leading each other somewhere we've never been.

We're going back to that day, finding where we left off, picking back up, finishing what we started, and discovering together where it will take us, realizing it's even better than we imagined, and knowing this time when we fall, we have somewhere safe to land.

There's no rush. He slowly explores me, experiences me, experimenting with touch and taste and texture, as if wanting to commit every detail, the very chemistry of me, into his senses and mind and underneath his skin, and remind himself of what he'd found that first time we kissed.

When he finally pulls back, my eyes lazily drift open. His face is close, blissfully blocking out everything else around us. He's all I can see, and all I want to. "I've been waiting to do that for two months," he says, his breath deliciously warm over me.

I smile and hold on tighter, absorbing the feel and nearness of him. He's been too far away for far too long. "Me, too."

Before he can say anything else, we both look over when we hear Ben whistling as he walks into the stable. "There you are," he says as he puts supplies on the shelf. Turning back, he grins when he sees me. "No wonder you wanted to get back here so fast. Hey there, Lexy."

Pulling free from Nick, I move around him to hug my uncle. "Hi." I'm breathlessly laughing as he engulfs me in his arms. He smells comfortingly the same; worn flannel and hearty earth and warm sunshine, predictable as the land and sky itself.

"It's really good to see you. So glad you're here." Releasing me, he looks towards Nick, an amused smile on his face. His eyes crinkle up in the corners in that endearing way I remember. "This guy has been missing you like crazy. You're all he's talked about for months."

Nick scowls, sending him a dark look. "Thanks a lot."

Ben laughs. "Don't mention it." He winks at me. "I'll let you two get caught up. Don't be too long," he says as he starts to head back out. "You know how Becca is about family meals. Great to have you back for a bit, Lexy." When he's gone, Nick and I are left alone again.

Facing him, I notice he has his hands shoved down deep in his pockets, his eyes on the ground. "Is that true what he said?"

He self-consciously shrugs. "Yeah," he mutters, not meeting my gaze. Is he embarrassed? My heart softens even more towards him.

Needing to touch him, I move back into his arms. "I missed you too," I confess, looking up at him, feeling him gradually relax against me. The vulnerability in his eyes makes me melt. This is so new and doesn't happen every day for lost, lonely people like us.

We've both been trying to figure out how to simply survive. "All the time. I couldn't wait to get back here to you."

His eyes hold mine in that way he knows how to do that makes everything stand beautifully still. "Good," he murmurs and kisses me gently, and it's just as sweet, and I wonder how my legs are holding me up. Lifting his head, he looks past me towards the door. "We better head to the house. Don't want your mama getting worried about you."

In another surprising gesture that startles and stuns me, he takes my hand. As he links our fingers, he seems to be absorbing the feel of me, the connection, the step we're taking, what it means for us. We've been on our own for so long.

His palm is rough against mine from the strain and scrape and splinters of ranch work, but the contrast is exhilarating, and I close my fingers around his. I don't want him going anywhere either.

"I told my parents where I'd be," I say as he leads me out into the warm evening.

"How's your mom doing with being back?"

I look toward the house. It's the only one around for miles. All the lights are on, a beacon in the dark. I hope it helps her feel safer. "It's hard for her. There's so much pain she hasn't faced here. And now she has to do it all sober."

Nick shakes his head and blows out his breath. "Yeah, that is going to be tough."

"At least she has her sponsor to talk to, and the AA meetings are required every day, so she has support."

"She also has you and your dad. I'll bet it helps that you're both here with her."

"I hope it does," I murmur, looking dreamily up at the night sky, glittering with stars. I've never seen so many as if the entire galaxy has swirled and gathered here just for us. The sun had still been setting when I went into the stable. "The moon is already out. I can't believe how full and bright it is."

Nick glances up, nodding. "Supposed to be a harvest moon tomorrow night. Only happens once a year. There's a place I like to go watch it out in your Great-Granddaddy Cade's field. It's so big and close it looks like it's sitting right on top of the land."

A bit awestruck, I smile at him. "I'd love to see that."

He smiles back at me, squeezing my hand tighter, and I wonder if he likes the security of belonging to someone. To me. "I'll be sure and find you. We can watch it together."

As he leads me down the worn path, it takes me a minute to recognize what it is I'm feeling. I've been so used to the worry, panic, and fear of the addiction that it's surprising to realize this sensation rushing through my veins is pure happiness.

Trusting it has never been easy, and I don't know if I've ever experienced it. It seems so effortless for other people, but it's been a foreign concept to me, unreal and out of reach, cruelly snatched away and stolen. I learned early never to get my hopes up, and the bottle and blackouts made sure I didn't.

And yet somehow, against all odds, and despite everything I've lost, I'm back on the ranch with Nick at my side, his hand linked in mine. Glory is safe and healthy. My mom is clean and sober. And my family is here together under the same roof for the first time in over twenty years.

My heart is full as I watch fireflies wink and dance, stars gleam as if guarding us, and the full moon smile as if it's listening and knows all our secrets.

And for this one moment, on this one summer night late in September, everything is how I always dreamed it would be.

Chapter Thirty-Three
VICTORIA

It's late, a little after one in the morning. I can't sleep. Jet lag and traumatic childhood flashbacks are not a great combination for a recovering alcoholic.

The house is eerily quiet and still, and I can feel the eyes of the past scouring each room, hovering, closing in, searching for me. As if it knows there's a score to settle and a long-overdue reckoning coming.

Stepping out onto the front porch, I take in a deep breath. The air is warm and fragrant, but it doesn't soothe or calm me. There's not even a breeze.

Wrapping my arms criss-crossed like caution tape around my waist, I stare out into the night, feeling a bit panicked by the open space. I miss the safe cocoon of rehab where I knew what to do and expect, and each day was regulated by routines.

I've been preparing for this trip for months, but facing what happened here on my own is a whole other test of my will.

I haven't been back twenty-four hours yet and already feel shaky. What if I can't handle it and I fail?

Unsettled, I feel a shiver crawl up the back of my neck as I weakly lower myself to the porch steps.

My only solace is, at least now, I'm not underneath them.

A lullaby mama used to sing to us when we were little floods back to me, the images harsh and sharp against my sober mind as I'm carried backward by time into a place I'm not ready to remember.

Rock a bye baby, in the treetop. When the wind blows, the cradle will rock. When the bough breaks, the cradle will fall. And down will come baby, cradle and all.

Over and over, the swaying melody plays through my mind, the sad, haunting sound of her voice warm in my ear. After daddy passed out and the coast was clear, she would come get us from underneath the porch and clutch us against her, humming quietly to comfort us even though she was the one bleeding.

With tears in her eyes and fresh bruises on her face, she'd promise everything would be alright, and we would say we believed her so she would stop crying.

The memory is so real and vivid it's as if I could touch her, feel the patched, worn cotton of her dress, her body trembling, the pungent sweat of her fear and desperation. I can't seem to shake the words or the brokenness in her eyes. I haven't thought of that song in years.

A lazy, sleepy groan catches my attention, pulling me out of the past and back to the present, and I look over at the old lab dozing under the porch swing. He's been keeping a close watch on me ever since I arrived. He seems to have woken himself up with his own snoring, and his eyes squint open to check on me before settling back into a nap. I feel oddly reassured having him nearby.

The screen door creaks behind me. I used to jump at the sound, knowing it meant he was coming. I'd learned early to have eyes in the back of my head and start running before his shadow was close.

My ears perk and tune in as I hear footsteps padding softly across the wood, but I don't have to turn around to know it's Becca. We've always felt and recognized each other's movements. Even when we were thousands of miles away from each other.

"I heard you get up. I made us some chamomile tea." She hands me a mug. A jolly fat man in an apron and chef's hat and the words *Kiss the Cook* is painted on it. "This was always mama's magic cure for everything. She swore it would help us sleep."

Needing warmth, I wrap the mug in both hands. "I don't want to sleep," I say, watching the steam curl up like ghosts. A few months ago, I was drowning out my thoughts with vodka and pills. Herbal tea seems like such a weak weapon against my pain. Plastic swords at a gunfight. "I don't want to see his face."

"I know," she says gently as she sits down next to me. I notice she's wearing an oversized Tennessee State football T-shirt that I'm guessing is Ben's and faded blue pajama shorts underneath. With her hair pulled up off her face in a messy bun, she looks like she could be in high school. She'd inherited mama's natural beauty and sweetness. I feel a hundred years older than her. It's comfortable enough out that we don't need layers yet. But the seasons are changing. "How was your AA meeting?"

This is now a typical conversation for me, I realize, tracing my finger over the smooth ceramic handle of my mug. I never thought it would be. Recovery has become all I think about and depend on. "Good. It helped."

"Nice that you can do it online. Especially all the way out here."

"Yeah, Andie sent me the link."

Becca blew on her tea, waiting for it to cool. "I like her."

"So do I." I shake my head. "Who would've thought?" In the glow of the porch light, I catch the concern in her eyes and feel guilty she still bears so much responsibility and is afraid to let me out of her sight. "Don't worry. I'm not going to drink. He's not going to win that easily."

Her legs are touching mine, and I wonder if it will forever be a habit for us to crouch and cling close. "I just know how hard it is for you to be back."

An ironic laugh escapes my lips. "Hard doesn't even begin to cover it." I look at her, thinking of all the times we hid underneath these very steps in our filthy clothes, bare feet, and hungry bellies, uselessly hoping and praying for something to change. "I still don't know how you're able to stay here."

"Where else would I go?" she asks, a weary acceptance in her voice as she holds my stare. "We grew up on this ranch. It's been in our family for generations. This is the only home I've ever known."

Resentment simmers beneath my skin. "This place was never a home. If you and mama hadn't been here, I would have left long before I did." On the edge of losing control, I force myself to breathe and deliberately find a focal point high above in the trees and stare hard at it to keep me from spiraling. My hands are shaking, and I hold the mug tighter. The heat on my palms is soothing, and the floral scent of the tea reminds me of my mother. Her kindness, her undying loyalty, her sacrifices, her weakness, and fear. It's all interchangeable. "How she stayed with him all those years is beyond me."

"Maybe she didn't know where else to go either. She was born and raised here just like we were."

"What is it about this land?" I ask into thin air. "It's like it owns us." She doesn't answer, and I don't expect her to as we fall into a throbbing silence. But I never minded the quiet with her. "Do you think he was ever sorry for what he did to us?"

Becca sighs. "I want to think so. Sometimes I wonder if that's why he drank so much. Because he couldn't face us or mama."

"I guess that's one more thing he'll never be able to tell us," I say, my voice dull. We both sit with the heavy helplessness of all the things still unresolved. Because there's nothing we can do, I look away, feeling how futile it all is. "Did you know his mama died when he was two?"

"I remember hearing that, but he hardly told us anything, and he wouldn't ever let mama talk about it."

"I did some research on our family tree while I was in rehab. It was one of our assignments to help us get to the root of why we drink. I went online and found out her name was Elizabeth, and she died of influenza. She was only twenty."

Becca winces, her eyes pained. "That's so young."

"Way too young," I agree. "His daddy was named William. After her death, they had to leave their farm. I think he'd already started drinking from the grief and couldn't keep up with all that had to be done. The bank came and claimed it. They moved around a lot, so the records after that time are a bit sketchy, but I read William died of cirrhosis a few years later."

"He was an alcoholic, too?"

"That's what the autopsy report said," I answer, shrugging one shoulder. "Daddy was only sixteen when he lost him. The records say William was of the violent kind and prone to bursts of fury and rages. He even went to jail one time for a bar fight."

Becca had been raising her mug, but her hand freezes mid-air, her eyes wide and stunned as she stares at me. "Daddy was abused like we were?"

"It sure sounds like it. There's not much on it though. But it makes sense considering how angry he was and all he put us through."

"You would think it would make him not want to hurt us since he grew up in it."

"Maybe all that happened hurt him too much, and something just broke inside of him. I can't remember ever seeing him happy or smiling."

"Me neither," Becca says, thoughtfully tapping her fingers against the side of her mug. "I only have memories of him being drunk."

"I read he had an aunt here in Tennessee that he lived with for a few months, but then he met mama when he came to find work on our ranch, and the rest is history. You know how she felt it was her responsibility to rescue the wounded souls of the world."

Becca stares down into the dust as she nods. "I remember. I don't know if that was her worst flaw or her greatest strength."

"Guess it depends on who she was trying to help."

"Not everyone wants to be saved," Becca murmurs. "Or can be."

I'm not sure if I respond. My mouth has gone dry. I fiercely hope I'm not one of those who are doomed.

"So that means daddy was an orphan," Becca says, shaking her head as she puts the missing pieces together. "That would be horrible to lose both your parents like that. No wonder he never wanted to talk about it."

"It was probably too painful." The air is heavy with unanswered questions and the heartbreaking realization of the suffering our father went through. I can't imagine this was the legacy he meant to leave for us. When does the destructive cycle end? *"Is it crazy that I feel sorry for him?"*

"No," Becca answers sadly. "I kind of do, too. He always seemed so lost."

"Do you wonder if some people just don't stand a chance in this world?"

"Maybe. Or they don't know how to accept the chance they're offered."

"Yeah, he hated asking for help. Thought the whole world was against him. And he never wanted to owe anyone anything."

"You're not like him, Victoria."

A shudder rumbles through me, and my breath rushes out as my deepest fear is spoken out loud. Becca has always been able to read my mind. I look over at her, strangely afraid of being seen. "How do you know?" I whisper and can hear my own desperation. I want so badly to be different and good and better than the nothing he told me I was.

"You got help. You're sober. He stayed in his pain, but you didn't. You're clean. You always were." Her eyes are pure and green, intent on mine as she leans towards me, our faces close just like childhood. "The abuse was never your fault. He just dumped it all on you because he didn't know how to deal with himself or his past. He was hurting, and he punished you for that. But you're not him."

I'm quiet as I let her words sink in. The logical part of my brain knows she's right. I learned this in recovery, faced him, the abuse, all the lies I believed, all the shame I carried, stripping myself down inside the raw, gritty exposure of my twelve steps. *Hurting people hurt people.* I can't even count how many times Andie said that to me, but the simple truth of those words rings out loud and clear over the conflict in my head.

Everyone comes from somewhere that has shaped them into who they are, I realize. And in some ways even decided it. We're all recovering from something and trying to come to terms with where our choices and crossroads have led us.

My most fervent hope for this trip is to get back to the girl I always wanted to be, the girl who sang and dreamed of the impossible. I came here to find myself again. It's the last place I ever wanted to look. But this land seems to understand me better than I do.

Sighing, I rest my chin on my hand and look out over the acres that stretch for miles in front of me. "Remember when we used to run out into the pastures and spin and spin until we'd get so dizzy, we'd fall down?"

Becca smiles, but her eyes are shadowed and bruised. "We'd lay on the grass and find faces and animals in the clouds. Then we'd climb Grandaddy Cade's tree and sit up there and watch the sunset."

"We couldn't come home," I say darkly. When the yelling would start, we would run for our lives out the back door, over the endless fields, to the far edges of the land where we'd be out of reach. So much open space, and we'd still been trapped. "I keep expecting him to come busting out the door, swearing and shouting at us."

She touches my arm to comfort me. "He's gone, Victoria. He can't hurt us anymore."

"He's constantly hurting me." I feel as if my skin is burning from the inside out. I have years of painful memories pent up in me. "He left us with so much damage. And he never once acknowledged it or showed one ounce of remorse. I'm so angry at him for that. How do you forgive someone who was never even sorry? And we're still here dealing with everything he did. What are we supposed to do with that?"

"I don't know," she whispers, tears filling her eyes. Her gold locket gleams in the moonlight, reminding me of our promises and secret pacts from long ago. "Hold on tight to each other, I guess." The air between us is tense and thick with our pain. There aren't answers for abuse and fear like this, and we both know it. It's unspeakable what happened to us. Saying it out loud is the only power we have left.

You are only as sick as your secrets.

Dragging my hands through my hair, I let out a heavy breath as if trying to purge myself of the toxins and poison of my past. I realize I'm shaking and clench my hand into a fist in my lap. I don't want him to win. He's not here. I don't have to fear him anymore. I may not have any absolution, apologies, redemption, or resolution. But I do have my sister, my husband, and my daughter. It's a comforting feeling having Becca next to me. Even after years of separation and silence, she's still the only one who knows me better than anyone.

I need to change the subject. My throat is hot and feels as if it's closing up, choking me. I sip my tea, trying to wash down the bitterness. "It was nice to finally meet Nick. I've heard so much about him. He's a handsome guy. Quiet though and a bit hard to read."

"He's just not used to you yet. He'll come around when he's more comfortable."

"He seems to feel pretty comfortable with Lexy." I can still see the relief in his eyes that she was finally back, and he didn't have to be alone anymore. It was as if everything had stopped for him when she was gone, but now he could start breathing normally again. I don't know how to feel yet about seeing that kind of intensity and need towards my daughter. And Lexy is just as fascinated by him. I'm surprised the house didn't light on fire with the two of them in the same room.

Becca laughs. "Yeah, but it took him a while. I think he had to realize he didn't want to lose her."

I picture his scar, white and jagged over his brow, and the sorrow that seems to follow him around like a shadow. "He's been through some things."

Pressing her lips together, Becca only nods. "Haven't we all?" she murmurs.

I expect her to say more, to elaborate, but she doesn't, and I can feel the warning not to ask or press. "They talked all the time while we were in California. It's nice to see her finally happy. I'm glad she had him to lean on in the middle of all that."

Becca gives me a knowing smile. "They've gotten pretty close over the last few months. She's been good for him."

"I like Ben." I can't help smiling thinking of him. He seems to have that effect on people. "He's very easy-going."

"Yes, he is," Becca says, and I notice her blush which somehow makes her even prettier. "He's the best guy I know."

"He takes good care of you," I say, grateful she wasn't stranded on her own after I left her to fend for herself.

"Yes, he does. I got lucky with him."

"Seems to me he's the lucky one," I tell her, and she gives me that shy, vulnerable smile only I am allowed to see. Trusting love has never come easily for the two of us. Seeing her this content and safe eases some of my guilt. We've both somehow found our way.

I quietly finish my tea. It's cooled now, but I realize mama was right. It does help a little, or maybe it's just the memory of her that does. We sit side by side on the step with our arms and legs touching and look out over the land we've both inherited.

The old lab stirs again and lifts his head, his eyes fixing on me. "You have a very strange dog," I tell her, watching him yawn widely and stretch out his front paws. I'm not sure why but it makes me feel better to have him close.

Following my gaze, Becca tenderly smiles at Abraham. "He knows who needs him. Hasn't been wrong yet."

"Is that why he sat by my feet at dinner?"

Becca laughs. "Yeah, probably. He's definitely a different kind of guard dog. Loyal as they come."

The protection is comforting, and I settle a little more into the surrounding dark. The air hums with insects, the croak of frogs, the soil breathing and stirring. "It really is beautiful here," I admit. "I just wish I didn't see him everywhere I look. It makes everything feel tainted."

"I know," she says, sighing. "There are some days I swear I hear him on the stairs, even think I smell whiskey in the house. I still have nightmares sometimes. But a lot of good has happened on this land in the last few years, a lot of healing with the horses. I want to think Ben and I have been able to change the course of the past a little bit. We took it back for ourselves. And it helps me to think that this land was never his. It has always belonged to the Montgomery family. He can't ever take that away from us." She reaches for my hand, and I have a memory of us clinging under the bed to one another, vowing to never let each other go. "I'm so glad you're here. It means he wasn't able to destroy everything."

"I promised I would come back for you." I hold onto her hand. I'm not going to let the past drive us apart again. "I'm sorry it took me so long."

"I knew you would one day." She gently touches my cheek, and my eyes meet hers. I suddenly feel nine years old again—two little girls against the world.

"I really want a drink right now," I confess, because with her, I know I can say anything. My entire body is clammy and aches from the craving.

She nods, her eyes full of understanding and compassion. I feel her hands grip tighter around mine as if to keep them from reaching for something I am not supposed to. "I know you do."

I can't have one. I'll never have another drink again. Sometimes it feels as if I lost the only thing that ever knew and loved me. But Andie said it's normal to miss it. She said even she still does sometimes. As long as we don't give in.

Exhausted from the strain of trying to cope sober, I lean my head on Becca's shoulder and close my eyes. I'm suddenly so tired, down to my very soul and bones. "Thank you for never giving up on me," I whisper.

She wraps her arm around me, brushes her lips over the top of my head, and rocks me just like our mama used to do on these same steps. And for the first time since being back on this land, I feel safe enough to rest.

Chapter Thirty-Four
VICTORIA

It's Tuesday. The sun is finally up. I made it through my first night back in Tennessee.

I wasn't sure I would. The last few hours in the dark felt painfully long and endless. Fitful, feverish dreams hunted me in my sleep. But it's morning, and I'm awake and still sober.

Breakfast is over, and everyone has scattered over the far ends of the land. To keep myself distracted, I wash the dishes, clean up the kitchen, sweep the floors, and fold the towels from the dryer.

Chores are now done, and I'm not sure what else to do with my idle, restless hands.

Lexy is doing homework. Richard is taking a nap. The time change and southern heat have drained him. I feel the craving crouching closer and don't want to give in. My phone is in my pocket, always within reach. I have Andie's number memorized.

I've come so far. Sixty-two days clean. That's not very long considering the months and years the vodka had its grip on me, but it's more than I ever thought I'd be capable of.

I'm going stir crazy in the house. The walls are closing in, memories resurfacing, too many at once, backing me into a corner. Feeling suffocated, I blindly fumble, clumsily pushing open the screen, and head down the back steps, relieved to be outside.

I need to be by myself on the land. I have to prove I can handle it. I want to face him on my own, lure him out of the shadows, into the daylight where neither of us has anywhere to hide. I have to go alone and confront the ghosts that still walk and wait for me here.

Rays of golden sunlight cast a hazy glow over the miles of green as I walk over the worn path in the grass. As a little girl, I used to imagine it was the yellow brick road that would lead me far away to a magical world where he couldn't find me.

I remember safer places on this ranch, ones where I managed to smile and laugh and pretend I was normal for a few moments.

I gravitate towards the stables where Grandaddy Cade taught us how to groom and care for the horses. He'd let us sneak them treats even though Grandma Rose didn't want them to have too many for fear of getting belly aches.

I pass the outbuildings where Becca and I played hide-and-seek. The hayloft in the barn where we'd climb up the ladder, lean out over the edge, and watch the world below.

I then wander over to my secret spot near the old forgotten well where I would play my guitar and sing and never worried about being discovered.

Standing in the middle of the field, I look around, searching for him. I listen to the whir of the cicadas, the birds chattering in the trees, the distant whinnying of horses, and the background echoing voices of Becca and Ben from somewhere off behind me. Sound carries far over the flatness of the acres.

I'm out in the wide-open, unprotected, with no weapons or shields, vulnerable, expectant, and watching. I won't back down. I'm no longer a child or a coward, and he can't chase me under a porch.

I wait for him to show his face and swing his shot. Bracing myself for the blow, I prepare to duck and dodge. He had a way of coming at me from out of nowhere. The blind corner of my peripheral vision that always caught the fist when I didn't turn around in time.

This land seems to have stood still while I've been gone, holding all the abuse and fear right where I left it. My last memory, my life itself, is frozen in mid-air as if the days have not moved forward, trapped in a plastic world inside a bubble. Everything has changed and yet is exactly how it's always been.

The years have passed, but they have not been kind to him. He is a bitter wrinkle in time during the long history of this ranch. His name taints tongues that dare speak of him. He is not remembered well, and I wonder if he ever regretted the destruction he left in his wake.

I pity him for what he missed out on by letting the alcohol overtake him. He could have had a family, a future, a safe home. A better life than the tragic one he knew growing up.

But he was unable to break free of his past or forgive himself for an abusive childhood that was never his fault. He didn't know how to be loved or love us. I wonder if he ever wanted to.

He refused to let us help him, his wounds and anger keeping him from admitting he needed us. The thought occurs to me that maybe he believed we wouldn't be there for him. That no one would, and letting us in would have made him feel too weak and small and defenseless. Just as he made us feel.

Targets. Punching bags. Doormats. Worthless.

Is that how he saw himself? Did he want to be that way, or did he think there was no other way? Was anyone ever kind to him? Did he wish he was different? Or had he believed his own father just as I believed him? Ironic to think we both were victims.

In the quiet, I hear the breeze whispering through the grasses, stirring the branches of the ancient oaks. I turn in a slow, full circle. He never comes out of hiding. Maybe for once, he fears me. I remain unharmed and untouched and unscathed.

He isn't here. Only the debris of his destruction is left like ancient, rusted-out relics and crumbled ruins—a desolate wasteland of his pain.

His suffering wreaked havoc over those caught in his crossfire as he flailed and failed and fought to outrun his demons. Sadly, he was never able to. And we were the ones who paid the price.

The brutal memories of his rages sear and scorch the fields, like gunpowder burns on a battlefield. We are the only surviving casualties of his war with himself.

He chose to die alone, in excruciating agony, shutting out Becca and mama even on his deathbed. I was already long gone. Did he think of me as he took his last breath?

I'll never know. He took all my answers with him. The only thing I have are faded scars on my skin and scattered, mysterious details of his terrible childhood. He left us behind to connect the elusive dots and figure out how to find ourselves in between the space and secrets he fiercely held against his whiskey-soaked chest.

Whatever it is I am looking for is nothing but dust. He no longer staggers and shouts and swears over these pastures. His bottles of Wild Turkey are long empty. His voice is silenced. His fists can no longer strike. He only exists now in nightmares and flashbacks. Even I have purged myself of him as the last drop of vodka was cleansed from my system. He has no hold on me anymore.

I thought this would be harder, sweatier, bloodier, violent. I'd been ready for war and death and to ruthlessly defeat him. A gladiator charging towards his enemy.

I wanted to take something away from him, just as he had done to me. I wanted him to pay. To be sorry. To suffer. I wanted to tell him to his face that I don't forgive him and how angry I've been. How much I've hated him. And demand to know how he could have hurt his own family the way he did.

But all I feel is heavy grief for a man who never was able to find his way out of the pit. He pulled us all down into it with him, and yet somehow, despite our childhood hiding under the bed and my own depraved years of drinking, we managed to claw free, still alive and breathing.

I walk aimlessly over the land he resented and cursed, not knowing where to go or what is supposed to happen next.

Frustration churns in my belly. Tears burn my eyes, making my throat ache and tighten.

I foolishly hoped he could give me closure, some shred of resolution, an apology, acknowledgment of what he had done to us. I've waited so long, but he's gone, and I have to look beyond him to find what I need.

I'm at the furthest perimeter of the ranch. There's nowhere left to go. I've searched everywhere and can't find him. One boundary marker over, and I'll be on the neighbor's farm. I can see their cattle from here.

Feeling defeated, I turn back and start the long walk back up to the house. It seems as if I have walked for five hundred miles and still ended up where I started.

The large old oak tree is a rippling mirage in the pastures where Becca and I used to lay out on the grass while we waited for him to pass out, and we'd count the stars in the sky. We'd climb to the highest branch we could where we were far out of his reach, and the moon seemed close enough to touch.

I remember this spot. Daddy never wanted to walk this far. And when he was drunk, he couldn't. Becca and I hid out here for hours, safely out of his grasp. We were nothing but a speck in the middle of the green. Two little needles in a haystack.

I hear singing and absently wonder who left their radio on. The voice is pure and pretty and hauntingly heartbreaking. I realize it's coming from a few feet away and follow the sound.

As I round the thick, gnarled trunk and get closer, I discover it's my daughter. She doesn't see me. Her eyes are closed as she plays, lost in a bliss I instantly feel and recognize. I wonder why she's all the way out here.

I didn't know she could sing. I've never heard her and feel a hot rush of guilt at missing out on another part of her I should have noticed and paid attention to. The blackouts have created incomplete gaps and holes where my life is supposed to be.

I hadn't realized she'd inherited the gift. It's strange that it's so beautiful. I didn't think I'd passed anything onto her that was worthwhile or good. Staying quiet, I stand behind her and listen.

The song isn't one I know, and I realize she must have written it herself. The lyrics are raw, honest, and painfully revealing. Am I the reason her voice is so sad and lonely?

She'd found her great grandmother Rose's guitar I left on the bed up in our room. I'd started playing again and writing songs in rehab, needing something constructive to do with my empty hands. I take it everywhere with me now.

I have the surreal sense of watching myself under the same tree, under the same sky, playing the same guitar.

Seeing it in her arms brings back bittersweet memories of my grandmother teaching me how to play and singing together on the front porch. It was one of the few times I can remember feeling genuinely happy on this ranch.

Lexy finishes her song, and her voice shimmers out like the glittering flutter of hummingbird wings, the final strum of the guitar echoing into the sunlight. Goosebumps shiver over my arms, causing the hair to stand up. I know I just witnessed something special.

"That was beautiful."

Startled, Lexy jolts, and her eyes fly open. I notice she looks surprisingly worried, as if I'd caught her with her hand in the cookie jar. My heart aches that she feels she needs to hide from me and realize it's why she's in the middle of this field. So no one can see or hear her. I used to do the same thing when I ran from daddy.

"I didn't know you were out here." Her cheeks flush as she looks down at her lap. "I'm sorry I borrowed your guitar. I should have asked, but I couldn't find you."

"I needed a walk. I don't mind you playing it. Can I join you?" When she nods, I come over and sit down next to her on the grass. The guitar looks natural in her arms, her fingers at ease on the strings. She's instinctively gifted, the genius of a prodigy as if it's second nature. Without being taught, she knows what to do, how to find those secret chords and notes that make the world stop and hold its breath in astonishment at the beauty she creates, and I can tell she's been playing for a long time, years even. How had I missed this? Why has she never told me? "It was you that sang to me while I was in the hospital, wasn't it?"

Still wary, Lexy hesitantly nods. "You were having nightmares. I didn't know you could hear me."

"I could," I tell her, wincing as I remember the violent thrashing of detox. And her sweet voice washing over me in the unbearable darkness, soothing away the bad dreams and sweaty spasms of the withdrawals. "It helped."

"Good," she says, her shoulders relaxing as the tension eases slightly. She looks past me towards the house. "Where's dad?"

"Taking a nap." I give her a half-smile. "Southern heat got to him."

"It definitely takes some getting used to." Lexy reaches for her thermos, opens it, and drinks. I hadn't thought to bring one. I wasn't expecting to walk out this far and realize how thirsty I am. My mouth is dry, my body drained. Noticing me watching her, Lexy holds out the water to me. "Do you want some?"

Nodding, I gratefully accept it. "Thank you," I say, taking a long, cool swallow. I guess I'm not as used to the southern heat as I thought. I don't live here anymore. It's the first time I'm realizing it. Somehow it feels as if I never left. I hand the thermos back, and she sets it down between us in case I want more. *Still taking care of me,* I notice and wonder if it will always be a habit of hers. "I didn't know you could sing like that."

The light dims from her as she becomes guarded again, and I'm saddened she still thinks she has to be so careful and cautious with me. As if I'm explosive or breakable or poisonous. Radioactive waste. Self-conscious, she fidgets with the guitar strap. "It's for one of my classes at school."

"You're taking music classes?"

"Yeah. It's a composition one." She shrugs, trying to be nonchalant, but I know nothing about this is casual. "I was just practicing."

"Sounds like much more than that. I like the song you were playing. Did you write it?"

"Yes," she answers shyly. I can tell she's not sure how I'm going to react, what I'll say, what else I will take from her. She's deliberately kept this from me. The sick reality sits heavily on my chest that she has been right not to trust me. I would have destroyed her, just as I had everything else that was important. I'd been too drunk not to. She's lost so much because of my addictions. "I've always wanted to play Grandma Rose's guitar. I remember watching you sing when I was little."

The memory feels like I'm remembering a stranger, as if the girl I used to be and who I am now were never in this same body. As if my life ended and then began again, and I became someone else entirely. Maybe I did.

"They don't make them like that anymore. The strings used to be made from sheep's wool." I laugh when Lexy's eyes get bigger, and she quickly lifts her hands off. "Don't worry; they were changed out years ago. The whole thing is hand-painted. Even those black roses on the front. It's a collector's item these days."

Lexy reverently traces her fingertips over the glossy wood. "It's beautiful. I like the way it smells. Like dreams."

She's right, I realize, touched at how awestruck she is. What a precious way to put it. So many hopeful souls have played that exact guitar. I was one of them. And now so is she. "Yes, it does. Your Grandma Rose taught me to sing on it. The first song I ever learned was on that guitar."

"What song was it?"

"*She's Got You* by Patsy Cline."

Lexy smiles. "I love that song. I don't know how to play it though."

"I could teach you some time if you'd like." I want to share this with her, a connection between two kindred beings. Music has a way of bonding people, even an alcoholic and her daughter.

"Yeah, that would be great."

Stretching out my legs, I lean back on my hands and look up through the canopy of branches. Even though we're sheltered under the shade, the air is still muggy and warm and smells of honeysuckle and delta-soaked soil. "This was always one of my favorite spots on the ranch."

Lexy looks up, sunlight dabbling over her face, her shoulders, the silky darkness of her hair. She seems at peace and content. I don't know how she found that here and envy her for it. She isn't haunted by this place as I am. "Mine, too. It's so quiet."

"And far away from everything." I look off over the fields. The barn and main house are barely a blip against the skyline. Blink, and you'll miss them. "We used to pretend we were at the edge of the world."

Lexy watches me closely, her eyes serious and intense. "You'd hide out here, wouldn't you?"

It's still such a bittersweet relief to be able to finally tell her. "Yes," I answer because there isn't anything else I can say. I have too many scars and sins to downplay the truth.

"I'm sorry this place hurts you so much."

"I am too." I want to ease the sadness in her eyes. "But the good thing about Granddaddy Cade's tree was that the branches were too high for daddy to reach us. And at night, if you look up there," I point to the blue sky peeking through, "you can see the constellations and look at the stars. There are so many out here. They don't shine as bright out in California."

"No, they don't," Lexy murmurs quietly, staring off over the pastures.

Something in her voice makes me look over at her. A wistful longing. An aching. My heart sinks low into my stomach. I know what she's thinking. I could feel the land pulling her back since the second we drove under the arch of her Great-Great-Granddaddy Beau's gate.

I'm afraid to ask, to say it out loud. I feel the question, the weight, and the consequences of her answer hanging in the air between us. She won't look at me, as if she's waiting for one of us to finally bring it all to light. But it's inevitable. Maybe this moment has been coming since the very first letter Becca ever sent. "You want to stay here, don't you?"

Lexy gradually, tentatively meets my eyes. She looks as if she's afraid to tell me, unsure of what I will do. That I'll relapse, spiral back down, fall apart, and fall off the wagon.

Tell each other the truth. I heard it every waking second in rehab. I'm thinking of getting it tattooed on my forehead. "It's okay, Lexy. I want you to be honest with me." Even if it breaks my heart.

Still apprehensive, she finally reluctantly nods. "I do," she answers, those two words sealing our fates.

What is it about this land? I wonder for the millionth time since arriving here. Once you step foot on it you can't seem to live without it. "What about college?" I know I'm stalling, but I'm trying to get my bearings. I need a minute. Things are changing too fast. I don't want to say the wrong thing. This moment feels very important and fragile. And I have to face it sober.

"There's a music school here I was hoping I could apply for."

My mind is spinning. I just got her back and am already losing her. "What music school?"

"The one at Vanderbilt. It's in downtown Nashville. Nick thinks I can get in."

Nick. Even the way she says his name is sweet. I wonder if she knows she's in love with him. I have a feeling he's a big part of why she wants to stay. He's not wrong. Her voice is stunning. She's even better than I was at her age.

And then it dawns on me, and I stare in amazement at her. "You want to be a singer?"

"Yes," she answers breathlessly, as if she can't help it, and the fever is consuming her from the inside out. Her eyes burn with that fire I know so well. I recognize myself twenty-five years ago.

Is this my redemption? I wonder, hope stirring. Has my healing been tied to my daughter this entire time? We have the same dream, the same talent. Is there something in my blood that is still pure enough to hand down to her? Did I manage to do one thing right?

"That's what I wanted to do, too. When I left here, I was going to be a star. I was convinced my name was going to be up in lights."

"I know. I remember hearing you sing when I was little. I thought you had the most beautiful voice in the world."

Her compliment flusters and embarrasses me. Shaking my head, I sigh, feeling the familiar rush, the nostalgia, and the ecstasy. It is an addiction in itself for me. "I loved it more than anything. My entire existence used to revolve around music, as if my life depended on it. I would eat, breathe, and dream it. When I was singing, everything would disappear. I could. It felt as if I were flying or made of lightning. I was free. And I could say things I couldn't say anywhere else. Singing let me be who I was supposed to be."

I'm so caught up I don't realize Lexy is staring at me as if seeing me in a new light, her eyes full of tears and glowing with that knowing only people with the same passion can understand.

"Yes," she whispers fervently. "It's exactly like that."

Bringing myself back, I see something in her face I've never seen before. For the first time in years, she isn't looking at me as an alcoholic, but as her mother. A musician, an artist, a singer like her. Someone she respects and can learn from and admires. Her equal. I've waited so long to be seen this way by her. "How would you apply for the school?"

She hesitates, but I keep my eyes on her, holding her gaze, trying to draw her out, and she finally gives in. "I already have an application," she admits quietly, carefully watching for my reaction. "I recorded a demo but haven't sent them in yet."

"When would you have to submit it?"

"November first is the deadline for next year's admission. My music teacher at school could write a reference letter for me."

A month from now. That's so soon. My palms are sweaty, and I fight the urge to grab a bottle. It's frustrating having it constantly out of reach and trying to cope without it. The taste is at the back of my throat. "You've thought this through." She's been planning this for years. Her entire life possibly. Just like I did.

Her face falls as the guilt takes back over. "But I won't do it if you don't want me to. I know we're dealing with a lot right now."

I look at her, at the excitement and dream burning in her eyes. I used to have the same flame and desire. It's unlike anything else on earth. I let daddy and the vodka bury it for years and have been lost ever since. Until now. "This is what you want?"

Lexy stares off over the land, her eyes full of love and longing for a place I have hated and feared. She managed to find a home on these acres, one I never gave her. She belongs here, more than I ever did. And it is her inheritance, just as her great-great-grandparents willed and wished when they settled on this ranch over a hundred and fifty years ago. She needs it the way they wanted her to, and maybe it also needs her.

"Yes."

The finality of her answer pierces through me, stealing my breath, but I know the decision is already made. I can't take her dream away. My past stole mine for far too long. I'm not doing it to my daughter. Not when she is so bright and hopeful. I understand her obsession, the yearning to pour your heart and guts into a song as if nothing else exists outside of the melody. I know better than anyone that asking her to give it up will destroy her and cause her to resent me. I couldn't bear it.

"Let me talk to your dad and see what we can figure out. In the meantime, you should send in your application."

She gasps and quickly turns to me, and I have a flash of her at two years old at Christmas, wide-eyed with wonder and staring at the pile of presents under the tree that seemed to have appeared from out of nowhere as she slept. She'd believed in everything back then. Santa and magic and castles made of snow. Before I took my first drink and taught her fairytales weren't real. "Are you sure?"

Tears are in my eyes, but I make myself smile and nod. I have to give this to her. Especially with that glow on her face. Have I ever seen her truly happy before? "You want to make the deadline, right?"

My breath whooshes out as she reaches for me, and I'm caught in a tight, fierce hug. My face is pressed into her hair, and I feel her arms gripping my neck. I lean in, desperately holding on, trying to get as close as I can, inhaling the flowery scent of her skin, absorbing the sweetness and innocence of her. She hasn't held me like this since she was little, as if she needs and trusts and believes me. I haven't let her or given her a reason to.

"Thank you, mom," she whispers into my ear.

Overwhelmed, I let the tears fall. This feeling is better than any drug or drink. Clinging to this moment, I make an internal vow that she will never lose anything else because of me.

She's still holding the guitar. I feel the neck jutting into my rib cage and reluctantly shift away, wiping my cheeks with the back of my hand.

Lexy lets go. She removes the strap from over her neck and hands my guitar back to me. Relieved, I take it, nestling it into my lap, the familiar weight feeling like a homecoming. It's become my security blanket. It always has been.

"Will you teach me the song Grandma Rose taught you?"

Feeling the glare of the spotlight shine and expose me, I blush and stammer a little. "I hope you don't mind if I'm a little rusty. I haven't sung it in years."

She gives me an encouraging smile, and I know there's no way I will say no with her looking at me like that. "It's okay."

I strum my fingers over the strings, and the surge of euphoria floods through me, over me, into the space between us, connecting her to me. I recognize the pull, the purpose, the necessity. It's instant, and I easily fall back into the world I chased and hungered for when I was younger.

I start to sing, and Lexy follows the melody, her voice blending in with mine, our harmonies melding instinctively and intimately on the air with the heat as if we've always been singing together. She effortlessly picks up my cadence and rhythm and adds her own spin to the classic song, and I'm again left staggered at how gorgeous her voice is. I've never been more proud of her.

As we sit and sing under my favorite old oak, I have the beautiful realization my life has finally come full circle, and I rediscover the girl I used to be. I'm somehow still here underneath the layers of yellowed, tarnished history. And I'm alive for the first time since I left him, and myself, far behind.

A sense of completion fills me, and I feel whole in a way I never thought was possible on this land as I pass down to my daughter the song her Grandmother Rose taught to me all those years ago.

Chapter Thirty-Five
LEXY

The porch swing creaks as I sway back and forth, staring down the dusty lane, watching the last rays of sunlight sink behind the stoic old oak trees. Scents of wild grasses, sweet hay, and irrigated soil hang heavily in the late evening air.

Highlighted against the skyline is the rustic shadow of my Great-Great-Granddaddy Beau's gate, the arch tall and proud and still defiantly standing even after all this time.

A sentimental sense of commitment and purpose fills me as I look out over the land I will now be able to call home. I'm next in our family line to watch over and protect and nurture the farmhouse, stables, barn, and fields that have been here for well over a century.

I've never had something like this before. Security. Safety. Somewhere to call my own. I feel as if I've been waiting to come back to this place my entire life, even long before I knew this ranch existed, and wonder if I was always meant to be here.

The light is almost gone. The harvest moon will be coming up as soon as it is dark. Nick isn't back yet, and I anxiously scan and search the hovering twilight for him. He's been gone all day.

I haven't seen or heard from him since breakfast this morning. I texted him, but he hasn't responded. I wonder if he forgot about sitting out and watching it together.

I haven't told him the news that I'm staying. I want it to be a surprise and do it in person. I'm curious what his reaction will be.

He missed dinner. One of the horses broke through a section of the fence, and a few had escaped onto the neighbor's farm. He and Ben have been bringing them back in and making the repairs. There's always the worry of them getting too near the road or being injured. I hope they were able to gather them all to safety. I spent the afternoon with Glory, so I already know she's out of harm's way.

I'm about to go back inside when I see him walking the worn path towards the house. He's carrying a blanket over one arm and a thermos. I wonder if he can hear how fast and hard my heart is beating as he comes up the porch steps. It seems to get louder and stronger the nearer he gets, as if it's leading him back to me.

I notice he showered and changed, his hair still a little damp and falling over his forehead, covering his scar. Odd how I can't seem to picture him without it. His pain is so much like mine, our wounds and loneliness binding us together.

"Hey," he says as soon as he's close enough.

"Hi." I'm already smiling as I push myself off the swing and walk toward him. I remember the first night he found me out here all those months ago. We were strangers then, guarded and defensive and far apart. And now he knows more about me than anyone. Funny how life can change so quickly.

"Sorry I didn't text you back," he tells me, his voice and eyes apologetic. "Day slipped away from us. Got back in a little later than we thought." He holds out his hand to me. "You ready?"

Nodding, I link my fingers with his, the feeling of completion immediate, as he leads me down the steps. He's here. Nothing else matters. "I thought maybe you forgot."

He looks over at me in that way only he knows how to do that makes everything on the edges of us blur and disappear. "I've been thinking about you all day, Lexy," he drawls, his voice low like a love note slipped secretly into my pocket, and a thrill rushes through me at the husky way he says my name.

Fireflies wink as if guiding us. Cicadas, crickets, and croaks of frogs call out from wherever they are hiding, seeming to surround us with their songs. Stars are starting to wake up and already crowding the sky as if coming to see the show. My mom is right. They do shine brighter out here. The horizon is darkening with hues of lavender and deep shades of blue that seem unreal in their beauty.

"What's in the thermos?"

"Hot chocolate," he answers. "I snagged some from the batch Becca made."

I beam at him. "I love how she makes it. She puts peppermint in it. It's delicious."

He laughs at my excitement. "I knew you'd like it."

"I do," I tell him, touched that he thought of it and that he notices little things about me when I am not even aware of it. This is the real him, I realize, my fingers tightening in his hold, the him I kept trying to get to underneath the deep layers of devastation and grief. Tender and sweet. He's irresistible. "The moon isn't out yet."

Nick looks up at the sky. "The sun just set. It'll rise in a bit."

"Did you get all the horses in?"

He nods. "Yeah, we did. And the fence is back up, so they can't get out again. For now, at least."

"Is it the part we worked on?"

Nick smiles. "No. Ours is still standing."

I smile back, remembering that sunny, sweltering afternoon a few months ago when we mended the fence line together. "That was one of my favorite days on this ranch with you."

"Mine too. I think of you every time I'm over on that side."

Surprised, I look at him. "You didn't seem like you wanted me out there with you."

Frowning, he glances at me. "That's what you thought?"

I nod. "You barely said two words to me. I felt like you just wanted me to leave you alone."

He's quiet as he studies me. "That's not what I wanted," he says softly.

"I could never tell what you were thinking," I confess, shaking my head. "It drove me crazy."

Nick seems to like that. I can see his mouth curve into a smile even in the dimming light. "Oh yeah?"

Laughing, I self-consciously shrug. "Yeah."

"I know the feeling," he murmurs, pinning me with that intense stare, making my world stand still. "I was constantly trying to figure you out."

It's my turn to be flattered. "Really?"

He nods. "But I think you understand me more than I do you."

Before I can ask him what he means, we reach the large oak in my Great-Granddaddy Cade's field. Nick lets go of my hand to spread out the blanket on the grass. Sitting down, he pats the ground for me to join him. He sets the thermos on his other side as if he doesn't want anything between us.

I sit next to him, close enough that our legs and arms and skin touch. Thick, gnarled branches drape over us, starlight peeking through. The night is comfortably warm.

"Why do you think I understand you better?" I watch his profile, memorizing the slope of his cheek, the curve, and stubble of his jaw, the length of his lashes as he blinks, waiting for him to answer.

He doesn't say anything for a moment, stretching out my anticipation, fascination, and curiosity. I would stay up all night to hear his voice. I think it's still hard for him to open up. I find it ironic that he thinks I'm the mysterious one. He's so quiet and elusive and likes keeping to himself. Talking about his feelings isn't something he's used to.

"You know how to read people," he finally explains. "You can feel their pain from a mile away. It was one of the reasons you always made me so nervous."

"How come I made you nervous?"

Stammering and struggling to find the right words, Nick opens his mouth, closes it again, then shakes his head. "I'm not very good at this," he mutters, staring off towards the fields where we spent dawn to dusk together months before. "It's as if you can see right through me or something. Like that day we worked on the fences. Every time you looked at me, I kept thinking of all the things I wanted to tell you. I knew you'd get it. And it would've been so easy with you, which was the whole problem."

"What problem?"

Flustered, he lets out his breath. Bringing his legs up, he rests his arms over them, clasping his hands. "You were changing everything, changing me. From the very first night I found you singing on the porch, I knew everything was going to be different."

"Do you wish I hadn't?"

He looks over at me then, his eyes dark and direct and a bit desperate as if the ledge of the pit is still right behind him, and I'm his only rope to safety. "No."

Reaching out, I hold onto his wrist, feeling his pulse throb under my fingertips, and tug him towards me until our lips meet. He seems surprised and doesn't even have time to close his eyes before I move back.

Confused, he searches my face. "What was that for?"

He seems so vulnerable and helpless. I can't help smiling. "You're just better at this than you think."

Shoulders gradually relaxing, he shifts his wrist I'm holding to where my hand moves back into his. His smile is sweet and shy, and my heart flips over in my chest. "Good to know."

I snuggle into his side, not leaving a hint of space or night or air between us. "You've changed everything for me, too."

He wraps his arm around my shoulders. "Are you sorry I did?"

Keeping my eyes on his, I shake my head. I want him to believe me. "No."

He kisses me again, a little longer this time, and I start to spin out, my fingers tangling into the ends of his hair, his hands moving under the hem of my shirt, just on the edge of where they shouldn't be, our breathing heavy, my mind and body weakening and leaning into him, warmth making my limbs weightless, the blanket a soft cloud beneath us.

But before I fully go under, he seems to get distracted by something and pulls back, leaving me dazed and breathless.

Turning his head, he points out over the fields. "Look."

Following his gaze, I look over and then gasp as I see the moon, large, full and bright, and seeming to land directly in front of us. I instinctively want to duck as if it unexpectedly fell from the sky like a meteor or a comet and is about to crash into me.

I'm not sure when it appeared or how I could have missed it. It's so close I swear I could touch it. Even though I know it's impossible, I still try to reach my hand out, but of course, it's thousands and thousands of miles away.

The glow seems to give off its own heat. A magical golden haze shimmers in the air as if the dust from the lunar surface has left a sheen over the entire earth, turning everything angelic, holy, supernatural somehow.

"It's beautiful," I say, stunned with wonder. "It looks like it's melting right into the land."

Nick grins. "I told you. There's nothing like it out here. Shame it only happens once a year."

Biting my lip, I look at him from under my lashes and decide it's time to share my news. "Well then, I guess it's good I'll be here next year to see it."

I watch as my words register, and he quickly turns to me. "What?"

I don't know why, but I'm suddenly nervous and fidget with the frayed seam of my jeans. "I talked with my mom today. I was out here practicing one of my songs for school, and she found me. She's never heard me sing before."

"What did she say?"

"That I'm really good." Overwhelmed, tears burn the back of my throat, and I blink as they cloud my vision. I'm still amazed at her response, at our conversation, at how years of mistrust and silence and hidden hopes and dreams had been broken wide open and revealed.

"You are."

I smile tenderly at him. He's the first I ever trusted with my secrets and believed in me. I will forever be grateful to him for that. "It's different hearing it from her. She used to sing all the time when I was little. I wanted to be exactly like her. She reminded me of a princess or a mermaid. She had the most beautiful voice I've ever heard. She still does." Sighing, I stare over the moonlit fields towards the house where my mom has come to face her demons. I can't see it from where we are but simply knowing she is nearby is reassuring. "I just want her to be proud of me."

Nick strokes my back, the heat of his palm radiating through the cotton of my shirt. "I'm sure she is."

"I hope so. I feel as if I have been waiting my whole life to be her daughter, but her drinking never let me. Until now. She taught me the song our Grandma Rose taught her when she was younger. We sang it together today on her guitar. I never thought in a million years that would happen with us."

"Sounds like you two made a lot of progress."

"We did," I agree, trying to wrap my mind around all that unfolded and came to the surface between us. "It's nice to finally be able to share something I love so much with her. She's the reason I can sing. I inherited my talent from her. And I think it means a lot to her to know that."

"That's really great, Lexy," he says, his voice sincere. "I know how much you've wanted this with her."

"I told her I want to live here and go to the music school at Vanderbilt. She said she supports my decision and told me to send in my application."

He gently nudges me in my side. "I've been telling you to do that for months."

I playfully roll my eyes. "I know. There was just so much going on though. But my mom said she understood why I wanted to do this. She has the same passion as me, so she gets it. I emailed my teacher today, and she said she would write the reference letter, so as soon as she does, I'll submit everything. I'm hoping I can make the deadline for next year."

"I already know you'll get in." And then it dawns on him. I watch his eyes shift back to me, widen, and focus on my face. "So, that means you're staying."

"Yes." I notice I'm holding my breath as I carefully watch his expression. As important as we've become to each other over the last few months, there's still something I can't break through on his end. A hesitation, a barrier, a line in the sand.

He still never says Megan's name out loud, and I don't ask. It feels too swollen and sore and sensitive to the touch. Almost as if neither of us knows what will happen or if it will break or tear us apart if we get too close to her.

So we talk around her, underneath her, in between her. She's on the outskirts, always in the shadows, right over his shoulder, up on a shelf just behind me, out of my reach, following and watching us.

I seem to have every part of him except that one place she holds. It's as if he's keeping us completely separate. I know letting someone else in is difficult for him, and I am hoping he will open up more with time.

But then he's slowly smiling, easing my doubts, the moonlight creating creases and lines and shadows over his features that have become so intimate and familiar to me. Even his eyes seem lighter, clearer against the ethereal backdrop.

"Good. I was hating the idea of you having to go again."

I quietly let out a relieved breath. "I won't leave you," I promise.

"You better not. I just got you back." He leans in and kisses me, and I taste his need and something else, something waiting, glimmering, the corner just peeking out, right under the surface that I can't quite get a grip on.

And I lay my hesitation aside, giving in to him, grateful to know he wants me here, letting it be enough for now.

He pulls away, but his face, his eyes, and his lips are only inches from mine, blocking out the rest of the world just beyond us. "Is it going to be hard for you to be so far from your parents?"

Still a bit light-headed, I let out a shaky breath. His kisses are addicting. "Yeah, it will. I'm going to miss them like crazy." I already feel the aching beginning to build at the thought of having to say goodbye in a few days. "But my mom is doing well with her recovery. And she and my dad are closer than ever now. She knows how much I love it on this ranch and how important singing is to me, so I think we will figure it out with each other. She did make me promise I would call and text her every day though."

"I'm sure she did." He tucks me against him, and I think of all the nights we will have like this now that this ranch is my home. "I'll bet Becca is happy you're staying."

I laugh and nod. "She is. Gave me the hugest hug ever."

I feel Nick's smile against my hair. The smell of him is so comforting. Soap, soil, grains, and horses. I'm surrounded by his body heat. Tilting my head, I look up at him with the moon casting a mystical, otherworldly light over the two of us and then go completely still as I realize I'm in love with him. Maybe I always have been since that very first night he found me in my most vulnerable moment singing on the porch.

The moment is surprisingly simple and pure; no fireworks or big bang or huge explosion. I've never been in love before and thought it would be more intense, a total eclipse or loss of sanity, a wild state of euphoria, a life-shattering epiphany and reeling revelation that swept over my body like a gusting wind, knocking me backwards off my feet.

But it's more like a delicate drifting, a feathery breeze, a gentle, floating free-fall through the air until I softly land in his arms. Easy, light, and effortless. A warm and lazy southern summer day, sipping cool lemonade in the shade of the porch. He's like the land itself. Consistent, predictable, faithfully loyal, and true. When I'm with him, I'm where I belong.

Catching me staring, he leans back, searching my face. "What's wrong?"

My lips part, the words straining, standing just on my next breath. But I can't find the courage to say them yet and close my mouth, swallowing hard to keep my emotions from bursting out. There's still a sliver of a question of whether he will let me be as important as Megan. I'm sad to admit I'm still not sure. What if he won't let himself love me? Or let me love him?

Losing my nerve, I shake my head and awkwardly look away, trying to hide my heart from his eyes. "Nothing. I'm just glad I'm staying."

He watches me a moment longer, and I'm relieved it's dark as I feel myself flush. My feelings are on my sleeve. I'm too exposed and am worried he's finally figured out how to see through me and knows there's more. But he doesn't push or ask, maybe he doesn't know how or dare, and I wonder if he's not ready for me to tell him yet either.

"So am I," is all he says.

We sit together in the crackling silence where there's too much being said underneath it, and I'm grateful to have a few moments to collect myself back from the cliff I almost tumbled over.

Breaking the tension, Nick reaches for the thermos, opens it, and pours hot chocolate into the lid. Steam drifts up; I can smell hints of peppermint, and my mouth starts to water, anticipating the taste. He hands it to me, and I close my eyes as I sip, absorbing the sweet flavor and warmth seeping through me.

"I was thinking you could ride Glory tomorrow."

My eyes fly open. Thrilled, I grin at him. "I would love that."

He laughs out loud, the sound echoing beautifully over the pastures. It's such a rare thing to hear it fully and openly from him. I can count on one hand the times I actually have. It's my favorite song on earth. "Thought you might. We can do it after breakfast."

He takes the lid from me, drinks the rest, then screws it back on, setting it to the side. As soon as his hands are free, he's reaching for me again, and I eagerly move toward him.

"I can't wait." Content and happy, I rest my head on his chest as we gaze at the yellow harvest moon that we won't see for another year. I'm curious how things will be then, where our lives will have landed. Autumn will be here in a matter of days, and everything will start to change.

There are so many thoughts and feelings burning through me, under my skin, waiting on the tip of my tongue, that I want to share, to confess, to give him. But Ben always says the best things in life are always worth waiting for. And he's right. They are. I will wait as long as it takes for Nick's heart.

Chapter Thirty-Six
NICK

The last person I expect to run into at six o'clock in the morning is Victoria making buttermilk pancakes.

I need to talk to Lexy. I barely slept. That's not unusual for me, but the look I saw in her eyes last night kept me tossing and turning. I wonder what she'd been about to say.

She didn't mention anything more about it, but there was that one split second between us that had my mind racing and my stomach churning. Something is coming, changing, whispering just on the edges of where I can't quite see.

With her name already on my lips, I come in through the back door and then freeze to a halt when I see Victoria standing at the stove, muttering to herself.

We're alone. The kitchen is quiet and dim in the early morning light. Brows raised, she looks over as the screen closes at my back, trapping me in with her.

I stand where I am, not sure what to do. We haven't had an actual conversation since they arrived. Just polite small talk here and there. Short sentences and one-word answers that I quickly excuse myself from. And there's always been the protection and distraction of others around. Honestly, I've deliberately avoided one with her. She makes me nervous. She seems to know things I haven't told her.

The silence is uncomfortable between us and much too loud.

"She's not down yet," she says, as she whisks batter in a bowl. "She was up late." Still stirring, she gives me a pointed look, and I instantly am five years old and in trouble for playing in the mud. "Didn't hear her sneaking in until a little after midnight."

Feeling scolded, I shove my hands into my jeans pockets, wishing I could shrink into the wall. I can't look at her. "She wanted to see the harvest moon," I mumble, and then hearing how stupid I sound, roll my eyes at what a fool I am.

Maybe I'm imagining it, but I think I notice her expression soften and her lips twitch and wonder if she's laughing at me. It's the kind of look a guy gets when it's clear he's got it bad for a girl.

"You take her out to Granddaddy Cade's field?" she asks as she pours batter onto the griddle. "That's the best place to see it."

"Yes, ma'am." I still can't quite meet her eyes.

"Good." She nods in approval. "And call me Victoria. You're making me feel old." She brushes her hair off her forehead with the back of her hand, leaving a trail of flour on her skin. I'm not sure if I should tell her. She's wearing the faded blue gingham apron I've often seen Becca wear. I know it belonged to their mama and is spattered with spices and stains from long ago.

Thinking she wants to be by herself, I motion back over my shoulder towards the door. "I can come back if I'm in your way." Aiming for a quick escape, I start to slink off when she stops me.

"You're not in my way. I was actually hoping for a chance to talk to you," she says. My hand on the screen, I grimace and silently curse my luck. But either she doesn't notice or doesn't care. I think she already knows she has the upper hand in the situation. Bacon is sizzling, and the smell is making my mouth water. "There's fresh coffee if you'd like some."

Glancing helplessly one last time at the back door, I realize I have no way out and inwardly sigh, resigning myself to the third degree I'm sure I'll be dragged through.

Relieved for something to do, I busy myself with pouring coffee into my mug, taking longer than I should, trying to delay the inevitable. But I can feel her patiently waiting me out as if she already knows what I'm thinking.

The quiet stretches, hums, and thickens, only the constant static and pop of the griddle filling the space between us.

Knowing I can't put her off any longer, I turn to face her and finally ask, "What did you want to talk to me about?" I instinctively brace my shoulders, expecting the questions of what a guy like me wants with a girl like Lexy. I already know I'm not good enough for her. I'm too messed up and damaged. Is that what this conversation is going to be about? Is she going to tell me to stay away from her?

Heavy hopelessness falls over me. I guess it was only a matter of time. My stomach knots up, and I look down at the scarred plank floor, anticipating the worst. I'm used to being alone but thought I'd no longer need to be with Lexy here.

"I'm not sure if this will mean anything coming from me, but I wanted to thank you for taking care of Lexy when I couldn't. She told me you were there when she got the call about...um...what happened..."

She trails off, cheeks flushing, and swallows hard. Quietly and very carefully, she plucks the strips of bacon off the griddle, putting them on a cloth, one by one by one. Her movements are shaky and robotic, as if she's fighting to stay in control. I wonder for a tense, panicked second if she's going to cry.

She doesn't finish her sentence. Maybe she can't. As if the overdose is still too tragic and traumatic and terrible. The awareness and intensity of it fills the room, making it a bit hard to breathe. My eyes slowly lift from the floor back up to her. She suddenly seems fragile, and I notice guilt and shame flicker over her face and feel a rush of pity for her. Becca often looks the same way when the painful memories start crowding in.

It occurs to me I've had this backward, and this whole time, she's needed my approval and acceptance. Forgiveness for her failings. Is she worried about what I think of her? Is she expecting my judgment and condemnation? Is she waiting for accusations?

A bit stunned, I notice my mouth is open and quickly close it. "You're welcome," I stammer, still not sure what else to say and hoping I don't come off as condescending. I wasn't expecting to have a conversation like this so early in the morning. And no one is coming in to rescue me yet.

A little more composed, she clears her throat. "I know you two have gotten close."

Uncertain where she's going with all this, I warily nod, trying not to give away too much. I'm still blown away that Lexy wants anything to do with me.

Opening up a drawer, she pulls out a spatula. "Everything is exactly where I left it," she murmurs, shaking her head as she looks down at the utensils. I'm pretty sure she's talking to herself. "You can find a spool of thread in the same spot from a hundred years ago."

"That's actually happened." I've found all sorts of old and odd treasures buried and tucked away in forgotten, dusty places.

She lets out a humorless laugh. "I'm not surprised." She flips over the pancakes. "You must be happy she's staying."

Does she blame me for taking her daughter away? Apprehensive, I sip my coffee, needing a barrier between us as I try and guess what she's getting at. "I am," I answer cautiously.

"I'm sure you heard she's applying for the music school."

"Yeah, she told me last night. She's too good not to."

Victoria pauses then and looks over at me. "Yes, she is." Her smile glimmers back, and I notice how in awe she seems. I don't think Lexy has to worry her mama isn't proud of her. "She said you've been really supportive. You think she'll get in?"

"I know she will," I say with absolute certainty. I'd bet my life on it.

"I have a feeling you're right about that." I notice a twinge of sadness, of longing in her voice as she moves over to the cupboard and pulls out a stack of plates, turns, and holds them out to me. "Will you please help me set the table?"

"Uh...sure." Grateful for a reason to avoid her gaze, I set my coffee cup on the counter and take the plates from her. Moving around the table, I put them in the usual places, making sure to keep Lexy's spot next to mine.

"Can you do me another favor?"

I think we both know I'm not in any position to tell her no. Without answering, I look at her across the length of the kitchen, expectant and waiting.

She waves the spatula over the pancakes. "I haven't made these in years and am not sure if they're any good. Do you mind taste testing them for me?"

The vulnerability is back in her eyes, and I again find myself feeling sorry for her. She just wants to get something right. I remember Lexy looking at me the same way. I finish arranging the silverware. "Okay."

Relieved, she reaches out her hand. "Give me your plate."

I do what she asks and watch as she prepares two pancakes and a few strips of bacon. My stomach is already growling. She gives it back, along with the mug I had set aside, and I take both from her. As I sit down, I wonder what I'm supposed to do if I don't like it. I don't want to hurt her feelings. She'll never let me be with Lexy then.

Turning away, she gets herself a cup of coffee. While her back is to me, I taste a bite, and the light, fluffy, buttery pancake melts in my mouth. They are better than Becca's, although, I'd never dare say it. I don't have to lie or pretend as I'm immediately flung back to my childhood on rainy Saturday mornings when my brother Jake and I stayed in our pajamas the whole day and made a fort underneath the dining room table. A sentimental nostalgia fills me for simpler days when I knew nothing of loss and death.

My senses are so overloaded I don't even mind when she sits across from me.

Holding her mug between her palms, she quietly studies me, searching, probing for something I'm not sure I have a choice in giving her. In the pink morning glow, her eyes seem greener and eerily wiser than they should, and she has a way of penetrating underneath the surface of things. *Like mother like daughter,* I think wryly. I see where Lexy gets it from. They both are way too perceptive. It's unnerving.

"You're really important to her," she says, but it sounds more like a question.

I had just put a bite of pancake in my mouth. Buying myself some time, I chew slowly, then swallow. But I know I have to answer her eventually. "She's important to me too," I awkwardly manage.

"She's been through a lot."

I hear the warning in her tone, and it's then I realize what she wants to know. If I'm going to hurt her daughter. If I will protect her, be there for her. If I care enough to do those things.

I want to promise that I won't ever break Lexy's heart, but all the declarations feel forced and much too small and juvenile, as if I'm trying to prove myself. And I'd be lying. I probably will hurt her. Not on purpose. But I'm still so new at this and haven't let someone get close in years. I'm not sure what I'm doing yet and am feeling it out as I go. How do I explain that I'm just now finding the courage and will to live again?

The thought crosses my mind that if anyone could understand the struggle, it would be her. It's the same thing she's doing, and she seems like someone who wants the straight truth more than simply saying empty words that mean nothing.

"I think you want me to tell you what my intentions are, but honestly, I don't have any big plans. I don't make those anymore. I know that's probably not what you want to hear. It's just how it is though. But if you're asking if she matters to me, she does. More than anyone has in a really long time." Still a bit overwhelmed by it, I have to force myself to hold her gaze as I lay my heart on the line. "I just want to be with her, but that's all I know for right now."

She's quiet as she watches me, thoughtfully tapping her fingers against her mug. I can't tell what she's thinking and realize I'm waiting for her to grant me permission to start over. "Taking it one day at a time?" she finally asks.

"Isn't that all any of us can do?"

Seeming startled by the idea, she blinks and stares at me as if the revelation is just now occurring to her. "Yeah, I guess it is." Her gaze lifts to my scar, holding for what feels like the longest, most excruciating minute I've ever sat through, searing through my skin and past and walls. She doesn't look away, and I go still, feeling my body tense and my insides burn hot. There's nothing I can do; nowhere I can go. I'm stuck and too exposed with no way to hide my deepest secrets. I wear the proof on the outside for the whole world to see. "I'm sorry for whatever it is you lost," she says so softly she almost whispers it as if she knows how raw the grief is.

My breath shudders out. I don't usually acknowledge it with other people. Megan is still off-limits. But for some reason, I let myself stay in this space with her. She has a way of bringing your pain out. I think it's because she's still trying to find a resolution for her own. "Thanks," I manage and can hear how unsteady and strained my voice sounds as if I got the wind knocked out of my lungs when she bumped against the unhealed scab. "You, too."

We look at each other across the table. I notice I don't feel defensive or angry around her. As if we are two survivors clinging to the same life raft, trying to find dry land in the middle of the wreckage we've been drowning in. An innate, silent understanding passes between us, and I wonder if the broken always call out to the broken. We all somehow find each other.

After a few moments, she sighs as if deciding something. I finally let myself breathe when she does and have the sense I just passed some sort of test. "You'll keep an eye on her?"

I very much understand the responsibility and trust she's handing over to me. "I will."

"Okay then." Eyes a little misty, Victoria nods as if the matter is settled. She rests her chin on her hand. "How are the pancakes? You cleaned your plate."

I look down and realize every last bite is gone. I didn't even notice I'd eaten it all. They tasted like she was trying to find her way back home, but I don't know how to begin explaining what I mean by that and am too embarrassed to try. "They're just right. I liked the bacon. It was sweet."

"A sprinkle of brown sugar. It's a little trick our mama taught us."

"Ben will love it."

She surprises me by laughing, and I'm relieved to hear the sound as some of the shadows ease away from her. "He seems to like to eat."

I smile. Ben's appetite is legendary. "Yeah, he does."

As if she knew we've been talking about her, Lexy walks in. The second she sees me, her face lights up, and she smiles as if I'm the only one in the room. I feel my heart stutter and my thoughts scramble. She's already dressed, and I know she's holding me to my promise to ride Glory. She's so excited I wouldn't be surprised if she slept in her clothes.

Trying to figure out what is going on, she glances curiously back and forth at her mom and me sitting together at the table. "Good morning," she says with a hint of surprise in her voice.

"Your mama made pancakes," I explain. "They're really good."

Lexy looks at her mom, and I feel the instant connection and pull as if Victoria is a magnet she helplessly gravitates towards. "You made breakfast?"

"I sure did." Pushing her chair back, Victoria smiles, getting to her feet. "Staying a good kind of busy."

Lexy stands close to her as if protecting her, and I wonder if she's aware of how she tracks Victoria's every move. I'm not sure if that habit will ever break. "Do you need any help?"

Victoria walks to the stove and hands Lexy the bacon. "Can you finish putting the food out before everyone comes in?"

Nodding, Lexy takes the plate and turns back towards me, setting it in the middle. When she leans close, I catch her scent. She smells how she always does; sweet and summery, and my gut tightens. "Save my seat," she says softly.

"I already did," I tell her, motioning to the empty chair next to me and then see the look from the night before coming back into her eyes when she smiles.

Caught off guard, I forget everything else, wanting to ask her what she's thinking, but then she seems to realize she's giving away too much and her expression clouds over with uncertainty and doubt, shutting me out of where we just were.

Confused, I open my mouth to say something, but her mom is calling her name, and she's moving away before I can find the right words, leaving me alone to sit and stew over what she's keeping from me.

Becca comes in from downstairs. "Wow. It's a feast in here." Walking to the stove, she puts her arm around Victoria's shoulders. "Thanks for letting me sleep in. I haven't been able to in years."

"I'm glad I could. I needed something to do. We still eat at seven sharp?" Victoria asks her.

"House rules," Becca answers, and they share a moment that is bittersweet and a little sad and intimate all at the same time. I'm still struck at how strong and necessary their bond is even after decades apart.

Ben comes in from outside, the screen banging behind him. Becca is always nagging at him to not let it slam so loud, but he has too much energy to help it. "I could smell breakfast cooking all the way out in the pastures." He sets his hat on the hook near the door. "Is that bacon?" Without waiting for an answer, he eagerly snags a piece from the plate and takes a bite, the crisp and crunch satisfying. "This is delicious," he says with his mouth full.

Victoria glances at me and winks, and I see why Lexy feels so protective of her. I understand how much she needs this. Some kind of normalcy in a place where there has been nothing but pain and fear and chaos. Maybe that's what we're all looking for here.

Ben gets a cup of coffee and brings it over, sits down, and starts talking to me about needing to get the stables and barn ready for the cooling weather. Only half-listening, I tune him out when Richard walks in. The kitchen is full of people and suddenly loud with laughter and chatter overlapping, colliding, and circling around me.

Walking towards his wife, Richard kisses Victoria, smiling as he brushes away the flour she streaked over her skin, and she blushes. "Good morning," he says.

She murmurs something I can't hear, their faces only inches apart. Lexy told me how they used to never be in the same room together and wouldn't talk for days. Now they can't seem to be separated for more than a few minutes.

Looking somehow younger and lighter than she did a few moments before, Victoria hands him a mug of coffee, and taking it, he joins us at the table, sitting directly across from me.

Both parents in one day, I think, trying desperately to fade into the background. *I'm on a roll.*

As Richard stirs in sugar and creamer, I notice he doesn't have one scar or callous on his hands. Even first thing in the morning, he looks like he should be on one of those glossy magazine covers. I can't imagine him mucking out stalls, but I bet he would if his daughter asked him to. They've gotten much closer over the last few months. "I hear you're going to help Lexy ride Glory today."

I guess it's too late to hope he didn't see me. Shifting uncomfortably in my seat, I remind myself not to slouch. He's taller than me, even sitting down, making me feel at a disadvantage. "Yeah. We're going out after breakfast."

"She's a big horse from what I've seen."

"She's a champion thoroughbred. Raced on the circuit for years."

"Think Lexy can handle her?"

I firmly nod. "I know she can. She's got a way with them. Glory will follow her anywhere."

"I'll have to take your word for it. I haven't spent a lot of time around horses." He sips his coffee, watching me as he lowers his mug. "I just don't want her to get hurt."

I'm not sure why but I think I hear a double meaning behind his words. I have a sneaking suspicion he's also talking about me. "I'll be sure and stay close."

As if knowing I need to be saved, Ben interrupts and starts talking about some movie he and Becca watched, pulling Richard's attention away from me. I'm grateful for the distraction, so I don't have to make any further conversation with him.

The sound of Lexy laughing makes me glance past Richard's shoulder over at her. Surrounded by her mom and her aunt, she looks beautiful and happier than I've ever seen her.

As I watch her, I have a flash of us sixty years from now in this kitchen, on this land, sitting on the porch swing, smiling and kissing her as we drink our coffee and eat buttermilk pancakes.

Realizing where my thoughts are going, sweat breaks out on the back of my neck, and I feel the blood drain out of my head. The noise fades away. I'm dizzy and have to brace my boots on the floor for balance as I sway slightly.

"What's wrong?" Ben asks me, his eyes concerned. "You look like you just saw a ghost."

Maybe I have, I think, dazed. The ghost of the life I almost had but then lost in a matter of seconds. I believed in happily-ever-after once. A long, long time ago. But then it all was ripped away from me.

Cruelly. Violently. Permanently.

And I've never been able to get it back. My ears are ringing. What if I lose Lexy too?

Richard is frowning at me. I don't blame him. I must look crazy. Shaking my head, I try to pull myself out of the gritty grip of that horrible night. My palms are damp and sticky, and I clumsily set my mug down before I drop it.

"Nothing," I murmur, again looking across the room for Lexy. Finding her, I stare hard, making sure she's still here.

Absolutely nothing is wrong. Everything is perfect. Not one problem or sign of danger in sight.

I'm not sure why it scares me so much.

Chapter Thirty-Seven
LEXY

I gently stroke the brush over the dip and slope of Glory's back and down her sides. The fans lazily turn above us, causing dander and dust motes to drift in the air, floating like tiny feathers on the slats of light peeking in through the cracks and gaps of the warped wood.

We're alone. I wanted to have a moment just between the two of us to connect with her before our ride and strengthen our bond.

She stands still and stoic as I move over the length of her, making sure there are no burrs or twigs caught in her coat. The stable is peaceful and hushed, the only sound coming from the distant echo of voices carrying in from the pastures.

Nick and Ben are out widening the training pen. I know what a big day this is for her, how her trust, heart, and spirit were broken by her previous owners. I want her to believe I will not hurt her as they did. She hasn't been ridden in almost a year and still bears the scars and trauma of abuse and neglect.

Coming around to the front of her, I brush over the broad width of her neck and shoulders. When she bends her head to sniff at me, I tenderly kiss her nose. "Hi, sweet girl," I murmur, smiling up at her. "Are you excited for our ride today? I'll be careful with you, I promise." She nuzzles my hair, and I know she is feeling comfortable and safe.

Going over to the supply shelf, I put the brush away, getting one of the blankets. Turning, I bring it back over to her and drape it over her back, smoothing out the folds and wrinkles. Nick told me it would help protect her against sores and chafing from the weight and rub of the saddle. I don't want to cause her pain in any way and not enjoy her first ride out.

Nick comes back in. He had already checked her hooves for roots and rocks and gave them a good, thorough cleaning. Pulling the saddle off the rack, he carries it over, and I help him put it on her. We don't say much, trying to keep Glory calm.

There's something reverent and ceremonial about the process of dressing her as we buckle the straps around and underneath her waist, as if we know we're in the presence of greatness.

I wonder if she remembers preparing for races, the excitement, and anticipation, the crowds, the cheers, the other horses straining and surging next to her, their breath on her neck, nipping at her heels, catching up, challenging her, competing against her.

Does she miss the victory? The dirt flying under her hooves, the steam and sweat glistening on her body, the wind through her mane, the clamoring attention, the smiles, praise, and admiration and respect as she was the first to burst and break through the ribbon of the finish line? Does she remember who she is? What she can do?

Sadly, she won't ever race again due to the severity of her injuries, but I want to give her golden days back to her however I can. She's lost way too much. Just as we have. She's still a champion and deserves better, more, everything, and I will do my best to make sure she has it.

We slip on her bridle, and Nick gently puts the bit in her mouth, being mindful not to clink it against her teeth. As he makes the final adjustments, I stand back a little and notice she looks like the world-renowned racehorse she used to be. She even seems to stand taller and prouder. A fierceness begins to glint in her eyes as if she's priming for a win. She's sleek and strong and majestic. She could make rulers and kings turn their heads and stare. My heart swells with pride and love for her. She's the most beautiful horse I've ever seen.

Nick hands me the reins. "You want to lead her out to the ring?"

A thrill shoots through me as I take them. "Yes," I answer, smiling at him. "Thank you."

He leans in and gives me a quick kiss, making my heart yearn to say things I'm afraid he's not ready to hear. "You'll do great." He looks over at Glory. "You both will."

Nodding, I take a deep breath. "Let's go." Clicking my tongue for her to follow, I lead her out of the stable, and she comes willingly, eagerly, as if she knows what the day has in store for her.

Carrying my riding helmet, Nick keeps an eye on us, making sure Glory stays on the path. He doesn't want her to startle or bolt. But she walks calmly, regally, and gracefully, experienced with star-studded arenas and prestigious racetracks. The southern sunshine glows over her like a spotlight as we walk towards the pen.

My family is already waiting for us, and I instinctively seek out my mom. I always look for her first, anywhere and everywhere.

Even when we were lost in the middle of nowhere, I never stopped needing her.

Almost as if she can read my mind, she glances over and locks eyes with me. When she smiles, my nerves quietly settle. It's still such a relief and surprise to have her here. I don't want to do this without her.

She grew up around horses, so she doesn't seem as concerned as my dad, who kept making comments over breakfast about how big Glory is and if I'm sure this is a good idea. I understand he just wants me to be safe and think it's sweet he's worried. I feel like we are finally a family.

Becca doesn't seem fazed at all and is casually leaning against the rail. She smiles and waves when she sees us. Ben gives me a thumbs-up sign as we pass them.

Nick opens the latch, and I lead Glory into the ring. He has me stop her in the middle next to the mounting steps, which will make it easier for me to get on her.

He puts the helmet over my head, latching it firmly under my chin. I had borrowed Becca's riding boots. "You ready?"

I've been waiting days for this moment, but now that it's here, I'm suddenly nervous. At over a thousand pounds, Glory seems much larger and more intimidating than she usually does. I look up at her powerful body towering above me. "I think so."

"Just relax and take a deep breath," he reassures me, tucking a stray strand of my hair back off my face. "She'll be clear with you what she's ready to do. If she only wants to walk, then just walk the ring. If she's ready to do more, follow her lead but remember you're the one with the reins. Be patient with her. She'll sense what you're feeling. And it's her first ride in a long time."

"What if I fall off of her?"

Nick looks at me, and I see nothing and no one else. "I'll catch you," he promises. "I'll be in here the whole time. You trust me?"

A ray of sun is slanting underneath the brim of his cowboy hat, catching his eyes just right, making the gold flecks glint. Fascinated, it distracts me enough that I forget about being anxious. "Yes."

"Okay. Now, you want to get on from her left. That's her mounting side, and she's used to it. She'll know what to expect."

He helps me walk up the steps until I'm standing next to her. He keeps a close watch as I hold onto the horn of the saddle and put my foot in the stirrup. Hoisting myself up, I swing my other leg over like he taught me.

Reminding myself to stay calm, I carefully adjust and settle myself in the seat, trying not to move too much or too abruptly. I don't want to spook or scare her. I can feel my family holding their breath, and everyone is very quiet as we wait for what Glory's reaction will be.

A full minute passes. She doesn't sidestep or rear up or try to buck me from her. There is no resistance from her at all, and I let myself ease my body more into hers.

The leather creaks beneath me as I look down at Nick from my perch on Glory's back. I remember Ben saying she was almost sixteen hands high. I'm not sure what that means. All I do know is the ground seems miles below my feet, and I feel my stomach do a little somersault. It's a good thing I'm not scared of heights.

"She's letting me ride her," I exclaim, beaming at Nick as I stroke Glory's neck to keep her steady and soothe her. "I can't believe it."

Nick grins up at me. "She sure is. I knew she wanted it to be you." He checks the straps on the saddle, making sure they are secure around Glory's body. "Remember to keep your shoulders back. Ride from your core." He pats his middle, and I automatically tighten my abdomen muscles. "You don't want to lose your balance if she starts to trot or gallop. Make sure your feet are in line with your hips."

I move my heels in the stirrups, aligning myself. "How's that?"

Nick nods. "That's good. Now take the reins and squeeze your thighs lightly against her and tell her to walk on."

Looking over the top of Glory's head, I do what he says. A small gasp escapes my lips as she instantly obeys and takes her first step forward. I pay close attention and try to match the flow of my body with hers as she walks the length of the pen. Her movements feel slightly hesitant as she finds her footing. "Good girl," I murmur as we complete our first lap.

"There you go," Nick says, tracking us. He's standing in the middle of the ring so he can turn as we do and is still close enough if something happens. I can hear how pleased he is with our progress. "You got this, Lexy. She knows what to do. Give her a minute to get the feel of it all again."

I tune everything out except Glory, listening to the crunch and clop of her hooves as she walks over the ground, the sway and rock as her body and muscles lengthen and shift, her size and strength supporting and carrying me. The reins feel natural in my hands, and I use them to gently communicate with her what I want her to do.

There isn't anyone else but us, the huge dome sky over our heads, the hazy morning light shimmering around us. We create our own language with each other, secrets only between the two of us, and she seems to sense my next thought and moves with me, for me, because of me.

The connection between us is intuitive and tender. To have this wounded, broken, beaten down horse come back from the brink, to have her let me get close enough to touch and ride her, is one of the greatest gifts I've ever known. I feel honored she's chosen me.

I think about my Great-Grandfather Cade, and the sensitivity and compassion he had with horses. I want to think I've inherited something from him, some innate ability and understanding. I wonder if I could ever make them dance the way he did.

And then, somewhere on our third time around the ring, Glory seems to remember her racing days and begins to trot, the pace somehow a perfectly choreographed prance as if the need to perform and compete is so deeply ingrained into her being she can't help herself. I rise and lower in the saddle with the rhythm of her gait.

She starts to pick up speed, her trot turning into a gallop, and the anticipation builds in me. I lean forward, preparing for take-off. I can feel her trying to break free, her body vibrating, straining, pushing against the fear and abuse that has held her back all this time.

"C'mon girl, let's go," I breathlessly urge her. "You can do it."

And then she's running, as if I cut her loose from invisible ropes, sprinting like lightning, a whirring, sudden surge of speed and power and resilience. It's no longer about training or instruction or technique. She's going on pure memory and instinct and God-given talent. She's remembering who she is, where she comes from, and what she was born to do.

We burst around the pen with the wind whipping through us, around us, over us, past us. The green of the fields and trees is an exhilarating blur, the faces of my family and Nick blending and disappearing into the landscape. If I ever thought animals could feel joy, I believe it now with Glory charging like freedom beneath me.

Her mane is flowing wild; her hooves pound like thunder over the ground, and I know I've never experienced anything more glorious or wonderful.

I let her do what she was meant to do and give her free reign to run, to fly, to be truly herself. And she helps me do the same. I'm laughing as we race around and around and around, faster and faster and still impossibly faster. It's unreal and unnatural, as if we're no longer in our bodies, and her hooves aren't even touching the ground.

All our pain is left far behind us in plumes of dust as if we're invincible, untouchable, unstoppable. It feels like nothing can ever catch us or tie us down or hold us back, and we somehow made it through the barrier of the sky and beyond the clouds. And we go higher and farther and deeper than either of us dreamed we could.

I don't ever want to come back down to earth as we penetrate through air and light and sound itself. This must be what it feels like to be made of magic or stardust or have wings, and my skin tingles from the heat and force of the momentum.

"Bring her back in, Lexy," Nick calls out, his voice a distant, thin echo in the rushing wind. "You don't want to wear her out."

I wish we didn't have to stop, but I listen to Nick and gently pull back on the reins, and Glory responds immediately. The world begins to come back into focus around us as we gradually slow to a trot and then a walk. I bring her to a triumphant halt where Nick is standing.

Still laughing, I collapse forward and wrap my arms around the back of Glory's neck, resting my head against her as we both catch our breath. I can feel her body trembling and heaving from the exertion beneath me. She is damp with sweat. I swear she's smiling. Closing my eyes, I inhale her scent. "Good job, Glory," I whisper. "You did it, girl. I'm so proud of you." She snorts in response, and I kiss her warm coat.

I feel Nick's hand on my leg, and I sit up. I'm smiling so wide my cheeks hurt. I don't think I've ever felt this alive. I look down at him. "Did you see us? Did you see what she just did?"

Nick grins up at me, and I can see how proud and awestruck he is. "The two of you were amazing." He keeps a hold on Glory's bridle to steady her. "You handled her so well."

"It was all her," I say, stroking her neck. "She knew what she wanted to do."

"Way to go, Lexy," Becca says, and I turn towards her. She's beaming at me. "How do you feel?"

I'm still shaking from the adrenaline and press my palm against my racing heart. It's pounding so hard and fast it feels like it's going to burst out of my chest. "Incredible. It was like flying. I don't think I'll ever come down."

I look at my mom. I want to know what she's thinking more than anyone. I watch her eyes. I always have. They are the most honest part of her. My breath catches when I discover hers are wet with tears.

"You were beautiful out there, sweetheart," she tells me. "It's like you've been riding her your whole life."

"Thanks, mom," I say, my throat tightening with emotion. I need this from her, her encouragement, and her support. I've been waiting years for her to be sober enough to truly see me.

I glance over at my dad, and he winks. I think he's relieved I made it without falling or getting hurt. "You were great, but I'll feel better once your feet are back on the ground," he teases, and I laugh.

"You two better get Glory back up to the stables and get her washed down," Ben says from the gate. "Rain is coming in."

Glancing up, I scan the sky but don't see one cloud. There's not even a breeze. Confused, I look back at my uncle. He catches my expression and grins. "Trust me," he tells me. I just smile to let him know I do.

Nick helps me dismount onto the steps. Once my feet are on the ground, I wrap my arms around him and kiss him, not caring that everyone can see us. "Thank you for giving me this today," I murmur, our faces barely an inch apart. "I—" love you. Startled, I catch myself just in time, hastily swallowing the words back. "I'm so happy," I stammer, flustered. My legs are a little weak and unsteady, but I'm hoping he thinks it's from the ride and not from me almost blurting out my feelings.

He frowns, and I see something in his eyes, a question, confusion, worry, a flicker of need, and something else that makes me go still in anticipation of what he might say. Does he know? I hold my breath, waiting, but then he seems to realize we're not alone and releases me, breaking our gaze, the intensity of the moment evaporating with the clouds of dust. "I'm happy for you. I told you she'd go anywhere for you."

And I'll go anywhere for you, I think, but don't dare say it. Instead, I smile at Glory. "She broke free today."

"Seems like you both did."

I look over at him as the truth of his words sink into me. "Yeah, I think you're right."

Nick opens the pen gate, and we lead Glory out of the ring and head back to the stable together. I reach for him, holding his hand as we walk up the path. I want to absorb the wonder of this moment a little longer. My heart is full as I look out over the miles of lush green pastures, still astounded at the rustic beauty and the reality that this ranch is now my home.

There are hundreds of stories that have been passed down around campfires and shaded porches from generation to generation on this land. Most of them are true, some far-fetched, some folklore, some too heartbreaking to even speak aloud.

I long to be a part of what is remembered here, to leave my mark on this place, to make a difference in some small way, and be included in the patchwork and tapestry of those who came before me.

I want those who inherit this land long after I'm gone to be told the story about how the local Horse Whisperer's great-granddaughter helped a broken-down racehorse named Glory break free from her pain, and we both somehow found our place next to the yellowed, grainy tintypes of my family history, standing on the shoulders of legends.

Chapter Thirty-Eight
VICTORIA

As my family walks toward the main house, I hang back near the training pen, watching the clouds of dust evaporate and settle over the ground where my daughter had ridden Glory moments before. Tracks mark and gouge the earth where they set the world on fire.

I can't seem to move from this spot. I'm still breathless and overwhelmed over what I witnessed.

Lexy and Nick are linked close as they head to the stables to wash down Glory before the rains come. They somehow seem as if they have always been together. Do they understand how alike they are? How their scars meet and match at their exact breaking points? Their pain and tragedy are like a scarlet velvet ribbon twining around their wrists, binding them to one another. A bittersweet ache fills me. I can feel the intensity of their need for each other even from a distance.

Richard begins to follow after Becca and Ben, joining in their conversation, instinctively reaching for my hand, his fingers grasping the empty space where he expects me to be. Realizing

I'm not next to him, he stops and turns around, a question in his eyes. I'm curious if he feels the void of a missing limb just as I do when he's not nearby. Does he know how necessary he is for my survival? How desperately I crave his presence?

When he comes up next to me, I can't help wondering if he is protecting me or if it's the other way around. We are incomplete and lost without each other. We always have been. He must sense I don't feel like talking yet because he stays quiet as we stand side by side, looking out over the land.

The beauty here is undeniable despite the heartbreak and bitterness that has stained the landscape. Time seems to slow down. There is no traffic, no rush, no crowds. Just open space and sunlight and sky around us. It's one of those rare instances where everything that needs to be said simply waits and holds until we're ready for it. I find myself wishing the rest of my life were as simple.

"Are you doing alright?" he finally asks.

Before I can answer, Lexy's laughter drifts over to us. It occurs to me that I have heard her laugh more in the last few days than I have in her entire life. I turn towards the sound, instantly recognizing it. I feel the yearning, that primal maternal love for our daughter. I would fight ferocious animals for her. She's over at the grooming area with Nick washing down Glory, the three of them celebrating in their own little circle.

"Did you see her today?" I ask, and I can hear the wonder and awe in my voice. "I've never seen her so happy."

Clearly as staggered as me, Richard lets out his breath as he nods. "She was incredible. I'm still blown away by what she did."

"I am, too," I murmur, shaking my head in disbelief. "I can't believe that was our daughter out there." I again think of her racing around the pen on Glory's back, her smile brilliant, her eyes bright and alive and glowing, her heart beautiful and free. A warm rush of pride washes over me, and I swallow back tears.

"This ranch has been good for her," Richard says, echoing what I'm silently thinking.

"Yes, it has." Even with so much of the past weeping over the fields, Lexy had somehow managed to find a whole new life here. A dream and passion and purpose. Love. She'd discovered the beauty buried beneath the ashes. "I thought there was nothing left in this place but violence and pain."

Richard looks at me. "What do you think about it now?"

I take a minute to process his question. I was dreading coming back here, certain it would be my undoing, and the pressure would cause me to unravel into an unrecognizable, sobbing heap on the scarred plank floor.

But I've withstood the onslaught of flashbacks from my childhood. Each blow that has come swinging towards me hasn't knocked me down. I'm still here, and I'm still standing. Daddy has not defeated me. And I survived this trip empty-handed, without one swallow of vodka. Temptation waited and lurked and tried to derail me, but I didn't give in. I consider it a huge victory.

I again stare at the sacred ground where my daughter and Glory had defied gravity and shattered through the sky. Each one of us had come away different from the euphoria of that experience. "When we got here, I had this idea that I was going to be able to take back everything daddy took from me. I was ready for a showdown and was finally going to tell him to his face what he did to us and make him admit it and apologize. I wanted to hear him say he was wrong. But he's not here." I scan the horizon, futilely waiting for a return that never comes. "I don't know why I thought he would be."

"Because he used to be. And he was when you left."

Thoughtfully, I slowly nod. Time moved on while I was locked away in a cold, dark room with nothing but my past and a bottle. People became ghosts. Bruises and scars faded. I look up, out, forward, away from where I last saw daddy's face and fists.

"But, what Becca said is true. He didn't destroy everything. There are still good things to be found on this ranch. There's still hope here. And it will be different for Lexy. She won't know the fear we did. She won't have to. He won't be able to harm her now. This place was never a home for me, but it has become one for her."

"How are you feeling about her staying?"

My thoughts are churning too fast, and I unsteadily pull my hand through my hair. A frantic mania starts to build within me whenever I scrape against the subject of my father. Fight or flight kicks in. "It's hard because of everything that happened to us, but I know how important this land is to her. I can't take it away from her. That would mean I'm still letting daddy control our lives, and I don't want to live under that kind of fear anymore. She's already lost too much because of me."

"What does Andie say about it?"

I can't help smiling at the mention of my sponsor. Andie has become so much more over the last few months. She has such a settling effect on me. I probably say her name more times in a day than I say my own. Her friendship and support are crucial to me. I don't know what I would do without her. I even miss my meetings back home with the comfort and reassurance of her at my side. "That she's proud of me. She said it's a huge step."

"She's right. It is. I'm proud of you, too. Are you? You should be."

Flustered and feeling exposed, I look away. It's strangely an embarrassing question to answer, almost as if I still think I need to ask permission to believe I did something right. I never thought I'd be able to say I'm proud of myself for anything. God knows I haven't done much to be proud of.

But I'm clean and sober now. I'm facing my demons. And over the last few days, I have felt something shifting, changing, and opening, a deep exhale of places inside me I thought were too damaged to be restored. I'm not the same person I was when I stepped foot under Grandaddy Beau's arch a few days ago. It's been a long time since I've wanted to be alive. Perhaps it's time I stopped believing daddy's lies and learned to love myself.

"I want to be." Sighing, I lean my arms on the rail, gazing out over the sun-kissed fields. "If you had told me a few months ago that I would be standing here and agreeing to let my daughter live in that house, I would have said you were crazy and laughed in your face. I never thought in a million years I would come back or be able to face any of it."

"But you are."

"I know. It's still a shock to me. But Andie reminded me that Lexy would have left for college eventually anyway, so she would have moved out regardless. I know how important the music school is to her, but I just didn't think all of this would happen so soon. I feel like I just got her back."

"She still needs us."

"But she also needs this." I gesture out over the pastures that are as much a part of me as my own skin. My eyes fall on Nick at the exact moment he leans in to kiss Lexy. The sweetness and purity of it melt my heart. "And she's in love."

Richard follows my gaze. "That's pretty obvious." His brow creases as he studies Nick. "Do you think he will be good for her?"

"He'll give her the moon," I murmur, thinking of Nick taking her out to Grandaddy Cade's field to watch it rise simply because she wanted to see it. I wonder what he's going to do once he realizes he's in love with my daughter. Something tells me it's going to be harder for him to let himself fall. His wounds are still very raw. I hope the landing won't be a crash.

Richard gives me a confused look. "What?"

I manage a smile. "Nothing." I watch Lexy smile adoringly up at Nick. I would swear I can hear her heart beating even from clear across the pastures. I somehow always could, no matter how far apart we were. "I think they are exactly what the other one needs. And I want her to be happy. Even if I have to let her go."

"She'll always be our daughter."

"But she's not a little girl anymore. We're starting over but not from the same place. I've wasted so much time."

He rubs my back to comfort me. "We're not losing her. And we'll be back to visit."

"Becca asked about having Christmas here." A small, slightly hysterical laugh involuntarily escapes my lips at what a normal thing that is to do. Could that be possible? "I never thought I'd have anything to celebrate on this land."

"It would mean a lot to Lexy if we came."

"I'm sure it would," I answer weakly. Family. Who would have thought we would become one in the middle of all this pain? We've all somehow found our way back to one another, despite the odds and decades of destruction caused by abuse and addiction. "I wonder if it will ever get easier to be here."

"I don't know," Richard replies, his expression tender. "Hopefully. It'll just take some time. And we don't have to decide right now," he reassures me, and I feel some of the tension ease out of my chest.

"We have to go back to real life soon," I warn him. "It's only going to be the two of us when we fly home on Monday."

He turns to face me, his blue eyes penetrating and suddenly serious. "Why do you say it like it's a bad thing?"

"It's just all going to be different."

"It needs to be," he says firmly, and I think he's saying it to remind himself as much as me. We've both made far too many mistakes with each other.

He's right. No more blackouts, slammed doors, days of excruciating silence, or sickening hangovers. Only him and I trying to figure out how to live together again with me sober for the first time in twenty years. One day at a time. Awake and aware of every minute and feeling and thought and craving. At least we will have the support of Andie and the AA meetings and our counseling sessions to help guide us.

"Yes, it does." Feeling a bit overwhelmed by the daunting task of facing the days ahead, I reach out to touch him, lovingly moving his hair back off his forehead. The waves are thick and sift silkily through my fingers. There's no one I'd rather go through this with. "Thank you for saving my life," I whisper, the words carrying on the sunlight over to him.

We've never talked about it. We addressed the overdose in family counseling, talking about the where, why, and how of what happened. But we were in a supervised group setting with everyone around and rules to follow. Never alone. Not face to face. This is different. This is personal. This is only about us and that horrible night.

He flinches, and I feel him freeze. His eyes turn dark and tormented, and he shakes his head, taking a step away from me. That familiar scorching guilt begins insidiously oozing its way back between us. I don't want it to separate us and quickly grab the sleeve of his shirt before he can slip out of my reach. I couldn't bear it if I lost him again.

"I didn't," he stammers, his words jumbled and tumbling over themselves. A flush rises up his neck, and I can feel him starting to spiral as the memory and fear get much too close. "I should have done more. I should have tried harder to get you help. I couldn't—"

I touch my fingers to his lips, stilling him, his words instantly fading into thin air with all our other regrets. "It wouldn't have mattered what you did," I tell him trying to offer an atonement for the guilt he's carried on his soul. "I didn't want to be saved. I didn't want to come out. I couldn't have faced it. I wouldn't have let you even if you had tried. I would have gone right back to drinking. Even more than before because I would have hated you for trying to make me stop. I wasn't ready then."

He searches my eyes, and I make myself stay and be fully seen. It's harder than I thought. I'm still learning how to be me. "But you are now?"

I helplessly shrug. "I don't know if anyone is ever really ready," I say truthfully. "Rock bottom can always go deeper. And there's always this idea that one more time will finally make the pain stop. But I want to live if that's what you are asking me. And I finally feel like I have something to live for. There's so much I would have missed out on, and I'm grateful you saved me, and that I'm still here. I never want to be without you. Or Lexy."

"I wouldn't have survived it," he says so fiercely that the force of his words steals my breath.

"I'm so sorry," I manage to whisper. I don't know what else to say. How do you make up for something so unspeakable?

He stares at me, and I'm reminded of our younger days when there was nothing but our feverish need for one another. It was wild and fiery and so necessary we could barely go a few hours without feeling each other's skin. "I am, too. For so many things."

I step towards him and close the distance. I hate that there is any space or barrier between us. We've had years of being apart, even if it was only two doors down the hall. I look directly into his eyes, holding them. I need him to listen and believe me. "I love you."

I watch as my words absorb into him, melting away his guilt, his body relenting and giving into me. The lines ease from his face, his shoulders loosen. He takes a full deep breath, perhaps the first one he has in years, and wraps his arms tight around me. "I love you, too. More than anything."

Leaning against him, I look over the acres of land and open fields. I can see why my daughter loves it. There is still a raw, resilient beauty that the abuse, fear, and addiction hadn't been able to touch or destroy. And the history, legacy, and traditions are everywhere in the old outbuildings, the Victorian farmhouse, and the unwavering commitment to staying true to the family that had settled here over a hundred and fifty years before. It's time to let her go so she can find her place here.

"We should head back up to the house," I say against his chest. Even after decades away, I still recognize the earthy dampness seeping up from underneath the soil, feeling the electric shift in the atmosphere. The hairs on my arms stand up. Lightning is going to strike soon. "The rains are coming."

Richard looks up at the cloudless sky. Sunlight shines warm and golden over his face. The wind hasn't even begun to kick up yet. "How in the world do you all know that?"

I glance at him from under my lashes. "City boys," I tease, smiling and shaking my head.

He laughs, the sound open and uninhibited and free, and I find myself laughing, too. It feels so good to finally let it go, to let it out, to share it with him.

He leans in and gently kisses the small scar above my lip where daddy had shoved me down the stairs when I was eleven for accidentally leaving the light on in the kitchen. So much pain to heal. These are the secret pieces of me that he now stands guard over, and I have finally found the courage to let him touch. It's such a comfort to be safely protected and known. "Let's not go anywhere without each other again," he says, linking our hands together.

"Deal," I promise. I scan the skyline again. The humidity feels heavier, thicker, charged. I can taste the moisture in the back of my throat. My ears are trained to hear the rumble of thunder long before it arrives. "We really do need to get inside."

He squints into the distance, still seeing no sign of a storm. "If you say so."

We're smiling like fools in love as I wrap my arm around his waist, and we walk up the worn path together towards the old farmhouse that no longer seems as haunted now that Lexy has made it into a home.

Chapter Thirty-Nine
NICK

J ust as Ben had said, the rain came through, one of those late summer storms no one could explain. White lightning flashed, bursting brilliantly through the gray, foreboding sky. Thunder boomed low, making the ground tremble beneath my feet.

I hate the rain. It reminds me of that night, the crash, Megan. It's been three years, but the smell of soaked earth takes me straight back to that same bend in the road as if I'm still stranded there.

I can hear the song on the radio, her screaming my name right before we hit, seeing my mangled truck wrapped around the tree, feeling the devastating shock as my whole world was destroyed in the blink of an eye.

The way the lightning streaks across the land reminds me too much of the flashing lights from the ambulance that took her lifeless body away.

As the clouds roll in and the sky grows darker, so does my mood. I've become irritable and short-tempered. I've slowly withdrawn, folding into myself until I'm silent and unreachable. I can't concentrate or seem to hold a simple conversation. Words and thoughts have become jumbled and disjointed.

Life has been too good the last few months. I'm actually happy. I've laughed. I have hope for the first time in years. I'm feeling again. The days aren't as heavy with Lexy here.

But I know all too well how quickly and easily I can lose what matters most. The rain seems to like reminding me that everything can be ripped away and how helpless I am to stop it from happening again.

An unexplainable sense of something not being quite right is nagging at me. The uneasiness is like an annoying tag on the collar of my shirt, scratching at the back of my neck, chafing and scraping up my skin.

Lexy is hiding something from me. I can feel it. She'll be smiling right at me, and then a strange distance creeps in between us. It's slight, invisible to anyone else, but I know it's there.

I keep thinking about the look in her eyes from the other night. I saw it again this morning after she had ridden Glory. She had been bursting with excitement and almost said something. I felt it humming in the air between us before she closed herself off.

Is she having doubts? Did she change her mind? I wouldn't blame her. I'm a mess and not a sure bet by any stretch of the imagination. I've got too much baggage. Maybe she decided she doesn't want to deal with it all and is going to cut me loose.

I walk into the storehouse, relieved to get out of the rain. I need a break from the grating noise and chatter that fills the main house. There are too many people, and the weather is stirring up too much of the past, and it's better for everyone if I'm alone.

I had quietly slipped out. I have to do something, anything to make the flashbacks of the accident stop. I'm not sure how long until Lexy notices I'm gone. She's still on cloud nine from her ride earlier and is celebrating with her family.

She'd been amazing out in the ring. Her technique and skill had been instinctive and natural. I barely taught her a thing, and she somehow knew what to do, as if she'd been handling champion thoroughbreds all her life. She'd definitely inherited her Grandaddy Cade's gift and intuition with them. She looked beautiful and alive. Free. She has so much potential and possibility waiting for her. The whole world is open to her. She can do and be anything she wants. Her victory reminds me that I'm dead weight and will just drag her down.

I didn't tell her where I was going. I can't be around her right now. It's not safe for me to be, especially with the mood I'm in. Plenty of places to hide though. It's a big ranch. And she won't expect me to be out here, which gives me a little more time to clear my head.

The rain didn't ease away the heat. Instead, it trapped it in, making everything even more muggy and humid. It wasn't a hard storm, but it has a power over me all the same. It's coming down in slow, steady sheets. There was a pressure in the air, an electric surge that makes my system feel edgy and charged. I'm on high alert like prey being hunted.

The wet makes the scents of grains, hay, and feed stronger. I can taste them on my tongue, inside my nose, and feel a small amount of relief at the familiarity. The light is dim and blurry through the doorway, and I purposefully turn my back on the rain and the painful memories it stirs up as if they are rising from the grave.

Trying to lose myself in what I know, I channel my frustration into heaving bags of feed onto the shelves. The sweat and exertion help distract me from the constant, incessant patter of rain on the roof. Each drop feels like needles prickling over my body. I swear it's going to drive me mad.

I'm towards the back when Lexy walks in. Every muscle in my body instantly tenses. I don't even have to turn around to know she's behind me.

"There you are," she says, and her voice sounds like musical notes in the static of rainfall. "I've been looking everywhere for you."

"Well, you found me." If she notices the hostility in my tone, she doesn't give any sign of it. She must have walked from the house. Her hair and skin are wet, so are her clothes. Her cheeks are flushed, her eyes bright. She's still smiling. I don't think she's stopped all day. It just makes my resentment towards her burn darker.

"What are you doing out here?"

"Had to get the supplies stocked that just came in before the rain soaked them," I tell her, wiping my damp hair off my forehead with the back of my arm.

She starts to step closer but then stops with a jolt as I shove a bag with more force than necessary onto the shelf. "Do you need any help?" Her eyes aren't as sweet and sure now. They are wary and watchful, cautious. I don't think she can read me, which is a first. I have the sick gratification that she finally knows how it feels.

"No," I answer too quickly, and even I can hear how harsh my voice sounds.

She frowns as she watches me, that same uncertainty I've been feeling for days crossing over her face. "What's wrong?"

"Why don't you tell me?"

"What do you mean?"

412

"Forget it," I mutter, and bend to pick up another bag. Why does the rain seem as if it's getting louder? I can barely hear anything over it.

Even with my back to her, I can feel her staring, her eyes burning through my clothes, straight into me. I wonder if she will finally realize she doesn't like what she's found. She walks towards me, reaching out to touch my arm. "Nick, what's going on?" I try to turn away, but she steps between my body and the shelf, trapping her in against the wall, forcing me to have to face her.

"I just don't feel like talking." Lightning flashes, making my vision waver and double, and I blink to clear away the haze. Her face looks distorted and fragmented. My breathing is heavy and jagged as if I've run a marathon, although I'm standing still. I wonder if I'm having a panic attack. I used to get them all the time the first few months after the accident. I would completely freeze and shut down. The walls would collapse and close in. Just like they are now.

"You're shaking," she whispers, her eyes alarmed and worried. She tightens her arms around my waist as if she knows I need her to hold me up. I hate that I don't trust my own strength. "You're scaring me."

She's about to demolish me, and I'm scaring her? What a joke. But nothing about this is funny. "I'm fine."

"You don't seem like it." She touches my face, her expression growing more concerned when she notices my skin is clammy. "Let's go back to the house." She tries to take my hand to lead me out.

Into the rain.

My stomach clenches, and I quickly pull my hand free. "I don't want to go back inside."

In the dim, shadowed light, her eyes are beautifully green as she studies me. I don't know why it makes me angrier. "Nick, please talk to me."

"I could say the same thing to you. You're keeping something from me, Lexy. I can feel it. What aren't you telling me?"

Instantly apprehensive, she shakes her head, avoiding my gaze. She takes the smallest step back, so small she thinks I won't notice, but I do. I catch everything she does. I have since she first showed up a few months ago. I can't seem to help it.

"I'm not hiding anything."

"Yeah, right." I let out a disbelieving laugh. "If you don't want to be with me, you should just tell me." I try to pull free from her, but she holds on tighter.

"I do want to," she insists, her voice rising, as she clings desperately to my arm. I can barely make out what she's saying over the relentless downpour. "You're all I want."

"Whatever," I mutter, stepping even further away from her. I hate the void that comes rushing in between us. I'm suddenly so cold. My chest is tight. And the rain won't stop falling. *Pitter-patter. Drip. Pitter-patter. Drip. Pitter-patter. Drip.* I want to scream and shout like a wild animal into the black sky. "You're lying to me about something."

"I swear I'm not. I..." she catches herself again, almost on the verge, the words hanging in the air in front of us, and I see her hesitation, her doubt, her mistrust. About her feelings for me.

"There it is, Lexy." I point my finger in her face, startling her, and see her eyes widen with surprise. "You what? Finish the rest of it." I want her to have the guts to rip my heart out so I can finally face the reality that this whole thing was doomed from the start.

"I love you," she blurts out, her voice trembling.

That's not what I expected her to say. I was prepared for a crash, but she instead did a one-eighty on me. I freeze as I watch her mouth form the words, almost as if it's happening in slow motion. They fall over me, the redemption and salvation of them, the terror of what they mean, what they will ask of me. The temperature in the room seems to drop ten degrees. I feel dizzy and disoriented from the abrupt shift in the atmosphere.

Her love is everything I had feared and everything I crave. And now, face-to-face with her, I realize I've been waiting for her to say it. I hadn't known how badly I needed her to love me, to know someone like her could.

We stare at each other as the thunder rumbles and the rain pounds down around us. I fiercely want to lean back into her and let her wrap me close and make all this pain go away. I know she could do it. I wouldn't even have to ask her. She'd know exactly what I need. She somehow always does. But I can't let her. I don't have anything good left in me. Sooner or later, she'd realize it. It's better that she sees it now. Before I end up ruining her life. Like I did to Megan. Like I do to everyone around me. I force myself to step back from her. She's instantly aware and straightens.

She reaches for me, everything she feels burning in her eyes. "Nick—"

I shake my head, back up out of her reach. "Don't." My mind is reeling from fear, from shock, from yearning. If she touches me, I'll crumble. "I shouldn't have let it get this far."

She flinches as if I slapped her. "What?"

"I just don't want you to get your hopes up."

"Why can't I?" she asks weakly.

"I'm not...we shouldn't..." I trail off when lightning splits the sky, and I hate that it makes me jump. I feel the urge to duck for cover, but there's nowhere to hide.

"Nick, please don't do this to us."

"Us," I repeat numbly, unsure if the word is a curse or a cure. This is what has been building up over the last few days. The inevitable talk about where this was going, what we were, what we could be. The pressure is unbearable. I need her to understand we may not have a future. How do I tell her I no longer believe in tomorrow? "That's what I'm talking about. You think there can be an us. But you're wrong. Forever doesn't exist. You want a fairytale, and there isn't one. Happily ever after isn't real."

She's pale. There are tears in her eyes. My stomach drops when I see the disappointment on her face as if she'd already had in her mind this is what I would do once she told me. I hate even more that she hadn't been wrong. "Yes, it is."

I back up. I can feel myself about to burst. She should get away from me before the damage hits. "No, it isn't."

"Why not?"

"Because people die, Lexy!" I shout, my voice echoing through the small storehouse as years and years of frustration and loss and grief erupt and spew like hot lava over the plank floor, scorching any middle ground we were standing on. "Nothing lasts. I had everything I ever wanted, and I lost it. What if I lose you, too?"

She goes quiet, still. I don't think either of us breathes. Thunder booms low and loud, rattling clear through to my bones, making my ears ring. She waits for it to pass as if she knows I can't cope when it's chasing me. "I'm here, Nick," she says softly. "I'm alive. I'm not going anywhere."

I shake my head. "You can't promise stuff like that. You don't know what could happen."

"But neither do you. Please don't throw this away. I won't leave you."

The wind has picked up, blowing through the doorway, swirling around us, making the warped wood lean and whine and creak. My brain is foggy, unclear. "It's not that easy, Lexy."

"So, what are you saying? That you're just never going to let yourself love me?"

"I don't know. I'm not sure if I can." I hear myself talking, but the voice doesn't sound like mine. I seem to have no control over what is coming out of my mouth. But my words crush her all the same.

I see her shrink into herself, withering right in front of my eyes. I did that to her. I hurt her. I made her cry. And I know I'm capable of so much worse. "I was never going to make it past her, was I?"

Triggered, my whole body jerks and shudders. She said it so quietly, so gently, but it still makes my breath rush out. We've never talked about Megan. We haven't dared. And this exact moment is why. This is reason she hasn't wanted to tell me how she felt. We must have both known it would shatter us. "I...I don't know what to say."

Shaking her head, she wraps her arms around herself. "No, I get it," she says wearily as if she's already given up. I don't know why the fear of that is more intense than the rest. "There was always going to be a line with you. And I can't cross it."

I almost tell her how much I need her, that I can't live without her, that she's the reason I breathe. I desperately want to rewind time and somehow find a way to take it all back, but I can't seem to move or say anything. The rain keeps falling and falling and falling, and she is asking me to believe in love again, and my past is wedging its way in between us, driving us further apart, and all I can do is stand there with my mouth open and no sound coming out.

I'd done it, I think dully. All her walls were torn down. I wasn't alone anymore. I had what I wanted, but for what? I'm still just as lost. I wonder if I'll ever figure out how to win this war I'm waging against myself. The shame is a chokehold around my throat.

When I still say nothing, Lexy sighs, and I can see her heartbreak and defeat like bruises on her skin. She's barely a wispy shadow against the gray sky beyond the doorway, as if she's dissolving right in front of me. I have the terrifying thought that she is. "You're wrong. We would have been happy. Who knows what it's like to lose everything more than us?" Her voice cracks as she turns away.

Panic strikes with the lightning, flashing over us. "Lexy, wait. I—"

"I don't want you to touch me," she says, stopping me in my tracks. Tears falling down her face, she hopelessly walks away. She's almost to the door when she looks back. "You're so afraid of losing me, but what you don't realize is that you already are." Without waiting for an answer, she walks out into the rain. I watch the curtain of it swallow her, just like it had done to Megan. Terror grips me, and I start to go after her, but then a gust of wind blows through, and I'm left paralyzed and blinded by the scattering drops pelting me in the face.

Cursing loudly, I turn away and pick up a bag of feed, angrily hurl it against the wall, causing it to rupture and scatter violently all over the ground. Thunder booms, vibrating over the earth until it reaches my feet as if it's searching for me. As if it knows I can never outrun it.

"I hate the rain," I mutter through gritted teeth and then bend down to start cleaning up the mess I made.

Chapter Forty
LEXY

Wrapped in a blanket, I sit curled up in the window seat, staring dully out into the darkness. Dawn will break soon. In the golden light from the small Tiffany bedside lamp, I can see the silhouette of my reflection in the aged glass. My face looks warped and rippled. I don't recognize myself. The pale girl looking back at me is nothing but a ghost.

It's eerily quiet and hushed. Even the birds have not yet come out of hiding from where they took shelter during the storm. I wonder if they are just as worried about what this day holds as I am.

I hadn't slept. The rain stopped sometime during the night. The air drifting in is fresh and clean and smells of musty old timber and soaked earth.

The clouds have cleared away from the sky. The wind has stilled. Everything is back to normal and deceptively calm. As if nothing happened yesterday. As if I hadn't gotten my heart shattered. All that is left are the debris and aftermath of our conversation, and my heart scattered for miles over the dirt.

Checking my phone, I notice the white numbers read 5:42. I had waited for him to say something, to come find me, hoping for a call or text, desperately praying he would want to risk trying for me, but he hadn't. I had almost run back out into the rain to find him, but was afraid he would push me away again.

The night had been much too long, and I cried harder with each hour that dragged by, his silence painfully reminding me that I may have just ruined any chance we had of being together. Who would have thought that loving him would be how I lose him?

Forever doesn't exist. Happily ever after isn't real.

His words had kept me up restlessly tossing and turning. I feel like they have branded my skin. Bitter tears burn my throat. I thought I'd cried everything out into my pillow, but my hurt is so deep and raw. I feel like he'd somehow broken me. I rub my hands over my bleary eyes. They are sore and swollen from sobbing.

He'd been different yesterday; silent, brooding, withdrawn, angry and on edge like a wild, caged animal. His movements and words had been sharp and rough, not tender like the night we watched the moon. He kept pushing at me, accusing me of lying to him and not caring. I didn't understand it. He seemed out of his mind somehow, like he was someone else entirely. I hadn't expected the sudden, abrupt shift in him. It threw me so completely off guard that I finally caved and said the one thing he fears most.

I knew it was a mistake. Even as I heard the sound of my own voice, felt my lips form the words, and helplessly watched the moment slip irreversibly away from me, I knew.

I keep coming up against Megan. We've never talked about her. And the horrible fallout from last night is why. Did I somehow know this is what it would do to us? That once one of us dared say her name, everything would break apart? What if we can't recover from the wreckage?

I understand that he still wrestles against the guilt over how he lost her. I would never tell him he had to forget or be so cruel to think he should just get over it. I know better than anyone how deeply and permanently damage can scar you.

He wasn't wrong that I've been hiding my feelings. I knew he wasn't ready. Maybe he never would be. I know he cares about me, and what a huge step that is for him, but risking saying he loves me is a whole other level entirely. It's so big and overwhelming and triggers every fear he has.

He's the first person I've ever said those words to. I've never been in love before, and it wasn't how I wanted to reveal it. I was hoping for a sweeter moment, one with moonlight and the fragrance of honeysuckle and his kiss on my lips. Not in the middle of a storm. I didn't realize the truth would create such a beautiful, devastating disaster.

All I want is to be a part of his life, too, and for him to let me into the place that continues to haunt and hurt and hold him where he is. I want him to trust me enough to share his pain with me. He has all of mine. There is not one secret he doesn't hold. Even the most fragile part of my heart is now in his hands.

I know how hard it is for him to allow people close to him. He's terrified to let anything change. And now I'm afraid he never will.

I don't know which is worse. Nick not loving me or him being in love with me, but not letting himself give into his feelings. Both are horribly tragic and lonely. And either way, I'm the one who gets hurt.

Doesn't he understand how rare it is what we have? Does he think this happens every day? The miracle of two wounded people like us finding each other and being able to fit our splintered pieces together and having them match so perfectly and completely? We've both been given a second chance. Is he really going to throw it all away?

I glance down at my phone again, anxiously willing something to come through from him. Still nothing. No message. No text. No call. No Nick. I want to weep.

I look over when I hear a quiet knock on my door. My heart leaps, hoping foolishly that it's him. "Who is it?"

My mom's voice echoes through the old, knotted wood. "It's me, Lexy. Can I come in?" I smother my disappointment. When I say yes, she opens the door, stepping inside. "I brought you up some coffee." Carrying two mugs, she walks over to me, handing me one. I offer her a feeble smile of thanks. I doubt it convinces her that I'm fine, but I don't have the strength to give more. She carefully studies me, concern in her eyes. "I saw your light on. You were pretty upset when you came back to the house last night. I just wanted to check on you."

I hold the coffee but don't drink it. The heat against my palms is comforting. I don't know how to begin explaining how I feel and wearily go back to staring out the window.

When I say nothing, she glances back at the door. "Would you like to be alone?"

Feeling lost and vulnerable, I desperately grasp for her hand, and she instantly takes it, almost as if she's relieved I need her. "No," I say, sounding like a frightened child. "Will you please stay with me for a bit?"

"Of course, sweetheart." As she sits down next to me, I notice her trying not to look at the closet where she and Becca cowered and hid or under the bed where they huddled and clung close. I can't imagine how traumatic it is for her to be in this room. She seems tense and jumpy as her eyes dart around, searching for somewhere safe. The haunted memories lay waiting for her in the faded wallpaper, scarred floorboards, Grandmother Rose's quilt, every shadowed corner. She was so brave to come back to this land and face her past. I am incredibly proud of her.

"The rain has stopped," she finally says, deciding on small talk, and I'm grateful. It's easier for now. Maybe for her as well.

I can still hear the sound of it beating on the roof as Nick told me he may never let himself love me. "Yeah," I manage hoarsely. I sip the coffee before the tears rush back up. It's warm and helps soothe the lump in my throat. "You're up early."

My mom shrugs and glances out the open window. "It's so quiet out here. I'm still not used to it. Too much space to think." Giving me a knowing look, she sips her coffee. "Did you get any sleep last night?"

Wincing, I can only shake my head. I can feel her waiting for me to say more, but if I mention his name, it will swallow and drown me. I again glance down at my phone in my lap, which stays excruciatingly blank and silent. "Are you and dad still going back to California tomorrow?"

She nods. "Yes. Why?"

"I was thinking I might go back with you."

"Really?" Her brows raise in surprise. "What changed your mind?"

I give her a bruised look. "You don't want me to come with you?" I know I'm probably overreacting, but everything is hitting me wrong. Even my skin feels chafed and sensitive.

"No, that's not it at all," she stammers, trying to keep up. "We would love to have you with us. I just thought you were happy out here."

Dragging my hand through my hair, I stare back out the window towards the rain-soaked lane that leads far away from last night, from Nick, from the words I can't take back. "With everything that has happened, I thought it would be good to be closer to you and dad in case you need me."

She leans forward, her eyes full of sorrow and regret. "Lexy, you don't have to take care of us anymore. I've made you responsible for things a daughter should never have to deal with, and I'm so sorry for that. I don't want you to put your life on hold for me. If you want to stay, your dad and I will support you. Becca and Ben are here. I know how much you love being with the horses. You want to sing, and there is a great opportunity to do that with the music school. Nick is here." She slips it in gently, carefully, but I still flinch.

I can't look at her. I'm too afraid I'll break down. I wrap the blanket tighter around me, some small, thin shield of protection from all this devastation. The thought of not being on this land with the horses, close to my aunt and uncle, and not seeing Nick every day is gut-wrenching. I can't imagine living anywhere else. But then I picture the dark look in his eyes when he said he doesn't believe in love anymore, and I don't know how I could stay. He seems to hurt me simply by breathing. "I just think it would be better if I left."

"Honey, what happened yesterday? Did you and Nick have a fight?"

A laugh escapes my lips, and even to me, it sounds a bit hysterical. *A fight.* More like a sudden, unexpected explosion of dynamite thrown in between us. I hopelessly look at her across the destruction and rubble. "Something like that," I murmur dully.

"Do you want to talk about it?"

I helplessly shrug. "I don't even know what to say. I'm still not sure what went wrong. Everything was fine, but I noticed he got quiet after our ride. He started pulling away. I was worried about him and went to go talk to him. I found him in the storehouse, but he was acting strange. I've never seen him like that before."

My mom frowns. "What do you mean? Strange how?"

I stare towards the direction of the outbuildings as if I can somehow find answers. But I can't see anything clearly yet. "He just was off. He wasn't acting like himself. He kept saying I was hiding things from him and lying about how I felt for him. He was upset and accused me of not wanting to be with him. I didn't know how to get him to believe me and ended up saying I loved him." My heart is so tired and feels like it's beating so slowly. I wonder if I would even notice if it stopped completely.

Her expression turns sentimental and tender, almost as if she already knew this was coming. "What did he say?"

My breath hiccups as the shock slams into me again. "That fairytales aren't real, and that love doesn't last," I whisper bleakly. *People die, Lexy!* I can still picture him, wild-eyed, sweating, his body shaking. Wincing at the harsh memory, I swallow hard. "He told me we don't have a future together. I thought he loved me, but he doesn't."

"I don't think him not loving you is the problem, sweetheart," she says softly, and I slowly lift my gaze to hers, desperate for a small shred of hope. Noticing the blanket has slipped off my shoulder, she tucks it tighter around me in a way that is maternal and reassuring. She used to do that when I was a little girl. Before the bottle took her from me. "Maybe he will come around."

"I don't think he will. He doesn't want to let me in." I brush at my tears with the edge of the blanket, but they are falling too fast now as my words pour out. "Everything has been going so well. I thought we were finally going to be happy together. I don't understand what happened, and he won't talk to me about it. I think I just messed everything up, and I have no idea how to fix it. What if I've lost him for good?" I can barely see her through the blur of tears spilling down my cheeks.

"Oh, honey, I think you just surprised him is all. Or he could have been dealing with something you don't know anything about. People say a lot of things they don't mean when they are scared and don't know what to do. But I don't think for one second that you're not important to him."

"That's the whole problem though," I insist, my voice choked by sobs. "The more important I am, the more scared he gets."

"Just give him a minute to figure it out," she soothes, gently moving my hair back off my damp face, her fingers gently threading through the strands. Her touch stirs a long-forgotten memory of her playing with my hair when I was sick to help me fall asleep. I have an overwhelming urge to lay my head in her lap. "Maybe you could just let it sit for a bit. Things might look different when the sun comes up. They usually do. You can take my word on that." Cupping my cheek, she brushes at my tears with her thumb. "We can talk more about it later once you both have had some time to think it over. And if you still decide you want to come back to California, then we'll all be on a plane tomorrow."

"Okay," I murmur, sniffling, still not convinced it will make any of this better. Liking having her close, I reach out for her, holding tightly to her hand. It's warm and soft in mine. I would recognize her touch blindfolded, even in a room full of people. She is completely aware, lucid, sober. Here. I never thought I would have a moment like this with her. "Thank you, mom."

She smiles, and I can't help but think how pretty she is, even in Becca's pale pink robe and her hair tumbling messily around her shoulders from sleep. Her face is calmer, her eyes no longer vacant and dead and tormented. Being out in the southern sun has brought color to her skin. She looks more at peace. She looks like her again. It seems at least some of her demons have been laid to rest.

She gets to her feet. "I'm going to go start breakfast if you feel like joining us in a little while." I think I nod, but I'm not sure. I feel dazed and numb. My head is throbbing and stuffy from crying. She takes my empty coffee mug from me. I didn't even know I'd drank it. "I'll bring this down for you. Ben made a fresh pot if you want more."

"Has Nick come in yet?"

She shook her head. "I haven't seen him since yesterday."

He's disappeared again, I realize. Because of me. Hiding out, running as far as he can. My whole body caves in. I think I understand what people mean now when they say they are lovesick. It's a horrible form of suffering from the agony of wanting someone you can't have. I'm nauseous, jittery, hopeless. How will I be able to stand seeing Nick, knowing he won't let us be together? I'm relieved it's still dark and I have a little time before I have to face him in the harsh light of day.

She walks across the room and turns to look back at me. "I don't think he wants you to go if that makes any difference." It would change everything, and we both knew it. She leaves me with that last thought as she quietly closes the door.

I desperately want what she said to be true, but even if it was, would Nick be able to let go of his fear of the past repeating itself to come towards me? I just need one reason, something, anything from him, and I will stay at his side until I take my last breath.

The kickstart and rumble of Nick's old beat-up Chevy truck pierce the air, the sound startlingly loud in the stillness. Jumping slightly, I lean over and look out the window in time to see his headlights cut through the dark as he drives away down the dirt lane towards the main road. I wonder where he's going this early. He hardly ever leaves the ranch. But then my heart sinks as I realize he's made his choice.

He's going to Megan's grave.

I don't even notice I've started trembling. My tears well up again, and I bury my head in my arms, trying to shut the whole world out. I have a horrible feeling my decision just got made for me.

Chapter Forty-One
NICK

"Where are you sneaking off to?"

I jump at the sound of Becca's voice. I didn't even see her come out of the darkness. Bracing myself, I look over at her trying to read her eyes but can only make out murky shadows. "You come out here to yell at me?" I ask wearily, expecting a lecture or an avalanche of questions I'm not prepared to answer.

"I should," she says, but she surprisingly doesn't sound upset. "You made my niece cry. But then I thought about it and realized what must've happened to you last night."

Denying it is pointless. I'm standing on the soggy ground, the soil squishing and sticking under my boots—the proof of my own self-destruction. Water droplets slowly drip from the canopy of leaves over our heads, spattering onto the roof of my truck. The rain has stopped, but the damage still lingers and waits just beyond the first rays of daylight.

"I can't talk about it yet, Becca." I hate that she's making it sound as if I'd had some sort of episode or have a screw loose.

Even if I had experienced a temporary breakdown, I still don't like the label attached to me. It's humiliating to be reminded of how flawed and sick I am. My face flushes, and I quickly open the truck door, hoping she'll get the hint and let me go.

"You don't have to tell me." She put her hand on my arm. "But please explain it to Lexy. She doesn't know what you go through or what triggers come up for you sometimes. It's nothing to be ashamed of," she says when I try to pull away. "You went through something horrible, and if anyone can understand that it would be her. But she thinks you don't care. She's been hiding up in her room since last night and won't come out."

The guilt is a hot, swift punch to my gut. I hadn't slept, and my scalp is caught in a steel-tight vice grip. I feel hungover even though I haven't had a sip of alcohol. The pressure behind my eyes throbs every time I blink. I keep replaying the moment Lexy said she loved me, obsessively rewinding it on repeat, uselessly wishing I could go back and do the whole thing over again so I could somehow make it right with her.

I can only remember bits and pieces of what happened last night. What I said. What she did. The shock and stress have left dents in my memory. It always happens like that. A complete and total shutdown. Everything goes blank. There are black holes and fuzzy gaps where the conversation should be.

Did I really tell her I couldn't be with her? That we don't have a future together? That I don't want her to love me? I feel sick. None of it was what I meant to say. Any other night I swear I would have responded differently, better.

Sanely.

But I'd been out of my mind, all my thoughts short-circuiting. As if a land mine had exploded in my brain. I should have known when the first cloud appeared in the sky I was in trouble. I had a false sense of security that I shouldn't have trusted. I haven't had anything happen in months. No nightmares. No flashbacks. No triggers. I thought I was past the worst of it. I've felt almost normal again. Being with Lexy has helped calm the chaos. Unfortunately, I realized too late that I was wrong and couldn't catch up to it in time to prevent the meltdown.

I was never going to make it past her, was I?

Lexy's question pierces through my fragmented brain, and I jerk as if she's right behind me. I can still see the confusion and tears in her eyes. The regret smothers me, painful and inescapable. She thinks she's not important. And it's my fault. This isn't who I want to be anymore. I don't want to keep hurting the people I care about. I hadn't meant to push Lexy away. I need her too much.

I had managed to get back to my cottage and locked myself inside. I desperately wanted to call her and apologize. But I wasn't sure what to say and couldn't get my mind in the right place to form a complete sentence. Every time I tried to say sorry, lightning struck, thunder rattled the windows, and my thoughts would scramble and spiral from the relentless flashbacks.

But now the storm has passed, the blind haze is finally clearing, and I have to face myself in the unforgiving light of day along with the consequences of the night before. Resurfacing is traumatic. The gravity of the situation and all the words I can't take back are scattered before me like the branches the wind blew across the pastures.

The second the last drop of rain fell and the sky cleared, I knew what had to be done.

"I'm going to talk to her, but I need to do something first." Resolved, I make myself look at her in the dim red glow of the dash light. "I owe it to both of them."

"Everything you want is here."

I again think of Lexy saying she loves me. My entire body fills with an aching yearning. I feel as if I've been waiting three years for her to say those words. Maybe I have. "I know," I murmur heavily. "But, I have to do this, Becca. It's time."

It's past time for a lot of things. To grieve, to mourn, to scatter stones and ashes, to let go and begin living and loving again.

Slowly nodding, she holds out a thermos of coffee for me, a peace offering. Surprised, I hesitate before taking it from her. I wonder if she already knew this is what I was going to do. "I understand. Promise you'll tell Lexy everything when you get back."

Once I return, I'm never leaving her side again. All I want is to do is fall into her arms. "I promise."

Getting into the truck, I set the thermos on the seat next to me. Becca leans in and lightly touches my cheek. Saying nothing more as if she senses I couldn't handle it, she steps back. I turn the key in the ignition, and the engine tiredly catches and rumbles to life as she closes the door. The ripped black leather seat vibrates beneath me, the windshield wipers seeming to groan as they sluggishly sweep back and forth to clear away the night's rain. The Chevy is older than Moses. Still as sturdy and reliable as the sun though. I put the truck in gear and pull out down the lane.

In the rearview mirror, I see Lexy's bedroom light on as if it's calling me back. My hands tighten on the steering wheel. I fiercely want to slam on the brakes, turn around and run upstairs and hold her, tell her I'm sorry, and beg her to forgive me for being so scared and screwed up and stupid.

But I need to lay my past to rest first. It's haunted me for far too long. I don't want my damage to hurt Lexy anymore.

Passing under the arch of the gate, I turn left and drive the familiar road out to the cemetery. It's not far, less than thirty minutes away, and I get there just as dawn begins to break.

Parking my truck, I grab a blanket from the seat along with the thermos and get out. The quiet here is unlike anywhere else and surrounds me like a cloak as I walk the path to the spot where Megan is buried. I'm always struck at how peaceful it is. You wouldn't think it would be with so much tragedy and the unshed tears people have yet to cry hanging heavily in the air.

First light cracks behind the smoky mountains, casting a hazy, haunting glow over the stone graves. As the sun peaks the horizon, the golden rays spread out and warm the earth, causing mist to curl and rise from the damp grass like wandering, searching spirits still not at rest. Water droplets glisten and sparkle like tiny diamonds in the trees overhead.

My eyes scan over the graveyard. *Strange how green the grass is here,* I think, in the middle of all this despair and death. I'm always amazed that anything manages to grow. I look out over the rows and rows of tombstones scattered over the fields. Some have been here for well over a century, the names and dates crumbling and eroding with age or from heartbroken fingertips trying to cling to what is no longer there. So much loss. So many people left behind trying to figure out how to live with the gaping hole the person left them with.

Guilt is a shadow next to me as I stand under the shelter of the magnolia tree and stare down at the little plot of grass. I can't make myself look at Megan's gravestone as if doing so would be like looking directly into her eyes. I haven't been here in a while. Two months to be exact. Since the morning I kissed Lexy. I used to visit every day. It was the only place I could come to feel I wasn't alone in my overwhelming grief. But I've felt too ashamed to face her.

The sadness is still there, but it's different in a way I can't quite put my finger on yet. The knife isn't as sharp and jagged in my chest. The pain is more like a dull ache, tender and sweet and sentimental rather than staggering. I didn't realize until now how the wound had mercifully eased. Faded slightly.

Setting the thermos and blanket on the bench, I turn and kneel down to somehow be closer to her, concentrating on carefully clearing away soggy, limp flower petals and leaves the rain had scattered around the bottom of the stone.

Finally, I lift my eyes and make myself look at the photograph engraved into the headstone. I had taken the picture myself. It was the last night I'd ever seen her alive. She'd only been eighteen. She is smiling over a cake full of candles. As if she had her whole life ahead of her. As if anything were possible back then. As if we still had more time together. She was so young and happy. Not ready to die. She looks like she should still be here. But she isn't anymore.

Letting out a ragged breath, I get to my feet and spread the blanket over the damp marble bench, sit down in front of the grave. Leaning forward, I clasp my hands between my knees.

If Megan were still here, I would tell her how sorry I am for what I've done with myself over the last three years. I know I'm not who I used to be. She wouldn't have wanted me to give up. But that's exactly what I did for far too long. I was so mad at everything and everyone. Most of all me.

I've spent all this time punishing myself for the accident, her death, my life. For surviving when she didn't. It never made any sense to me. It still doesn't, and I've never been able to come to terms with the senseless futility of that. I haven't known how to forgive myself.

Three years have gone by since she died. Has it been that long? How is that possible? Where did all the time go? It feels like I just lost her, and if I waited long enough, she'd walk through the door.

I wonder if Megan would recognize me now. I'm completely different from the person she knew. The grief and guilt have changed me, worn me down, made me older, wearier, jaded, and bitter. My own madness worked against me, chipping away at my mind and skin and soul until I didn't look anything like who she used to love.

As the days and weeks bleakly bled and blurred one into the next, I had gotten to the point where I was so hardened and angry that I believed I was no longer capable of loving anyone. I didn't care anymore. There was no point. I questioned why I was even here and gave serious thought to ending it all. I kept my heart bricked up behind a wall of thick concrete. It was the only way I could protect myself from being completely demolished by the overwhelming pain.

But then Lexy showed up. I can still remember the strange sense of relief I felt when I opened the front door and instantly recognized myself in her. As if she came looking for me.

Lexy kept her promise. She never once asked me about Megan. I've deliberately kept the two of them separate in my mind. It helped me feel less guilty. I wanted to tell her. There were so many times I'd almost poured out everything about that night, the accident, the chronic, constant struggle of living with so much agony and trauma. She'd have let me, and she would have understood. I have no doubt in my mind about that. But even accepting her empathy and comfort would have felt like a betrayal.

By keeping Megan removed from what was happening with Lexy, I was somehow able to keep them both. I was so afraid of wanting to let go. I didn't think I had the right to. I thought it meant I didn't love Megan enough. It felt selfish and cruel. The devastation has become such a huge part of me over the last three years. I didn't know who I would be without it and thought that hanging onto the grief was a way of still holding on to her.

Opening the thermos, I pour coffee into the lid and sip it as I watch people drift in and out, wishing and waiting, mourning, heads bowed, silently praying and pleading with Heaven for signs or miracles or reprieve as they quietly cry and lay flowers at the foot of the graves of their loved ones. And they all leave empty-handed with the same helpless realization that the person they lost is never coming back, and they have to figure out how to go on living with the void left behind.

Megan is never coming back. She's not here, not the girl I knew and loved. No matter how hard I try, I can't remember her voice as clearly now or how she smelled or how she felt in my arms. I guess I took for granted that those parts of her would stay permanent and vivid and within my reach. But without me barely noticing, she's become whispers in the wind. Flitting images that disappear much too quickly before I can grasp them.

We will never be those people again, and we will never be able to recapture what we had. Our lives as we knew them are over.

Chapter Forty-One

Forever. It's the first time I've been able to admit it.

I close my eyes and let the thin rays of sunlight soak into me. I need the warmth. I need something to prove I'm still alive and breathing as I say the words I've dreaded speaking aloud for the last three years.

"You're gone."

They hang, heavy and suspended, in the air in front of me. I keep my eyes closed and wait, wishing she could somehow prove me wrong. When I open them, the first thing I see is her grave, and I'm again forced to face the undeniable finality of her mortality. And my own. The small dash that connects the beginning and much too short end of her life. It wasn't long enough, and it wasn't fair. I stare at her name engraved on the stone. Her death is there right in front of me with no escape.

I wait for the waves of devastation, bracing myself for the crippling, breathtaking sadness to crush me to the ground. But the vicious, bottomless hole doesn't feel as hopeless or painful. The suffocating depression is lifting. I'm finding my way back to the surface and can withstand the loss of her without being sucked under and drowning.

I can't say when the shift happened. I wasn't trying to let go. I never would have. But, somewhere in the last few months, I've stepped further away from where we used to be. From where I last saw her alive. It happened so slowly that I didn't realize how far I'd gone until I finally paused and turned around and see that Megan is nothing but a shimmering shadow in the distance. There's a chasm between us now, a wide canyon I can no longer get across as I've allowed myself to be pulled to the other side.

Now, in the quiet starkness of Megan's grave, I finally let myself accept the truth.

I'm in love with Lexy.

The realization makes my breath rush out. The air around me feels fragile and too bright, as if one quick move could shatter this crystallized layer of ground I'm standing on. It's been so long since I've loved anyone else. I'm almost afraid to believe in it again. I don't want to lose it.

I don't know when I fell in love with her. Maybe it was the first time I heard her sing on the porch or watching her break through to Glory, or the morning she fell apart in my arms after finding out about her mom's overdose or staying up all night telling each other things no one else knew about us.

There are a hundred little looks, words, touches, and moments between us. I hadn't realized I'd been collecting them all, storing and saving them, holding on tight to them. Each one was so seemingly simple, but they had changed me in ways I hadn't understood until now.

Lexy loves me. She believes there's something good and worthwhile underneath all my damage and despair. She's seen the worst of me and still wants me. The fear and wonder of it leave me feeling weak and breathless. I can still picture the exact moment she'd said it, how her voice had trembled as the rain threatened to tear everything apart. She'd been beautiful, vulnerable, pure, and sweet, everything I could ever dream of. And I'd turned around and broken her heart. I'd pushed her away out of my own trauma and panic and fear.

I hate that she'd been afraid to tell me, not trusting what I would say or do. I feel even worse that she'd been right and that I reacted exactly as she knew I would. The instant she penetrated my deepest scars, we imploded.

But what I didn't realize until now is that she just saved me. The broken rescuing the broken. She's given me the very reason I need to let go. Her love is the life rope I've been waiting to have thrown out to me to lead me back into the land of the living.

She was right in what she said. She's here and is offering me a second chance. If I dare to take it. I'm painfully aware that I could lose her in a matter of seconds. Neither of us can foresee what will happen, and we can't predict the future. But the thought of not being with her right now and never seeing her smile again, hearing her sing and laugh and say my name, frightens me more than what potential loss or tragedy might steal her from me.

I don't know how long I sit at Megan's grave. Hours pass. The thermos of coffee is long empty. The sky is clear and blue as the first day of October finally makes its arrival. The earth is still slowly spinning on its axis, just as it's supposed to. The world has not ended.

I understood when I drove out here that this time was different. I came to say goodbye and finally lay her to rest. I'm ready to move on and let her be free. I want to be fully alive again. I owe it to Megan to keep going, and to myself. She wouldn't have wanted me to die with her. But that's what I did. I became a walking corpse, burying myself six feet under the suffocating weight of grief.

I'm one of the straggling few left at the cemetery. I've spent far too long in the underground of the dead. Not even Megan is here anymore. I will never forget her as long as I live, but she's now just a memory. One I will carry with me wherever I go. She will always be the first girl I ever loved back when we were younger, and the days were easier, and we were innocent in a way I'll never be again.

It's time to leave. I need to get to Lexy. I have to tell her I love her, too. I don't want to live one more second without her.

Standing, I fold up the blanket, tucking the thermos under my arm. Kissing my fingertips, I tenderly brush them over Megan's gravestone. "I'll see you soon," I tell her because that's what we always used to say instead of goodbye.

Feeling lighter and more hopeful than I have in years, I get in my truck and drive back to the ranch towards a girl who has changed the course of all our lives simply by finding a stack of letters.

Chapter Forty-Two
LEXY

H e's been gone for hours. Almost the entire day. No call. No text. Not one word.

Tears slowly slide down my face as I stand at Glory's stall. Every few minutes, I glance anxiously towards the door hoping Nick will come through it and come back for me. But he never does.

The stable is quiet, and I am relieved to be surrounded by the stillness and solitude. I don't want to be around anyone right now. I can't handle it. I'll completely break down.

I took my mom's advice to get some space and perspective and give Nick a chance to figure things out. But the longer he's gone, the more heartbreakingly clear it becomes that I'm waiting in vain. I ruined everything last night by telling him how I felt, and now I've scared him off.

Even as every nerve in my body screams and rages against it, I know it's time to face the cold, hard truth. We're over; nothing but ashes. Nick doesn't love me and isn't going to let us be together. He's not ready to move on from Megan. And his silence is proof of that.

I know what I need to do. I just wish I didn't have to.

I can't stay. I don't want to leave, but I don't think I have any choice. It will hurt too much knowing Nick doesn't feel the same. How will I face him every day, be close to him, but not able to share my heart with him, and constantly be reminded he doesn't want to give me his?

Sniffling, I wipe the tears with the cuff of my sleeve, but more keep falling. I can't seem to stop them. Sensing my distress, Glory bends her head to sniff at me, and I cry harder and lean into her, burying my face in her warm coat. How am I going to leave her? She won't understand. The ache is unbearable. I thought I finally found where I belonged.

I can't put it off any longer. I have to let my parents know I'll be flying back with them in the morning. They need time to change the reservation. Already homesick and painfully lonely, I kiss Glory one last time before wearily turning away.

I've only taken two steps when Nick walks in. My entire body jolts as if an electric shock surged through me. Paralyzed, I stop where I am.

"Hey," he says hesitantly, and I can feel the weight of his stare burning into me. My stomach knots up, and I suddenly want to run and hide. I didn't have time to wipe the last traces of tears away. All my pain is in plain sight, making me feel much too vulnerable. My heart feels as if it's pounding out of my chest through the cotton of my shirt into the space between us. I notice his movements are careful and cautious. As if he's not sure what I'll do and is testing how far I'll let him come. "Becca said you were out here."

Even his voice hurts me. I love the low, deep drawl of it. The thought of never being able to hear it again makes me want to curl into a ball and weep. I can't find the strength to say anything. I need to get away from him, or I'll shatter into pieces. Avoiding his eyes, I step around him to go back to the house.

"Lexy, wait." He reaches out and grasps my hand as I try to get past him. His touch sears my skin. Why is he putting me through this?

"I have to go." I'm amazed I'm able to speak. My throat is hoarse and strained from crying. "I need to start packing."

I see him freeze, which surprises me. My system is so overly sensitive that his every move makes me flinch. I thought he'd be relieved. He doesn't have to worry about me making him feel guilty over Megan anymore. "Packing? What are you talking about? Why are you packing?"

"I've decided I'm going back to California in the morning." I want to hate him for all of this, but I'm too desperately in love with him. I already miss him, and I haven't even left yet.

His eyes flash, change, darken. They are almost black, just like they were last night. A muscle in his jaw clenches. Is he angry or terrified? I can't tell. The gold flecks are gone. I instinctively want to back up from the intensity. He shakes his head, and I feel his grip tighten on my hand. "No. You can't go."

"I get it, Nick." I can hear how dull and detached my voice sounds. I feel numb, empty, nothing. He's killing me so softly. "I saw you leave this morning. I already know you've made your choice. You don't have to tell me." I silently beg him not to. I can't take it.

Before I can walk away, he quickly steps in front of me, blocking my path to the door. "It's not what you think. I went there to say goodbye to her. I choose you, Lexy."

His words aren't registering. Confused and dazed, I get distracted by the collar of his shirt. The edge is frayed, the threads splitting at the seam. He's probably had it a long time. He's always looked good in that color blue. "But, I thought you said…"

"I know what I said," he interrupts impatiently, and I jump, breaking out of my fog, and my eyes fly up to his. He seems panicked, desperate, and on the verge of losing control. "Please don't leave. I won't make it if you go, and neither will you. You know you won't."

I can't seem to figure out what is happening. Nothing is making any sense. A few minutes ago, I was devastated, certain it was the end of us. Now he's choosing me? Has he changed his mind? I can't keep up. I'm suddenly exhausted. Lack of sleep and the stress of waiting and wondering and not knowing work against me, and I throw up my hands in frustration. "Why would you even want me to stay?"

"Because I love you," he blurts out, his voice louder than it should be. The words are rushed and frantic and urgent, tumbling recklessly out of his mouth. He's winded as if he took a fast punch to the gut.

I'm speechless. My mouth falls open. All I can do is stare at him. I don't think I remember to blink. "What?" I can't move even as he steps closer. His jeans brush against mine.

"I love you, Lexy," he says again, more quietly and gently this time, and I watch his lips form the words to make sure they are true, the beauty of them washing over me.

I can't feel my legs and wonder vaguely if I'm in shock.

When I say nothing, only continue to gape at him, he lays his hands on my shoulders, leaning in so he's eye level with me. "Breathe, Lexy," he murmurs.

His rippling face comes into focus, and I obediently do what he says, my breath seeping shakily out between my lips, drifting over him and fluttering strands of my hair. "But you told me we couldn't be together," I finally manage. "That you didn't believe in love anymore."

Regret is like a heavy cloud around him. I can see his sorrow as if huge black wings are chained to his back. "I didn't mean it. I'm so sorry."

"You scared me last night," I confess, thinking of him shaking and sweating, his eyes wide and wild. "I've never seen you like that before."

"I know. It scared me, too." Frowning, he breaks our gaze and straightens. He seems tense and a little uncomfortable, as if he's working up the courage to admit something. Apprehensive, I watch him carefully. I'm still trying to process what is happening. "Ever since the accident, I get these...um...panic attacks, I guess you could call them. I just blank out and shut down. I can't think or breathe or do anything. It was raining the night Megan died, and now whenever it does, it's like I'm right back on that road watching the crash all over again, and I get stuck there. It just hits me sometimes from out of nowhere. I couldn't get ahead of it in time. I just...I don't like the rain," he mutters, trailing off. He awkwardly shoves his hands into his pockets. "I must sound crazy."

I gasp a little at her name. He's never said it before. It feels sacred and forbidden somehow. The air is hushed, holy, and reverent. I'm very aware of what he's trusting me with and what it changes for us. My every defense crumbles, and I instantly move towards him. I wish I had known what was happening to him, how helplessly surrounded he was by the flashbacks, fear, and trauma.

I notice he's shifted away as if embarrassed or ashamed. I can't let him disappear again and pull him back, wrapping my arms around his waist, giving him somewhere to fall apart. A safe emergency crash landing. "No, you don't. You're not crazy at all. I'm so sorry you go through that. It must be awful."

He slowly lifts his gaze back to mine, searching my eyes for a couple of seconds before letting out an unsteady, shuddering breath. I feel his arms, at last, come around me, watching as the tension gradually leaves his face, his mouth, eases off his neck and shoulders. As if the weight of the world is crumbling away. The gold flecks are back. It's a relief to see them. "I really wanted to tell you about that night, but it's all so big, and I didn't know what would happen once I said it out loud, and I felt too guilty. So I just kept it to myself."

My heart wrenches as I slowly nod. "I understand," I reassure him, holding on tighter. "I can't imagine how hard it must be to carry that much pain inside of you." I think of the damage the storm caused, wreaking havoc over the land and with us. We almost didn't make it back to each other. "I guess last night wasn't the best time to tell you how I felt, considering what you were dealing with."

"Or you were just in time."

"What do you mean?"

He absently plays with the ends of my hair. He's gotten into the habit of doing that. I'm not sure if he's aware of it. I remember him saying he likes how soft it is. "I was thinking today that it's been like this with you right from the start. Since the very first day you got here. I was so messed up I couldn't see straight. I was barely alive anymore. But then I opened the door, and there you were." His voice is tender, his eyes never leaving mine as if I'm anchoring him where he stands. "Every time I turned around, you were right in the middle of the pain, and it was always exactly when I needed you to be there. Even if I didn't know it yet. It's as if I'd been waiting for you to get here, and I was just holding my breath until you showed up."

"I was so worried I had ruined everything with us."

He shook his head. "You haven't. You didn't do anything, Lexy. It was all me." His expression is pained, apologetic. "I swear I wanted to talk to you last night. I kept trying to think of something to say, but the rain wouldn't stop, and my mind wasn't right. I knew I needed to deal with everything first. I didn't want to hurt you anymore. Megan was so important to me, and I owed it to her to say goodbye in the right way. It's time to lay her to rest. For her and for me. I don't think the pain of it ever fully goes away, and I can't promise that what happened last night won't happen again. It's never really gone, and I still have nightmares sometimes. But you've made things better and a little easier. And I don't want to lose you. I finally feel like I'm ready to start over." He pauses, unsure and vulnerable, as he searches my face for a sign, my feelings, his future. "If you still want to start over with me."

I smile brilliantly at him as I nod. If this is a dream, I never want to wake up. "I do."

I'm still saying the words as he kisses me, and we fall into each other. He tastes different, sweeter somehow, as the salty, metallic sting of grief and death is soothed away. We hold nothing back. The kiss is hungry and feverish, as if he's pouring out years of unspoken pain into me. His hands are everywhere, pressing me against him, tangling into my hair, as if he needs to touch every inch of me to prove we're both still alive and here and real.

There are no longer any secrets between us, no barriers or walls, no past or ghosts haunting our every glance and hope and heartbeat. For the first time, it's only the two of us.

After a long while, when my pulse is thundering, and my limbs are trembling, I finally break the kiss. Breathless, I pull back and look up at him. His skin is flushed, his breathing heavy, his eyes dark and full of need. He's so warm and close it makes me dizzy.

Very gently, I reach up and lightly trace my fingertips over his scar. The edges are jagged and harsh, the skin sensitive to touch, and the emotions it stirs up still very raw. He immediately goes still and sucks in a sharp breath. The moment is intensely exposing and somehow more intimate than any kiss we've shared. I meet his eyes, and we stare at each other with his deepest pain in my hands. I feel like it's the first time I'm seeing him. His wounds are beautiful to me.

"I love you, too," I finally tell him, holding his gaze so he will believe me.

His face slowly breaks into a smile, the one from a long, long time ago, before the accident and years of loss stole his hope, and my heart swells with wonder as I watch him come back to life. Overwhelmed, he doesn't say anything, maybe he can't, as he pulls me back to him, so tight and fierce it steals my breath, but I don't mind.

I lose track of time as we stand in the quiet, surrounded by the scents of hay, seed, grain, oiled leather, and the musk of horses. The sun will set soon. Shadows are creeping along the dusty ground, crowding out where light used to shine.

"We should probably get back," I murmur, my lips pressed against the curve of his neck, but make no move to leave the shelter and heat of his arms. "I need to let my parents know I'm staying."

Nick glances over my head at the door. "I have a feeling your mama already knows," he says. "She's way too perceptive. Just like you."

I think of my conversation with her earlier. She'd been right. Everything worked out. I can't wait to tell her. She's the first person I want to know. "I get it from her." It's one of many things I'm realizing she's passed down to me.

"You sure do. You both know how to read minds. It's spooky." I'm laughing as Nick kisses me once more. Straightening, he takes my hand. "Come on." He leads me out of the stable. "Dinner will be ready soon anyway. You know how Becca is about us not being late for family meals."

"House rules." We're both smiling as we walk hand in hand up the old, worn path.

I look out over the lush miles of green, the weathered outbuildings, the horses peacefully grazing, the arch of my grandfather's gate standing tall against the darkening October sky. I remember the very first day I walked underneath the thick timber posts all those months ago. I knew nothing of Beau and Adelaide Montgomery who originally settled here, or how following in their footsteps would help me discover my own purpose, heritage, and legacy.

When the sun rose this morning, I thought everything was hopelessly lost. I was afraid I would have to leave this land, my family, and Nick far behind. I was convinced my dreams were over.

But life can change in a split-second or an hour, or even forty-two minutes.

And as the sun sets on another day on this beautiful ranch in Tennessee, I've got Nick back at my side, right where I hoped he would be. And he loves me. And I love him. And I am home.

The old farmhouse comes into view as the path weaves and winds through the wild grasses, faithfully guiding us back as it has for over a hundred years. All the lights are on, the golden haze glowing out into the pale lavender evening. As we get closer, I see my family in the kitchen, preparing dinner, setting the table, talking and laughing, and simply enjoying being together.

We are almost to the back porch steps when it suddenly dawns on me that I am no longer an alcoholic's daughter.

For the first time in my life, I just get to be me.

Made in the USA
Las Vegas, NV
24 January 2023